THE STATE AND THE WORKING PEOPLE IN TANZANIA

Edited by
ISSA G. SHIVJI

The State and the Working People in Tanzania ·

© CODESRIA

ISBN 0 906968 12 7 (paperback)
    0 906968 13 5 (hardback)

First published in October 1986 by CODESRIA,
B. P. 3304, Dakar, Senegal

Typeset by Grassroots, London NW6 6PS
Printed in England by Whitstable Litho, Kent

The State and the Working People in Tanzania

CONTENTS

Notes on the Contributors

Issa Shivji is an Associate Professor of Law at the University of Dar es Salaam. Author of *Class Struggles in Tanzania* and *Law, State and the Working Class in Tanzania,* his main research concern is in the theories of state and law.

Harrison Mwakyembe is doing post-graduate work at the University of Dar es Salaam and is a teaching assistant at the Faculty of Law. He researches in administrative and constitutional law and has written a novel and worked as a journalist.

Aggrey Mlimuka graduated from the University of Dar es Salaam where he is now pursuing his Masters and teaches at the Faculty of Law. His research interests are in constitutional law and has previously worked as a journalist.

Palamagamba Kabudi is teaching at the Faculty of Law, University of Dar es Salaam and doing his post-graduate work in constitutional and labour law. Previously he worked as a journalist with a Kiswahili daily published by the ruling party, *Chama cha Mapinduzi* (Tanzania).

Wilbert Kapinga is an Assistant Lecturer at the Faculty of Law, University of Dar es Salaam where he specialises in teaching labour and family law. He is currently completing his Masters work.

Henry Mapolu is a consultant in Industrial Relations at the Eastern and Southern Africa Management Institute, Arusha, Tanzania. Formerly he lectured in sociology at the University of Dar es Salaam and later worked as a training officer at the Friendship Textile Mill, Dar es Salaam. He is the author of several articles on the agrarian question in Tanzania.

Shamshad Naali is a Senior Tutor at the Cooperative College, Moshi, Tanzania. A graduate of the University of Dar es-Salaam where she did her LL.B. and LL.M., she has also worked as a corporation secretary.

Chris Peter is an Assistant Lecturer at the Faculty of Law, University of Dar es Salaam. His interests range from international law to theories of state and law and his research has included work on refugees and human rights in Africa.

Sengodo Mvungi worked for several years as a journalist with the Party newspaper *Uhuru/Mzalendo* before he joined the Faculty of Law, University of Dar es Salaam. He was an active participant in student struggles during his undergraduate days. He is currently completing his Masters dissertation.

PREFACE

The Tanzanian state is among the few in Africa which has hitherto managed to maintain a liberal image while at the same time establish a virtual organisational hegemony over its working people and popular classes. This is no mean feat and calls for explanation. Yet the scholars and academics dominated by the ruling ideology of developmentalism (see the introduction) and blinded by uncritical Tanzania-phobia have failed to provide any meaningful explanation. Radical scholars too share the blame. They were too occupied with either the economistic theories of underdevelopment or the revisionist theories of the centrality of the productive forces to unravel the development of the state. So they too, albeit using their own jargon ('the key link is the productive forces!'), were no less dominated by the ideology of developmentalism.

It is only with the deepening economic crisis that the scene is beginning to change. As people realise that developmentalism has failed to bring any real economic development, they are beginning to ask certain fundamental *political* questions. So politics, as it were, is making a come-back, and this is an absolute pre-condition for the development of popular struggles. Mass politics cannot find expression in independent organisational forms unless the hegemony of the state is explained, understood and challenged. This is the task undertaken by the contributors of this book.

Many of the contributors of this book are young intellectuals who write with passion and commitment. Their major concern is to contribute towards the struggles of the working people in their historical task of transforming the neo-colonial, imperialist-dominated African societies to a new democratic and nationally independent Africa. And they have found that their concern cannot be expressed within the restrained and pretentious jargon of the established academia. We are honoured to be part of the committed and unconventional 'scholarship' exhibited in this book.

Issa G. Shivji,
University of Dar es Salaam,
May 1985.

1. INTRODUCTION: THE TRANSFORMATION OF THE STATE AND THE WORKING PEOPLE

Issa G. Shivji

The Burning Issue

The central theme around which the contributions in this book are woven is the question of state: the organisation of the state *inter se,* its class character, the relation between the state and the working people and the direction in which these inter-relationships have evolved since independence, over two and a half decades ago. To comprehend the state in its varied aspects and relationships is to comprehend the *politics* of a social formation. Marx characterised the state as a 'table of contents' of social contradictions[1] and Lenin called it the 'organisation of the ruling class'.[2] Indeed the focus on the politics of Tanzania from the standpoint of the working people is a necessary antidote to the economistic developmentalism which has hitherto constituted the central element of the ruling ideology. Let us explain.

The central element in the dominant ideological formation in post-independence Africa has been, what we call, the ideology of developmentalism. The argument of this ideology is very simple: 'We are economically backward   to develop and develop very fast. In this task of deve'   the luxury of politics'. Therefore politi   while economics come to occupy the   terrain. The whole ideological discourse among the ra   ng class and between the ruling class and the masses is conducted within the framework of developmentalism. And academic scholarship follows suit. Even marxist scholars and 'politicians' echo the ideology of developmentalism albeit in their own vocabulary. The key-link, they say, is the development of productive forces. Class, class struggle and the question of state are the fond pre-occupations of neomarxists, argues one of the leading marxists.[3] The question for the true marxists presumably is one of strategies and tactics of economic development!

The fact that politics are displaced from the dominant ideological terrain does not of course mean that politics disappear from real life. As a matter of fact, developmentalism is the ideological guise under which the new post-independence ruling classes consolidate themselves and their alliance with imperialism. Conversely, it is under this ideological rationalisation that independent politics of the working people are suppressed and ultimately co-opted. The *organisational* manifestation of the process of consolidation of the ruling class on the one hand and the suppression of mass politics on the other is the emergence of an *authoritarian* state as the organisation of the ruling class. This goes hand in hand with the statisation of popular organisations such as trade unions, peasants' associations, professional bodies, and so on.

The contributions in this book are an attempt to document, analyse and seek out the implications of the process of the emergence of an authoritarian state in Tanzania. Whereas the rise of the authoritarian state is almost universal in post-independence Africa, it has taken different forms in different concrete situations. In one respect, the process in Tanzania has been almost unique in that it took place under the ideological hegemony of the ruling class without the overt and direct intervention of coercive apparatuses. Therefore, all the more need to analyse and understand the general tendencies discussed above in their concrete manifestation in Tanzania. The issues and themes addressed by the authors in this book may be grouped under three major headings: state power, state apparatuses and working people's struggles and organisations.

State Power

The transition from colonialism to neo-colonialism was marked by a change in the class character of the state; forging of new class alliances within and a realignment of relations with imperialism. This process took place in the context of and within social struggles in the course of which the state was transformed from a despotic colonial state to an authoritarian neo-colonial one.[4]

During colonialism the commercial and the merchant bourgeoisie composed mainly of the immigrant nationality (Asians) provided the compradorial base to the ruling metropolitan bourgeoisie. Although they played a strategic role within the colonial economy, they had little share in state power. On independence, the petty bourgeoisie, which had led the independence movement, inherited the reigns of the state. Between 1961 and 1967 this petty bourgeoisie underwent significant differentiation in which its state-based section emerged as a state bourgeoisie.[5]

In the first five years of independence there were intense struggles between different factions of the petty bourgeoisie. In the course of these struggles the former compradorial class was displaced and a new compradorial ruling class emerged. This new compradorial ruling class may be said to be composed of two factions: the state bourgeoisie and the private bourgeoisie (particularly the private industrial and commercial bourgeoisie). The state bourgeoisie plays a hegemonic role in the ruling bloc while the petty bourgeoisie—particularly in the ruling party—plays a supportive role. The relation between the state and the private bourgeoisie on the one hand and that between the compradorial bourgeoisie and the petty bourgeoisie on the other is characterised by unity and struggle.

The high point in the emergence of the state bourgeoisie was the Arusha Declaration of 1967 which nationalised important means of production and declared *Ujamaa,* a variant of petty bourgeois socialism, the official ideology of the state. The nationalisations also expressed the end of the hegemony of British capital and the multilateralisation of relations with imperialism. The organisational hegemony which the emergent state bourgeoisie had begun to establish with the banning of the trade union movement in 1964, the formation of the new army in the same year after the mutiny and the establishment of a one-party state a year later, now received a further fillip with the consolidation of its ideological hegemony through the Arusha Declaration.

Although petty bourgeois in its character, *Ujamaa* objectively served the interests of the state bourgeoisie. For the next ten years the organisational and ideological hegemony of the state bourgeoisie reigned supreme while its relative autonomy from imperialism was at its greatest.

In the middle seventies, certain external factors—rise in oil prices, world recession, drought—exacerbated the internal contradictions inherent in a neo-colonial economy. For let it be said, both before and after the Arusha Declaration the *economic policies* [6] pursued by the regime were not fundamentally different from those of many other African governments. They were predicated on increased cash crop production for export; import-substitution industrialisation[7] with high import content and loans and foreign 'aid'[8] to build the infrastructure to service the export-oriented economy. Increased cash crop production of the late 60s and early 70s was based on greater acreage under cultivation and intensive labour input. Without technical and chemical inputs like tractors, fertilisers and pesticides, of course, such agriculture has very limited potential. Its technical limits began to be expressed in soil exhaustion and falling yields.

Meanwhile, the state during this same period, had intensified its exploitation of the peasantry which was made to yield greater and greater surplus to support the ever expanding state bureaucracy and the voracious appetite for capital, both local and foreign. This too began to manifest its *social* limits in such phenomenon as passive resistance by the peasantry—withdrawal from the market; resistance by the peasantry to growing of cash crops for exports; use of parallel market, and so on. The cumulative effect of these limits is reflected in the fall in the volume of exports. Compounded by the notorious adverse international terms of trade and the accumulating debt-service charges, the economic crisis manifests itself in the chronic shortage of foreign exchange. This in turn reduces the capacity to import the necessary inputs for the highly import-dependent industries resulting in industries working below capacity, shortages of consumer goods and ultimate laying-off of workers. As if all this was not enough, the 1978-79 war with Uganda, whereby Tanzania undertook upon itself to 'liberate' that country, was almost the last stroke in the crisis. Since then the economy has entered into an ever deepening vicious circle of shortages, inflation corruption and crippling inefficiency.

The economic crisis has also become the backdrop to the increasing loss of hegemony of the state bourgeoisie. Widespread cynicism has replaced the ideological consensus of the previous decade. These are some of the first signs of cracks in the ideological hegemony of the ruling class. Within the ruling bloc it is expressed in the form of greater contradiction (more struggle rather than unity) between the state and the private compradorial bourgeoisie as the latter flexes its muscles and is able to wrench more and more concessions (witness the recent so-called import-liberalisation and legalisation of what was, only two years ago, called racketeering and economic sabotage).[9] Internationally, the relative autonomy *vis-a-vis* imperialism begins to constrict as donors are able to exert even greater pressure and erstwhile imperialist agencies like the International Monetary Fund and the World Bank begin to call the tune in no uncertain terms.[10]

The economic crisis is undoubtedly developing into an overall crisis. And even though appearing to be distant and still undefined, political rumblings are on the horizon. Politics, so to speak, are coming back to the stage. We shall return to this point in our conclusion. But, for the moment, let us turn to the second set of issues addressed in this book.

State Apparatus
The class struggles outlined briefly above have had profound expression on the level of the state. The transformation of the state has taken place both on the level of state power—its class character—as well

as in the reorganisation of the state apparatuses. Indeed, in life the two are inseparable and are separated here only for the purposes of analysis.

Within a bourgeois democratic state, parliament is the central organ which at once legitimises the political rule of the bourgeoisie as well as provides an arena for resolving intra-ruling class struggles. Whereas it is true that bourgeois democracy is ultimately the political dictatorship of the bourgeoisie, it nevertheless provides the working people with freer channels for their own political expression. Hence the form in which bourgeois dictatorship is expressed—from fascist to democratic—is not unimportant to the working people, including the working class. Working class organisations and their ideologues, while exposing the *class* character of democracy, have always defended and fought for it against fascist and authoritarian enroachments.

In this regard Mwakyembe's discussion in this volume on the role of the Tanzanian Parliament and the electoral process is very significant. He elucidates the historical process through which the parliament as a representative organ within the state lost its power and prestige. He, and Mlimuka/Kabudi in the following Chapter, argue that both power and prestige have shifted to the National Executive Committee of the ruling party, first the Tanganyika African National Union and later the *Chama cha Mapinduzi* or the CCM.

It seems to us that these two contributions highlight the double-shift in power within the state apparatus. Within the state, power is concentrated in the executive arm[11] while prestige and political legitimacy are shifted to the NEC of the Party. Within the Party, power has been increasingly concentrated in the central committee whose membership has over the years decreased in size. At the same time, there being a significant overlap and interchange of personnel between the central committee and the top echelons of the state executive, power is exercised by the common single pinnacle at the top. Undoubtedly, the NEC and the Parliament, but much more the NEC, still provide the forum and arena for the expression of different factional interests and tendencies within the ruling class and the supportive petty bourgeois class.

In the sixties Parliamentary debates often reflected arguments for western type democracy expressed by its petty bourgeois members and objectively representing the interests of the private bourgeoisie. In the NEC, on the other hand, the 'left' petty bourgeoisie have argued for greater statisation under socialist rhetoric objectively representing the interests of the state bourgeoisie. No wonder then that the dominant ideology in Tanzania partakes of a strong populist flavour whose base is essentially a petty bourgeoisie. Mlimuka/Kabudi discuss the judicious use that the ruling class has made of the 'left'—particularly the marxist 'left'—at various times to bail it out of crisis and maintain its legitimacy.

Before we leave this section a word needs to be said about the role of the military[12] and the legal machinery. Tanzania is one of the few African countries in which the colonial army was completely dismantled. This was done in 1964 after the army mutiny which was put down with the assistance of British troops. The new army was recruited from the youth league of the ruling Party and screened by the Party. Since then the Party has had a formidable presence in the army through its political commissars while members of the officer corps have often found themselves being appointed to government—executive posts from Ministers down to Area Commissioners. Simultaneously a significant number of party loyalists in top echelons have received formal military training in the top-notch military academy in the country and bestowed with military ranks. The strategy of part militarisation of the civilian regime[13] and part politicisation of the military may have played an important role in the relative stability of the civilian rule in the country.

Law and legal machinery too ultimately reflect and reinforce the peculiar character of the ruling compradore bourgeoisie. Its weakness and flabbiness as a *bourgeoisie* find expression in lack of independence and impartiality of the judiciary while its authoritarian character as a *ruling* class manifests itself in lack of ideological notions of 'rights' as a central element in legal ideology. Indeed law assumes a typically *instrumentalist* character while legal ideology has little role in the dominant ideological formation.[14] This is of course very much unlike the 'juridical world outlook'[15] of the western bourgeoisie.

The western bourgeoisie was born in a revolution which destroyed the essentially status and tradition-based feudal order. It ushered in a bourgeois order; individualising and atomising society and replacing status with contract and tradition with legalism. The individual commodity-owner of the market-place appeared as a legal subject[16] in law, a bearer of rights and duties. The central place in bourgeois ideology is occupied by legal ideology whose core element is the notion of 'right'.[17]

In the neo-colonial situation, on the other hand, as we have seen, both politics and legal ideology are displaced from the ideological terrain by the ideology of developmentalism. Law becomes simply and without mediation the *instrument* of control and power and has very little *hegemonic* significance. Legislation is about enabling the state and state organs to exert unquestionable power rather than about individual rights. And both as a matter of law and practice the powers of the executive cannot be or are rarely challenged in courts or if challenged stand little chance of success. This is due to a combination of factors such as the widely-worded law which leaves little room for judicial activism; timidity and mediocrity on the part of judges accompanied by loyalty born out of pressures and expectations of favour from the executive.

These general characteristics have been as marked in Tanzania as elsewhere.[18] There are some faint signs of changes with the general changes in the political climate which we shall discuss in the concluding section. Meanwhile let us recapitulate the third major issue—working peoples' struggles and organisation-discussed by the contributors in this book.

Working People's Struggles and Organisation

The transformation of the state and changes in the class configuration discussed above have been a process grounded ultimately in the social struggles of the working people. The organisational hegemony of the ruling class manifesting itself in the rise of an authoritarian state has been predicated on the simultaneous suppression of the organisational initiative of the working people and the destruction of their independent organisations. Thus the organisational capacity of the working people is stunted and coopted by the state. Independent politics of the people lack expression, or at least, lack organisational expression. Often they are channelled into forms which are innocuous from the point of view of the ruling class. In this book these processes are discussed with regard to the working class, the peasantry and students by Kapinga, Naali and Mapolu and Peter/Mvungi respectively.

The Working Class

Its small size and relatively recent origins notwithstanding, the working class in Tanzania has a brilliant chapter of struggles. It was in the 40s that some of the most concentrated collective struggles were waged by the dockworkers culminating in the banning of their union.[19] The second phase of a decade of strikes from 1955 to 1964 saw the rise of a massive trade union movement which became the first victim of post-independence intra-petty bourgeois struggles of the early 60s. In 1964 autonomous trade unions were banned and their place was taken by a state-sponsored and state-controlled single trade union. At the same time, workers were robbed of their most important weapon of collective struggle—the strike—as strikes were made virtually illegal. Since then the workers have yet to make a come-back in any significant organisational form.

Without their own independent organisation even such advanced workers' struggles as were witnessed between 1971 and 1975, 30 tend to dissipate. There is little doubt that during its ideological and organisational hegemony, state control of the working class reigned supreme. Kapinga shows how law has been used since independence as an instrument of control. And whatever concessions the state may have made to the working class in the form of certain material benefits, these have been at the expense of its organisational autonomy. Ultimately therefore even these benefits have been eroded since there has been no organisation to defend and protect them.

Notheless, the economic crisis has already begun to eat into the hegemony of the ruling class. Certain forms of resistance, protest and challenge are already evident. These are yet in their first stages and it is difficult to say what forms these will assume ultimately. But it is clear that the working class will have to recapture its organisational initiative and rebuild its organisational capacity. It is inevitable that the first steps in this direction will be some form of autonomous trade unionism. While this is a necessary and a welcome phase, the character that working class struggles and organisation assume during this crucial period will heavily depend on the general politics in the country and particularly the development of an overall democratic movement.

The Peasantry

Henry Mapolu highlights the central contradiction in a neo-colonial, semi-patriachal formation—the contradiction between the peasantry and the state as a representative of imperialist finance and local compradorial capital. The peasant constitutes the major source of surplus and as such is made to yield maximum surplus product.[21] To maximise the rate of exploitation of the peasant producer, capital lets him retain ownership of the means of production and control over the labour process so that capital may be free from bearing the costs of peasant reproduction. But this in turn means that unlike a worker who yields surplus value by sheer operation of economic forces, the peasant has to be constantly subjected to extra-economic coercion so that he continues yielding surplus to capital. The major extra-economic force is state coercion. The contradiction between the relative autonomy of the peasant labour process and his role as a producer of surplus value for capital is therefore the main element in the relation between the state and the peasantry.

During the colonial period, state-coercion was limited to the level of production while the private merchant took care of distribution. The colonial experience of centralising surplus through marketing boards was generalised by the post-independence government and further experiments were made with such forms as villagisation and so-called decentralisation. Meanwhile, the private merchant was displaced first by state-directed cooperatives and later by state-controlled crop authorities which replaced cooperatives altogether.

Whereas the cooperatives had some semblance of historical legitimacy and democracy, crop authorities had neither. They were undisguised extentions of the state bureaucracy with even greater inefficiency, insatiable appetite for embezzlement and without any accountability to the peasant producer. No wonder even the proverbial tolerance of the peasant begins to reach its limits. In absence of organisation and direction, peasant resistance takes on typically individualist and primordial forms as documented by Mapolu. Yet the super-exploitation[22] of the peasantry which forces it to live sub-human existence constitutes the material basis for any new democratic movement.

The changing organisational forms through which the state exerts extra-economic coercion for extracting and centralising surplus from the peasant forms the central theme of the story told by Shamshad Naali. She documents the development from the cooperatives to crop authorities paying particular attention as to how this is reflected in law and how law in turn is used as an instrument of control in the relationship. She concludes by touching on the recent half-hearted measures to reintroduce cooperatives in an attempt to arrest the spawning inefficiency of the bureaucratic crop authorities. Yet it is clear that the state bourgeoisie would not allow genuine, democratic and independent cooperatives as is shown in the numerous controls built into the 1982 legislation re-introducing cooperatives. That brings us to the story of student struggles.

Student Struggles

Unlike workers and peasants, students are not a productive group. Indeed, in our societies they form a privileged section. Until recently, university students in Tanzania were being prepared essentially to join the high echelons of the state. Yet given their peculiar position in the ideological apparatus, they are exposed to a cross-current of various ideas and ideological tendencies. It is in these apparatuses that various ideological tendencies (representing the material interests of social classes in the society) lock in struggle. At the University of Dar es Salaam, which until recently was the only university in the country, ideological struggles have found dramatic and most concentrated expression. Peter and Mvungi in their contribution—probably the only one of its kind written so far—have traced the development and main contentions of ideological struggles at the University.

Readers of this Chapter and others who have even slight acquaintance with the University of Dar es Salaam may marvel at the fact that such intellectual/ideological discussions have been possible or permitted on an African campus. This once again is a reflection of the consistency with which the Tanzanian state has approached independent opposition politics. As far as university intellectuals are concerned, the state has been fairly liberal and tolerant towards theoretical debates, yet, at the same time, it has as consistently and firmly put down and nipped in the bud any *political* and *organisational* expressions of these debates. As Peter and Mvungi show, from the 1966 demonstration against compulsory national service to the 1978 demonstration against fringe benefits and privileges of 'leaders', the state has unhesitatingly used coercion to maintain its hegemony. Thus liberalism towards theoretical/ideological debates on the one hand and total suppression of political struggles on the other has allowed the state to project a tolerant/liberal image internationally while maintaining its hegemony internally. Consequently, in spite of their renowned ideological/theoretical contributions the students/ intellectuals of the University of Dar es Salaam have little to show in the political battlefields. Few states in Africa can boast such a record as Tanzania's in their relation with left intellectuals/students: in a rare feat, the Tanzanian state has managed to have its cake and eat it too—at least during the last two decades.

Finally, we need to say something on the subject which is conspicuous by its absence in these contributions. This is the role of the petty bourgeoisie as part of the working people. The absence of treatment of the petty bourgeoisie as a distinct social class and objectively as part of the working people is not accidental. It falls within the long tradition of radical writings and debates in Tanzania whereby the term petty bourgeoisie is, more often than not, used in a politically derogatory sense (as opposed to accurate scientific) to describe the compradore bourgeoisie, the ruling class. In other words, theoretically, no clear distinction is drawn between a bourgeoisie and a petty bourgeoisie.[23]

This theoretical confusion no doubt has some material basis to it. We may identify two important bases. Firstly, the compradore bourgeoisie, particularly its state bourgeois faction, emerged from the petty bourgeoisie not long ago; therefore it is easy to blur the demarcation between the two. Secondly, the petty bourgeoisie has been a supportive class of the ruling compradore bourgeoisie; this too makes for lack of clarity on the issue. Yet it is extremely important to distinguish between these two separate classes.

When we talk of the petty bourgeoisie we are referring to that social class which largely lives by its labour—therefore like the proletariat it does not exploit but unlike the proletariat it owns and controls its own means of production. In its ideal definition therefore the petty bourgeoisie is neither an exploiter nor exploited. Of course, in real life the situation is much more complex. But it may be said that all those groups which more or less fall in the *middle* position between the bourgeoisie and the proletariat, and social groups akin to them, are part of the petty bourgeoisie. For instance, in our situation the urban petty bourgeoisie would include such groups as shopkeepers, vendors, craftsmen, and so on, in distribution and production sectors and middle and lower level intelligentsia (groups akin to those aforementioned) such as clerks, office workers, civil servants, teachers, and so on. Space does not allow us to dwell further on the theoretical treatment of this issue. It is sufficient it to touch on certain aspects which make the petty bourgeoisie a very important social class.

Objectively the petty bourgeoisie is part of the 'people' as opposed to the ruling compradore bourgeoisie which is allied with imperialism. Although hitherto it has been supportive of the ruling class during the latter's hegemony, the petty bougeoisie is beginning to be hit by the economic crisis. It is likely to be the most articulate in its opposition. Yet in history the petty bourgeoisie always has provided a social basis for both the extreme right (fascist) and extreme left (adventurist) currents. While it plays a significant role in mass struggles and democractic movements, the petty bourgeoisie is incapable of providing a firm revolutionary leadership. These are some of the generalisations derived from historical experience. The least that can be said therefore is that there is an urgent need to address the question of petty bourgeoisie in Tanzania concretely and specifically on historical, ideological, political and organisational levels.

Conclusion: A Reawakening of Politics?
We opened this introduction with the argument that the ideological terrain has been hitherto dominated by the ideology of developmentalism. That politics—that is independent politics of the masses—were pushed to the background. Under this, the ruling class consolidated itself, establishing its ideological and organisational hegemony while the state emerged as an authoritarian state. In short, depoliticisation of the masses constituted the politics of the ruling class.

However, this state of hegemony seems to have entered a period of transformation with the severe economic crisis. The economic crises have, as it were, blown the lid off the ideology of developmentalism. The truth is that the economic crisis has revealed that no real and sustained economic development has taken place since independence but meanwhile people have lost their political freedom as well. This realisation,—which may be coming slowly and joltingly but is surely coming—we believe, marks the beginning of a re-awakening of politics. In Tanzania, a year-long debate (see Mwakyembe) on constitutional changes, to a certain extent, demonstrated this re-awakening. The central thrust of the debate was the demand for democracy. No doubt, this demand took different forms, for democracy does not mean the same thing to all social classes and groups in a society.

For the state bourgeoisie, constitutional changes garbed in the language of democracy, only meant a few *technocratic* changes in the organisation of the state apparatus. The compradore bourgeoisie, on the other hand, shouted loudest about the privatisation of the economy while making only half-hearted political mutterings such as multi-party system and freedom to own private property. The petty bourgeoisie was typically divided but dominantly tended to go along with either the state or the compradore private bourgeoisie. The demand for complete freedom of association, popular and independent associations such as trade unions, peasant associations and so on was weakest reflecting the unorganised and weak state of the popular masses. Nonetheless, the debate was a turning point. Yet, given the aforementioned weakness of the popular classes, the immediate politics of the country in the wake of the current economic crisis, by and large, will be shaped by the sharpening contradiction between the state and the private compradore bourgeoisie.

This contradiction expresses mainly on the economic plane and may be summed up as between statisation and privatisation of the economy. The economic crisis coupled with indefensible inefficency and corruption of the state bureaucracy puts the state bourgeoisie on the defensive while the private compradore bourgeoisie—objectively backed by such erstwhile imperialist agencies as the IMF, the World Bank and various funding organisations/agencies—is on the offensive. It is wringing concessions from the state with a vengeance and concessions of the worst kind from the stand-point of the long-term interests of the *national* economy. The policies lying behind the package adopted in the 1984/85 budget—so-called import liberalisation, introduction of school fees, cutting-off of agricultural subsidies, devaluation and redundancies—will undercut even the neo-colonial import-substitution industrialisation of the 60s and early 70s. Indeed, as it is being shown, these policies are in the narrow interests of the worst kind of compradores, currency smugglers (who have now become respectable importers of foreign luxury goods) commission agents, local representatives of foreign commercial firms and so on. And even the small 'national' bourgeois manufacturers of local shoes, garments, processed food-stuffs and so on, are now being compradorised as they fail to compete with imported goods, on the one hand, and find mere *distribution* of foreign goods even more lucrative, on the other.

What of the political effect of this contradiction? The private compradore bourgeoisie under imperialist hegemony is incapable of any sustained struggle for genuine democracy, even bourgeois democracy. Thus, in our countries experience has shown that economic *privatisation* does not necessarily produce political *liberalisation*. More often than not, the contrary is true. This is because the private compradore bourgeoisie will not be able to deliver even some basic needs of the popular masses. And lacking in any political legitimacy, it will inevitably resort to naked force to subjugate people. The authoritarian state built by the state bourgeoisie will come in handy in this regard—without its ideological hegemony this time. (It is not surprising, for instance, that the spokesmen of the private bourgeoisie were not interested in any talk about independent mass organisations during the constitutional debate).

While therefore the immediate politics of the country remain uncertain—or at least do not seem to be favourable from the point of view of the people—there is little doubt that much ground has been cleared and is being cleared for expressions of popular struggles— the only sure way for the emergence of mass struggles, mass independent organisations and mass revolutionary potential. These are the necessary prerequisities in the shaping of a new democratic revolution.

NOTES

1. Quoted in Lenin, V.I., "What the 'friends of the people are' and how they fight social democrats," *Collected Works* (Moscow: Progress Publishers, 1971), Vol. I., p. 162.
2. Lenin, V.I., *On Trade Unions* (Moscow: Progress Publishers, 1970), p. 307.
3. Babu, A.M., *Africa Events* (London), No.1.
4. For a more elaborate discussion of this see Shivji, I.G., "The Reorganisation of the State and the Working People in Tanzania", in *Socialism in the World* (Beograd: 1984), No. 45, pp. 156-78.
5. For a discussion of class struggles in post-independence Tanzania see Shivji, I.G., *Class Struggle in Tanzania* (Dar es Salaam: Tanzania Publishing House, 1975).
6. There is a host of literature on the economy of Tanzania. For a bird's eye-view of the same (and a comprehensive bibliography) see Coulson, A., *Tanzania: A Political Economy* (London: Oxford University Press, 1982).
7. For a critique of import-substitution industrialisation and export-oriented economy generally see Shivji, I.G., et. al., *Tanzania, the Silent Class Struggle* (Dar es Salaam: Tanzania Publishing House, 1973).
8. Tanzania probably receives the highest per capita foreign aid in Africa. As a matter of fact, she has become *more* dependent on foreign aid *after* the Arusha Declaration policy of self-reliance. The annual average of loans and grants between 1967 and 1983 was shs. 1771.5 million, 18 times more than the annual average of the six year period before the Arusha Declaration, see *Class Struggles in Tanzania, op. cit.,* p. 161 and *Uhuru,* July, 3, 1984 for the post-Arusha figures.
9. The 1984/85 budget, among other things, permits Tanzanians with foreign currency abroad to import certain goods. And Tanzanians with foreign currency locally may buy goods from exclusive foreign-exchange shops. Indeed imports and

possession of such luxuries as videos is now freely permitted. Not long ago these very practices were held out as racketeering and sabotaging of the national economy. Thousands of suspected 'economic saboteurs' were rounded up in 1983 under the Economic Sabotage Act, tried and sentenced by specially constituted tribunals. Indeed, as is always the case when such exercises are conducted for ulterior political motives by a corrupt administration, the 'big fist' escaped the net while small ones were made scape-goats. Hardly a year later, as one satirist put it, the economic saboteurs of yester-year had become economic saviours of today as they began to flood the market with consumer luxuries bought with foreign currency previously spirited away to foreign banks through the black market.

10. The long-drawn out 'dialogue' between the IMF and the Tanzanian government on the latter's application for a loan and the former's insistence on conditionalities may soon become a legend. As the Tanzanian government willy-nilly makes small and not so small concessions, the IMF comes up with even harder conditions. And the pressures from within, particularly from compradore elements and their academic spokesmen, to accede to the IMF conditions are becoming spokesmen, to accede to the IMF conditions are becoming stronger every day. For the alignment of forces within the administration on this issue see Singh, A., "The Present Crisis of the Tanzanian Economy: Notes on the Economics and Politics of Devaluation", in *Law Review* (Dar es Salaam: Faculty of Law), Vols. 11-14.

11. Cf. Shivji, I.G., "The State of the Constitution and the Constitution of the State in Tanzania", *Eastern Africa Law Review* (Dar es Salaam: Faculty of Law), Vols. 11-14.

12. See Shivji, I.G., "The Reorganisation of the State...", *op. cit.*, for a fuller discussion.

13. See Swai, F.S., *The Integration of the Military to the Political System in Tanzania*, M.A. Dissertation, Unversity of Dar es Salaam, 1982 (unpublished).

14. For a fuller discussion see Shivji, I.G., "Law in Independent Africa: Some Reflections on the Role of Legal Ideology", in *Ohio State Law Journal* (forthcoming).

15. Engels, F., "Juridical Socialism", quoted in Tumanov, V.A., *Contemporary Bourgeois Legal Thought* (Moscow: Progress Publishers, 1974), Ch.I.'

16. For an interesting discussion on this aspect see Pashukanis, E.B., *Law & Marxism: A General Theory* (London: Ink Links Ltd., 1978).

17. Cf. Scheingold, S.A., *The Politics of Rights: Lawyers, Public Policy, and Political Change* (New Haven & London: Yale University Press, 1974).

18. See Shivji, I.G., "The State of the Constitution...", *op.cit.*, and Peter, C.M., & Wambali, M., "The Socio-economic and Political Context of the Judiciary: the case of Tanzania," (mimeo.) for a somewhat charitable view of the judiciary.

19. For a comprehensive treatment of the development of the working class in Tanzania see Shivji, I.G., *Law State and the Working Class in Tanzania* (London: James Currie Publishers, forthcoming).

20. These are popularly called post-Mwongozo struggles as they came in the wake of th Party document called *Mwongozo* (or Guidelines). For the discussion of these struggles see Mapolu, H., & Shivji, I.G., *Vugu-Vugu la Wafanyakazi Nchini Tanzania* (Kampala: Urban Rural Mission, 1984) and Shivji, I.G., "Working Class Struggles and Organisation in Tanzania, 1939-1975", in *MAWAZO*, Vol. 5, No. 2 (Kampala: Maherere University), pp.3-24.

21. Shivji, I.G., "The Exploitation of Small Peasant," in Das. A., et. al., (eds)., *The Worker and the Working Class* (Delhi: PECCE, 1983).

22. *Ibid.* See also, Ellis, F., "Agricultural and Peasant-State Relations in Tanzania", (University of East Anglia: Mimeo, June 1982). Ellis, for instance, shows that the share of producers in the final sales price of export crops declined from 70%

to 42% between 1970 and 1980. At the same time, export taxes from these sales accruing to the central government rose form 6.5% (average 1971-1972) to 19.9% (average 1978-80), a more than two-fold rise. Respective figures for the surplus accruing to parastatals were 26.0 and 37.0%, (tables 1 & 2). He shows similar trends in the case of staple food crops sold to the National Milling Corporation.

23. My own work *Class Struggles in Tanzania* fails to draw the distinction between the petty bourgeoisie and, what I then called, the bureaucratic bourgeoisie (or the state bourgeoisie, the term used in this paper).

2. THE PARLIAMENT AND THE ELECTORAL PROCESS*

H. G. Mwakyembe

Introduction

On Monday the 11th of December 1961, two days after attainment of juridical independence from Britain, a parliament complete with the Speaker's golden mace, a Sergeant-at-Arms, a Clerk, Order Papers and so on, characteristic of the British House of Commons, was officially inaugurated by Prince Phillip, the Duke of Edinburgh in Dar es Salaam on behalf of Queen Elizabeth the Second of England. Tanganyika's Independence Parliament, with all the above outward trappings of liberal democracy, was a creature of a British piece of legislation—the Tanganyika (Constitution) Order in Council of 1961[1] (hereinafter referred to as the Independence Constitution) which proclaimed Tanganyika to be a multi-party parliamentary democracy with parliament as the central institution of government.

The Independence Constitution in fact introduced into Tanganyika the British system of government commonly referred to as the 'Westminster model', a model of parliamentary or liberal democracy which colonial Britain indiscriminately bequeathed to all its dependencies on the eve of their independence. The practice and procedure in the preparation of this article.
of the Independence Parliament closely conformed to that of the Commons House of Parliament of Great Britain and Northern Ireland. Likewise the position of the constitutional monarch in England (who

---

* This Chapter confines itself to the parliament and the electoral process in Tanganyika (Tanzania Mainland) from 1961 up to 1964. The discussion on the subsequent period naturally touches on Zanzibar as a result of the union between Tanganyika and Zanzibar to form Tanzania in April 1964 which brought about the union parliament. I am greatly indebted to Comrade Kwey T. Rusema, currently a member of the Bench, for his research assistance in the preparation of this article.

is the head of state but ceremonial and almost wholly non-executive) became the model for the post of Governor-General at independence. So was the position of the Prime Minister who wielded real power. He was, just as in Britain, the head of the political party commanding support of the majority in a popularly elected, representative legislature. The principles of prime ministerial and cabinet system, the sovereignty of parliament, loyal opposition, electoral system based on one-man one-vote, the independence and impartiality of the judiciary, civil service and armed forces, made up the substance of the Independence Constitution.

The Independence Parliament, as already noted, was the central institution of government vested with supreme powers by the Independence Constitution. It was envisaged that it would exercise direct control over legislation and indirect control over the actions of the executive. Under the Westminster model, parliament is said to be both omnipotent and omnicompetent in respect of legislation i.e. there is no constitutional restriction on its authority, courts are bound to enforce without question any law that it enacts, and other law-making bodies in the country exercise their powers only so long as parliament authorises them to do so.[2] As Dicey puts it, parliament "can make or unmake any law".[3] The only thing it cannot do is to bind itself.

In respect of its direct control over the executive's actions, parliament is said to have ultimate control by virtue of the convention that ministers are responsible to parliament, both for cabinet decisions and for the functions of their departments. This is what is called the doctrine of ministerial responsibility which covers collective responsibility for cabinet decisions and individual responsibility for the work of departments of each minister. The principle behind the collective responsibility is that members of the government should present a united front to parliament in defence of their policies and that if parliament refuses to support the government on an issue of importance, the Prime Minister and all his ministers have to resign. On the other hand, the essence of the convention of individual responsibility is that the minister in charge of a department is personally answerable to parliament for all the actions of his department. He has to see to it that relevant decisions are applied fully by the officials under him since in parliament he is the one to answer for his department.

The legislature and judiciary in the liberal democratic theory of government are regarded as checks or brakes on the executive. The functions of the judiciary are, *inter alia,* to declare the law where parliament has not been sufficiently explicit and to prevent any tendency towards arbitrary government by applying the law impartially and independent of any outside interference.[4] This explains why the doctrine of separation of powers bears immense significance in the liberal democratic system of government. According to French philosopher, Montesquieu, it is based on the principle that justice and man's liberty would be at stake if the same man or body, ''whether those of the nobles or of the people, exercised the three powers that of enacting laws, that of executing the public resolutions and of trying the causes of individuals''.[5]

The Independence Constitution was accompanied by legislative provisions for the regular holding of general elections as well as spelling out the lifetime of a parliament. This in a nutshell was the system of government which Tanganyika adopted at independence, a Westminster model which to the constitution framers in London, was the best to uphold democracy in post-colonial Tanganyika.

It is important to note at this juncture that parliamentary democracy or representative government did not fall as a bolt from the blue even in Britain itself. It was a product of more than three centuries of intense struggles by the lower classes (during feudalism) which were constantly demanding greater control in their political life and a greater stake in the economy. The protracted struggle was waged against the feudal nobility and later absolute monarchs whose wide and unlimited political powers not only curtailed individual freedom and rights, but also militated against the overall growth and advancement of society. Having crushed the nobility, the absolute monarchs also had to go. After a concerted campaign against absolutism, which in some societies in Europe ended up in a serious blood-bath, the monarch in Britain was forced to strike a compromise with the rising bourgeoisie (who spearheaded the struggle) under which the monarch retained only nominal power while surrendering real state power to the victors.

The boroughs, which were the political institutions of feudalism suppressing the rising bourgeoisie and keeping them outside parliamentary control of state power, were eliminated with the passing of the 1832 and 1867 Reform Acts. The combined effect of this was the extension of the franchises and the granting of qualification for candidacy to the bourgeoisie on the basis of property. The bourgeoisie ultimately got hold of the British Parliament thus marking the triumph of parliamentary democracy over feudal absolutism; a democracy which the victors projected as genuine and universally ideal in that every citizen 'participates' in the business of government. The parliament was put forward as a 'popular' organ enjoying legislative supremacy and composed of legislators 'freely' elected by the people as their representatives, hence directly responsible to the electorate. It is apparent from the foregoing discussion that parliamentary democracy like any other type of democracy was an evolution of human experience (in this case the bourgeoisie) in struggle.

Relevance of the Westminster Model to Tanganyika
Some "radical" scholars looking at Tanganyika's independence constitutional arrangements have forcefully argued that since democracy was borne out of struggle and inextricably connected with the material conditions in society, it could not simply be imposed or transplanted from one area to another or treated as an exportable item. Democracy, they argue, is one of the forms in which the dictatorship of one class over others in society is politically expressed and parliamentary democracy is no exception. They contend further that the struggle for parliamentary democracy in Europe was fundamentally for the political elevation of propertied elements rather than for securing genuine freedom and individual rights and all parliamentary democracies as a result are characterised by a manifest contradiction between the declared 'rule by the people' and the actual domination of the exploiters. It is argued therefore that parliamentary democracy had no relevance whatsoever to the interests of the oppressed and exploited strata of the people of Tanganyika and was bound to work to their detriment.

Before one considers the substance of the above reasoning it is important to investigate the factors which led colonial Britain to promulgate the Westminster model for its dependencies shortly before their political independence. Were these political developments in the late 1950s a sequel of the people's struggle against alien rule and denial of democratic liberties or simply (as some apologists of British imperialism try to explain) part of the Crown's gradual and long-term political programmes in British Africa towards representative and responsible government?[6]

Whereas colonial Britain indeed tended to demonstrate a strong concern for bequeathing the Westminster model to its dependencies at zero hour, its own rule in the colonies was in complete disregard of the colonised people's basic human rights and democratic liberties. The essence of the colonial system was despotism which characterised the imperialist stage of capitalism.

The development of capitalism in Europe witnessed the emergence of giant monopoly firms operating by constantly fighting to gain control over raw materials, markets, means of communications and new profitable areas for investments. The scope for expansion within their national boundaries became limited and the need for spreading out became compelling. "Expand or burst was the dictum", as Babu aptly puts it.[7] The only 'safe' way for capitalism to resolve its internal contradictions was to go international and the well-known scramble for less developed Africa, Asia and Latin America ensued. To maintain undisturbed domination over the seized territories and ensure their maximum exploitation in peace, imperialist nations patched up their differences in Berlin in 1885 and established full state power over the acquired territories. Colonial territories henceforth became appendages to the metropolitan home market for manufactured goods, sources of raw materials, reservoirs of cheaper labour and areas for the investment of capital.

In each territory a colonial state was installed to keep the colonial people in political subjection and create suitable conditions for their utmost exploitation. A string of laws was enacted to force peasants to cultivate cash crops (for feeding industries in the metropole). Laws were passed outlawing strikes, banning or restricting trade unions, disallowing or limiting political parties, suppressing criticism, banishing or arresting political leaders, laying down lowest possible minimum wages and sanctifying systems of land tenure which robbed the peasant of the best land.[8] In short, colonial rule in Tanganyika and other territories was characterised by total absence of democractic institutions and ideals cherished in the bourgeois world. As Lenin once said, "imperialism is indisputably the 'negation' of *democracy in general,* of all democracy..."[9] Even the much talked about Legislative Councils (LEGCOs) established in British colonies with their often exaggerated semblance of representation, were more extensions of Governors' offices than representative institutions.

A Legislative Council for Tanganyika, the function of which was to deliberate government measures, was established on 1 October, 1926 under the Tanganyika (Legislative Council) Order in Council.[10] The council was unrepresentative and a preserve of Europeans and Asians only while Africans' participation was confined to tribal authorities.[11]

Colonialism with all its repressive apparatuses could not keep the local people in perpetual passive inertness and obedience. It faced mounting resistance in all the subject territories. The victory of the Russian workers and peasants over the Tsar in 1917 worked as a catalyst to the struggles against alien rule in the colonies. The year 1919 alone saw, among others, the 1 March uprising in Korea, the historic 'Fourth of May' movement in China, the formation of the Ceylon National Congress and a wide-spread upsurge of strikes and demonstrations in India which were met by the British colonial authorities with sadistic brutality.[12] In 1920, apart from the big 'December Boycott' movement in Burma, organised political movements sprung up in Egypt, Tunisia and South Africa as well as a spate of strikes in Kenya and the Rif rebellion in Morocco. By the end of the Second World War in 1945, a great wind of change was fast sweeping across the world. The escalating struggles for national independence in the colonies saw India and Pakistan in 1947 winning their political independence with Burma, Sri Lanka and Indonesia following suit. Between 1948 and 1959 alone, further victories were registered in China, North Korea, Vietnam, Tunisia, Guinea, Ghana and Cuba to mention but a few. What is of significance in these developments is that a number of these countries which were basically agricultural and semi-feudal, smashed their outmoded economic systems and set out on the road to socialism thus strengthening the socialist alliance in the world.

With the expansion of the socialist camp, the global anti-colonial movement and the growing awareness of the colonial people for independence, imperialism's sphere of exploitation continued to shrink. In East Africa, the post World War II period was punctuated with unprecedented unrest, demonstrations and wide-spread strikes in opposition to colonial oppression and exploitation. In Uganda, peasants and workers burnt down administrative buildings and houses of local chiefs in protest against high taxes, poor crop prices and the oppressive system which denied them democratic rights. From time to time police action had to be brought against the 'rioters' and in 1949 along over 1,724 arrests were made.[13] The situation in Kenya was worse.

In Tanganyika, apart from the various forms of struggles which the people resorted to, wage-earners who had started organising themselves into trade unions especially after the Second World War gave the colonial government hell. In 1951 for instance, about 12,775 man-days were lost due to industrial disputes involving strikes. In 1956, a year after formal registration of the Tanganyika Federation of Labour (TFL) which had 17 independent trade unions affiliated to it, the number of man-days lost rose to 58,066 involving over 17,695 workers and by 1960 it shot up to 1,494,773 man-days involving 89,495 workers.[14] Colonial Britain, already weakened by the severe economic bruises it had suffered in the Second World War, was forced to yield to the people's pressure for change in its overall policies. In fact, the colonial government had started to effect some cosmetic reforms in Tanganyika as early as 1945 in order to contain the growing anti-colonial sentiments in the territory.

On 24 November, 1945, it appointed two Africans (both chiefs) for the first time as unofficial members to LEGCO.[15] The aim was apparently to fool the people that they were being represented in the day to day running of the colonial government. By 1948 there were four Africans (three chiefs and a Dar es Salaam school teacher) sitting on the unofficial side of LEGCO,[16] giving the council what was ironically termed 'balanced representation', meaning that the combined Asian and African representation equalled the European.

Despite some further inconsequential reforms such as the appointment of a speaker and a slight expansion of its membership, the council remained a ridiculously clownish institution mocking the very bourgeois notions of representative democracy. Whatever role it was supposed to play, the Governor as the sovereign's representative remained the supreme source of legal and political authority. He could rule without consultation if he chose to, subject only to general instructions of the colonial office. Meanwhile the people continued to struggle for the right to rule themselves and to organise themselves in political parties as well as elect their own representatives.

It was during the second half of the 1950s when the colonial state facing serious political tension in the country decided to do some further face-lifting of its tool, LEGCO, by passing the Legislative Council (Elections Ordinance) of 1957,[17] under which Tanganyikans for the first time in over 75 years of (both German and British) colonial rule, were allowed to elect their representatives the following year. The 1958-59 general elections, however, were carried out in a restricted franchise which required Africans to meet several criteria to be eligible to vote (i.e. eight years of education, a minimum age of 21, an annual income of shs. 3,000, literacy in English or Swahili, or being an office-holder under government appointment). The elections were undoubtedly a desparate attempt to inject some legitimacy into LEGCO. The number of elected members in the council was 30, but they were outnumbered by the *ex-officio* and nominated members.[18]

As independence approached, some further changes were made following recommendations of the Ramage Committee (known by the name of its chairman Sir Richard Ramage) which was appointed by the Governor in 1959 to study revisions of the electoral practices. Its recommendations which included slight extension of the franchise[19] and abolition of representation on the basis of race, were adopted by the colonial government. As a result, the new 81-member council constituted after the second general elections on August 30, 1960, (in which the Tanganyika African National Union (TANU) led by Julius Nyerere won an overwhelming majority of votes) had 71 elected and only 10 nominated members. Out of the 71 seats however, 10 were reserved for Europeans and 11 for Asians. A month later in September 1960, the British conceded responsible government in Tanganyika followed by constitutional talks in Dar es Salaam chaired by British Colonial Secretary Ian Macleod from March 27 to 29, 1961. It is at this meeting that the colonial government managed, among other things, to push through the Westminster model.

From the preceding account, it is quite clear that Tanganyika's political independence and that of other colonies, was a product of the people's protracted struggle against alien rule and denial of democratic rights. It was not, as it is sometimes presented, a result of an orderly and generous abandonment of alien rule by imperialist nations. Having failed to crush the people's struggles by brute force, imperialist powers realised that their days of direct colonial plunder were numbered. Thus they made a tactical retreat by conceding to some of the people's demands in order to maintain their domination in new forms. For they very well knew that any intransigence on their part would have meant further escalation of the people's struggles which would have eventually brought to power 'pro-communist' governments (as had happened in the case of China, North Korea and Vietnam) to the detriment of imperialist interests. The granting of political independence to Tanganyika and other colonies was but part of the concessions made by the colonialists as a result of the people's ever mounting pressures. This was accompanied by the bequeathing the Westminster 'package' embodying most of the liberal democratic ideals. There were, however, other ulterior factors behind the 'package' which help to explain the keen enthusiasm which gripped colonial Britain in the final days of its rule in bequeathing it to Tanganyika.

Realising the inevitability of Tanganyika's independence, the colonial power became extremely apprehensive for the security and rights of its companies, nationals and other immigrants who had flocked into the colony in search of easy money and life and had over a period of time acquired a great deal of wealth and property. What compounded its worries was the fact that it had, like other colonial powers, built an oppressive state structure in the territory which was bound to work to the detriment of the minorities at the hands of an indigenous ruling class. A way had to be found for their protection. To the British imperialists, the Westminster model or parliamentary system of government (with its emphasis on one man-one vote, rule of law, the notion of government and a loyal opposition and so on) provided the only feasible way out. In drafting the Tanganyika Independence Constitution, the Colonial Office in London made sure that it had entrenched clauses which guaranteed some rights, liberties and security of the minorities and their property. The British knew that none of the nationalist leaders at the constitutional talks would dare raise any hell about the provisions, since they coincided with some of the people's demands for democracy.

We do not dispute that parliamentary democracy is essentially a bourgeois institution. Neither do we dispute or pretend not to see the delusiveness of political independence. Our contention however is that political independence and parliamentary democracy were part of the political developments in the late 1950s in Tanganyika which should not be looked at in isolation from people's struggles. That without these struggles, none of these developments would have taken place in the late 1950s and Tanganyika would have remained for years an entombed territory. It is our assertion therefore that these developments were a sequel of the people's struggles and did not run counter to the people's interests. To dismiss these developments as spurious, is to ignore the strategic importance of democratic struggles at the political level. Political independence could not of course disentangle Tanganyika from the claws of monopoly capital, but it broadened the way for people's higher struggles for democracy at all levels, including the economic. Lenin pointed out that, "the domination of finance capital does not in the least nullify the significance of political democracy as a freer, wider and clearer form of class oppression and class struggle".[20]

While we know that parliamentary systems of government have always been characterised by a manifest contradiction between the declared 'rule by the people' and the actual domination of the exploiters, it is also true that they provide a broader framework of political freedom and independent social and individual activity. Self-determination or political democracy in general was but the people's partial or limited demand which was necessary in creating a much more conducive climate for the achievement of further and fundamental democratic rights. What was expected of the Tanganyika nationalist leaders therefore, was to build a sound democratic tradition in the country upon attainment of independence, a tradition which could not, as we have shown, be evolved under the oppressive colonial rule. It was as a matter of fact a mandatory duty on the part of the TANU government, for democracy has always been a *sine qua non* for any healthy economic and political development. Whether this duty was diligently discharged is an issue we look into in the next sections.

The Independence Parliament
The Independence Parliament operating on Westminster lines[21] took off without an effective loyal opposition as a result of TANU's land-slide victory in the 1960 general elections which saw the political party snatching all but one of the 71 Legislative Council seats.[22] Even the remaining seat was won by an independent candidate, H. Sarwatt, who is reported to have been an active TANU member. Thus other political parties, especially the United Tanganyika Party (UTP) which took part in the elections but was severely beaten, were virtually unrepresented in the Independence Parliament. The absence of an effective opposition in the Independence Parliament (which consisted of the National Assembly and the Governor-General on behalf of Her

Majesty)[23] did not have much effect on the House's role and authority.

Constitutionally the central institution of government, the Independence Parliament's supremacy, was acknowledged by both the ruling party and the executive branch of the government by words and deeds. There are several cases which bear ample testimony to this fact such as the decision to turn Tanganyika into a Republic. A recommendation to this effect was first made by TANU in January 1962 at its National Executive Committee (NEC) meeting. According to MacAuslan, "it was at that meeting that it was also announced that TANU had recommended to the Government that Tanganyika become a republic as soon as possible, and the government had accepted that recommendation".[24]

The Government then presented the matter to the National Assembly. A motion was first introduced in the House inviting the government "to draft such amendments to the Constitution as may be necessary to provide that Tanganyika becomes a republic within the Commonwealth as soon as possible". Introducing the motion in the National Assembly, the Prime Minister said, "It would obviously be wrong for the government to spend time in considering the form which our new republic should take if in fact the members do not want a republic at all".[25] The motion was passed on February 15, 1962.

Secondly, a Government Paper entitled "Proposals of the Tanganyika Government for a Republic" was published and submitted to the House for deliberation. The Prime Minister, introducing the proposals in the House, spoke of parliament as being "the voice of the nation and fount of authority which must remain sovereign". He went on stating that "if the proposals contained in this white paper are approved by the National Assembly at this sitting, as I hope they will be, legislative provision will be made at this sitting of the Assembly for the President-Designate of the Republic of Tanganyika, and on December 9, 1962 Tanganyika will become a Republic within the Commonwealth".[26] The proposals were debated and finally agreed on in the National Assembly on June 28, 1962.

The above constitutional issue clearly demonstrates the status of the Independence Parliament *vis a vis* the Party and the executive. It is apparent that in spite of the Party's resolution, the government could not proceed with the matter without the assembly's approval. This means that if the Assembly had rejected the motion, the government would have undoubtedly dropped the matter. The position of TANU during this period reflects the positon of political parties in the Westminster model.[27] Msekwa aptly observes that, "Parliament was thus seen not only as the supreme law making body in the land, but also as the institution whereby people through their representatives, were to exercise their supreme authority in decision making".[28] Msekwa, the first black Tanganyikan to hold the position of Clerk to the National Assembly in 1962, testifies that the Independence Parliament was held in high esteem by members of the executive and the general public.[29]

The Assembly's Standing Orders provided for the appointment of standing and select committees to scrutinise any particular aspect of government activity such as public expenditure which was entrusted to the Public Accounts Committee. The House's control extended further to the consideration of budget speeches and annual estimates of revenue and expenditure by government ministeries. Back benchers could as well introduce private member's bills although this opportunity was not fully utilised by the MPs.

Pratt observes that each cabinet minister was individually responsible to Parliament for the administration and the detailed policies of his ministry; members of the cabinet were collectively responsible to parliament and to the country for the major policies of the government.[30] The Governor-General was obliged to follow the advice of the Cabinet, except in cases where by law he was enjoined to act on the advice of some other person or body and in certain situations, in which he was expressly directed to act on "his own deliberate judgement".[31] The Governor-General was also obliged to dissolve parliament if it passed a resolution of no confidence in the government and the Prime Minister did not resign within three days. But if the resolution was one passed within 14 days of the commencement of a new session following a general election and he considered it might be attributed to changes in the membership of the Assembly caused by the election, he had the option, instead of ordering a dissolution, of removing the Prime Minister.[32]

The Independence Constitution in short created a situation which could not allow the government of the day to fool around. Almost every government proposal before the House was subjected to rigorous scrutiny, frank and fearless exchange of views among parliamentarians.[33] The Prime Minister and his team were kept on their toes. The Speaker was in no better position, for apart from keeping the fervent discussions within acceptable limits, there were just too many interventions from the back-benchers to keep pace with. "So many interruptions would do nobody any good", complained the Speaker at one point, "I would suggest that the Minister without Portfolio continues now".[34]

One of the most important and heated debates since independence was on the proposal we touched on earlier of making Tanganyika a republic. The MP for Rungwe, Mwakangale—one of the firebrands in the Independence Parliament—was not happy at all with the provision of Tanganyika becoming a Commonwealth member upon assuming the republic status. "I have several times referred to the Commonwealth as another form of British Empire, another imperialist bloc, one of the biggest capitalists, exploiting us even though we are independent",[35] Mwakangale argued. He was challenged by the Prime Minister, Rashidi Kawawa (who had taken over from Nyerere when he resigned from premiership in January 1962 to devote his full attention as President of TANU) to substantiate the "allegations on the Commonwealth". For to President Kawawa, the Commonwealth was in fact a "wonderful comity of nations".[36]

In reply, Mwakangale said the Commonwealth was headed by the Queen of Britain and that Britain was against the independence of the then existing African colonies which included Angola and Portuguese East Africa (Mozambique). On top of that, Mwakangale argued, Britain was a member of the North Atlantic Treaty Organisation (NATO) which he called an imperialist military bloc. The MP said there was no need for Tanganyika to remain in the Commonwealth headed by people who helped gangsters to massacre "our people in Angola". He saw the Commonwealth as a means of disuniting Africa by forming blocs, the English bloc, the Casablanca group, the Monrovia group and so on. "I say Sir, there is no need to remain in the Commonwealth",[37] he concluded. Nyerere, seated in the House as a back-bencher, took the floor admitting that Mwakangale's speeches always provoked him. He took time to explain the matter arguing that he was a supporter of the Commonwealth and African unity, and that if African unity was endangered by the move, Tanganyika would pull out of the Commonwealth.[38]

Nyerere's charisma as the brain of the TANU movement did not help much in holding back the radicals. Other MPs, Tumbo (Mpanda) and Kundya (Singida)[39] maintained Mwakangale's stand against the Commonwealth. The Mpanda MP went further to express concern over the wide powers of the executive President to misuse it.[40] Another MP argued that it was improper to make provisions for the wide powers by taking into account personalities. "'Power of the President ought to be reduced. We must not base our decision on our good leaders like Nyerere and the Prime Minister. They will go. And the Constitution will continue for a long time. Such power to be given to one person is dangerous".[41]

Nyerere rose to rationalise the strong presidential power: "Any government in the world is a dictator ... It has all the coercive means, it has the police, it has the armed forces; and it is incredible when one thinks of it ... *And yet an individual can push these out of power, and elect someone else to go and control the armed forces*"[42] (emphasis added). The question how and under what proposed constitutional provisions would an individual manage to push the powerful chief executive from power, was tactfully avoided by the back-bencher. With the backing of reactionary elements in the House obsessed by expectations of more material rewards under the proposed republic, the Act to Declare the Constitution of Tanganyika[43] was ultimately passed by the Constituent Assembly[44] on November 23, 1962 with most if not all the controversial provisions attacked by some radical MPs virtually intact. The Act placed the country in an irreversible process towards concentration of power in the executive and erosion of people's democratic rights.

The Republican Constitution

Preparations for the first Presidential Election under the President Designate (Election) Act of 1962, started on June 18, 1962 with the registration of voters throughout the country. A total of 1,800,000 voters in 50 electoral constituencies were registered. There were two candidates contesting for the seat—Julius Nyerere (TANU President) and Zuberi Mtemvu (President of the African National Congress—ANC) who prior to independence was TANU's Provincial Secretary, but broke away to form the ANC which resolved to adopt a more radical approach to the independence question.[45] The election held on November 1, 1962 saw ANC candidate, Mtemvu badly beaten by TANU's Nyerere who obtained 1,127,978 votes as against 21,276 polled by his opponent. Nyerere became the first executive President of Tanganyika under the Republican Constitution and assumed office on December 9, 1962.

It is important to take note of the fact that the arrangements for the inauguration of the Republic involved retention, for "an interim period"[46], of the National Assembly in its then existing form.[47] The full republican changes in relation to the Assembly were to be effected only after the expiry of that period. After expiry of the 'interim period', the Assembly was to comprise 107 elected members and, until parliament otherwise provided, not more than 10 nominated members. We now proceed to argue that the coming into effect of the Republican Constitution marked the beginning of the weakening of parliamentary authority *vis a vis* the Party and the executive as well as a noticeable departure from the Westminster model.

Indeed, the assurance given earlier by the government that the proposal to have an executive President would in no way derogate from the authority or status of parliament,[48] stood in contrast to the position which the Republican Parliament found itself in. First of all, we note the tremendous broadening of power and scope of the government and an increase in the authority of the chief executive under the Republican Constitution at the expense of the legislature. Under the Constitution, the President becomes the Head of State[49] and Commander-in-Chief of the Armed Forces;[50] the executive power of the republic were vested in him and (unless otherwise provided by law) in the exercise of his functions he was to act in his own discretion, without being obliged to follow advice tendered by any person.[51] He was thus not bound by the British convention inhibiting the chief executive from acting otherwise than in accordance with ministerial advice.

The Constitution empowered the President at any time to dissolve parliament[52], the power which under the Independence Constitution rested in the Governor-General and could only be exercised where the National Assembly passed a resolution of no confidence in the government and the Prime Minister did not resign within three days.[53] To inject further impotence into the National Assembly, the Republican Constitution robbed it of its vital weapon to control the actions of the executive i.e. the vote of no confidence. Therefore under the Constitution there were no other circumstances than the effluxion of time (or according to Article 34(4) of the Constitution the President's refusal to assent to a Bill which had been re-presented) that could bring about a general election. After all, there was no mention in the Constitution of collective ministerial responsibility which was expressly made part of the Independence Constitution,[54] a lacuna which left the Assembly without any effective remedy against the government as a whole for decisions of which it did not approve.

The relationship between the Cabinet and the Head of State was also qualified to inject further authority into one man. The Constitution restricted the advisory functions of the Cabinet to ''such matters *as may be referred to it* under any general or special directions of the President''[55] (emphasis added). Looking at the previous Constitution, there was no such limitation on the initiative of the Cabinet, which could proffer advice to the Governor-General on any topic whatever relating to the government of Tanganyika.[56] Worse still, under Article 17 of the Republican Constitution, the chief executive could even control the agenda for the Cabinet meetings! The next Article i.e. 18, vested in the President almost absolute power over the Civil Service of constituting and abolishing offices, and making appointments to such offices, and promotion, termination of appointment, dismissal and disciplinary control of persons appointed to such offices.

During the debate on the government's proposals for a republic in the Assembly, Nyerere—aware of the enormous powers he would be wielding upon being elected President—assured the MPs that ''Commonsense, decency, intelligence and good sense'' would prevent any abuse of such wide powers on the part of the President to be. He went on to say, "if he tries (to misuse the powers), the people of Tanganyika would simply say 'NO'. . . that 'NO' is really what is going to be a safeguard against these powers, which I accept are terrific powers".[57]

This is a typical instance of employing sophism. To start with, one is asked to believe that what the would-be President would consider as commonsense or decent, would necessarily be commonsense or decent to his fellow petty-bourgeoisie and the workers and peasants alike. Secondly, one is also called upon to believe that in a society split into distinct antagonistic classes, a simple 'NO' (which is not even provided for in the Constitution) can be an effective safeguard of the ruled. Even if the so-called 'NO' safeguard was plausible in the context of Tanganyika, the question is through which organ would the people register their so-called 'NO'? There was none, for the only organ through which the people could at least air their grievances effectively—the Parliament—was already muzzled by the 1962 Constitutional changes.

Apart from the above powers provided for in the 1962 Constitution, the President enjoyed additional powers flowing from other pieces of legislation. The Preventive Detention Act[58] to start with, which was based on the principle that "the executive, especially in the circumstances of a new nation such as ours, must have the necessary powers to carry out the functions of a modern state",[59] gave the President sweeping powers of detention without trial that could not be challenged in any court of law and the detainee could only appeal to an advisory committee the decisions of which were not binding.[60] The legislation represented a return to the autocratic system of government which existed in the colonial era.

The President also gained the power to 'deport' citizens from one part of the country to another and 'to expel' undesirables under the Deportation Ordinance[61] and the Expulsion of Undesirables Ordinance[62] both being pieces of colonial legislation adopted by independent Tanganyika. The Emergency Powers Order-in-Council of 1939 also gave the chief executive prerogative to declare an emergency.[63] This list is not easy to exhaust, but important to note here is that all the above powers and others, were conferred upon the President in the widest discretionary terms possible and they were all extremely subjective. The Assembly's authority was relegated to the sidelines and as if this was not enough the Constitution further imposed restrictions on the House with regard to certain financial measures,[64] a development which ran counter to the liberal democratic concept of parliamentary sovereignty discussed in detail earlier. As McAuslan correctly observes, this restriction on the Assembly was intended to ensure that parliament imposes "only that taxation which is in accordance with the wishes of the government".[65]

The 1962 constitutional changes did not only heap wide powers on the President but also initiated, albeit indirectly, a movement towards party supremacy and consequently the entombment of the National Assembly. Although the position of the party *vis a vis* the National Assembly was not altered by the 1962 constitutional changes, the movement cannot be said to have been unexpected. For all MPs and top members of the executive were TANU members and the most powerful man in the country was also the TANU President. Thus TANU was in every respect running the show in the country.

The decision to make Tanganyika a *de jure* one-party state bears enough evidence. A resolution to that effect was passed at the meeting of TANU's National Executive Committee (NEC) in January 1963, authorising the TANU President to set up a commission which would deal with the matter.[66] NEC's resolution was a month later endorsed by TANU's Annual Conference in Dar es Salaam which directed the government to give statutory recognition to the one-party system of government in Tanganyika. The Commission's report was later submitted to an extraordinary meeting of the TANU Annual Conference (attended by Afro-Shirazi Party delegates) held on June 1 and 2, 1965 which gave a final approval to the recommendations therein. A Bill for a Constitution based on the proposals was thereafter drafted and presented to the National Assembly in July and passed to become law on July 10, 1965 on which date Tanzania became a *de jure* one-party state. This constitutional issue demonstrates the beginning of a change in government procedures for seeking a mandate to produce major changes. No motion was introduced in the National Assembly to invite the government to present proposals for the desired changes in the Constitution. What we saw instead, was the Assembly being simply required to rubber-stamp what was already decided by the Party.

It is interesting to note that even the attitudes of the members of the executive branch especially the ministers, exhibited a marked change. Conscious of the wide powers vested in their immediate boss and the fading status of the Assembly, ministers adopted an authoritative tone. Unlike in the Independence Parliament, it was now the ministers who were arrogantly interrupting MPs' speeches. Why? Simply because MPs no longer posed a threat to their positions. Apart from that, with the 1962 constitutional changes, ministers felt more and more accountable only to the President. For instance in the February 1963 session, the MP for Mpanda, Mbogo was arrogantly interrupted twice by the Minister for Agriculture and the Vice-President who was leader of government business in the House[67] when he criticised abuse of power by government officials. Vice-

President Kawawa went so far as calling the Honourable MP for Mpanda a 'liar' for accusing government officials of not being accessible to the people.[68]

During the same session, Kawawa lashed out at the MP for Kilway, Baghadelleh for disputing a Minister's statement as crooked. "It is not the procedure of this House to refer to answers given by the government as lies. Tell the truth if you know it",[69] Kawawa fumed, forgetting that he had earlier used the same derogatory word 'liar' in reference to the MP for Mpanda. The Vice-President gave the MPs a stern warning against blaming the government instead of co-operating with it to "build the new nation". The above and numerous other cases demonstrate clearly the confidence of the executive in the country's hierarchy of power. The MPs, on the other hand, were also realising fast that the honeymoon was over.

Reasons Behind the Swift Dismantling of the Westminster Model
The disturbing question at this juncture is what gave rise to the dismantling of the Westminster type of constitution? The answer lies in the class character of the state and the ruling class in post-colonial Tanganyika. We stated earlier that in a colonial situation, it is the dominating foreign power which runs the entire show in the subject territory through the use of the colonial state. The colonial state as we have already shown does not in any way constitute a separate state from the imperialist state. For with the colonisation of a particular territory, the colonising power extends certain apparatuses of the imperialist state to its colony which keep the colonial people in political and economic servitude.[70] The colonial state or rather the state in the subject territory therefore, remains simply as an extension of the imperialist state in the hands of the ruling class of the colonising power. In pre-independence Tanganyika likewise, the colonial state was nothing but part of the British imperialist state with the metropolitan bourgeoisie as the ruling class. By state here, we mean an organ for the maintenance of the rule of one class over another.

Tanganyika's attainment of political independence in 1961 altered considerably the class character of state power in the country. Fundamentally, it severed the direct and overall political subordination of the country to imperialist Britain on the basis of state power being in the hands of the colonising power. Tanganyika was therefore no longer a colony but a separate national state with the petty bourgeoisie who led the independence campaign constituting the new ruling class. The creation of a separate state however does not suggest that Tanganyika was free from the economic domination of finance capital. But, as Shivji puts it, "it does mean that the state power in this state is no more directly controlled by the ruling class of the former colonising power".[71]

This "economic aspect" however, has fascinated a number of scholars in Africa who have as a result come out with controversial discourses on the question of the state in former subject territories. These scholars, capitalising on the economic dominance of finance capital, forcefully argue that political independence in the neo-colonies did not bring about any change in the class character of state power.[72] They contend that the ruling class remains the financial oligarchy in whose hands all capital is concentrated at a global level. As an economically dominant class in the capital world, this group of financial magnets controls and dominates the economic and political life of both neo-colonial and imperialist states.[73]

The implication of this thesis which flatly denies any concept of relative autonomy of politics within the dominated social formations is that all political developments in the neo-colonies (such as the dismantling of the Westminster Model in Tanganyika in 1962) should be taken as a direct dictation by this ubiquitous ruling class. This global ruling class, the international financial oligarchy, should be seen as well as the immediate enemy for the working class in the neo-colonies to marshall its forces against.

We refrain from dwelling at length on this school lest we lose trend of our main discussion. It is sufficient to point out that the main theoretical weakness of this school stems from its failure to appreciate the strategic importance of democratic struggles at a political level. For it considers political independence, or the establishment of separate national states, as unachievable from the point of view of finance capital, a proposition which Lenin considered as emanating from "sheer confusion".[74]

Armed with this discredited proposition, the exponents of this school fail to grasp concrete political movements in the neo-colonies and resort to subjectivist explanations. To them, with the rise of imperialism all bourgeoisies are "negated" or "destroyed" by the financial oligarchy.[75] Thus in all dominated social formations there exists, apart from the proletariat and the peasantry, the *petty bourgeoisie* who constitute an impotent class of intermediaries for finance capital.[76] And these petty bourgeoisie have nothing to do with the state power with the exception of providing personnel for the state apparatuses!

Such an analysis surely gives rise to a static evaluation of indigenous classes in neo-colonies and obscures the way in which these classes reproduce themselves. Thus the proletariat is called upon to ignore the identifiable, local and existing enemy (for he is simply a 'robot') and lead a revolution against "an unseen, abstract international ruling class".[77] Such serious theoretical weaknesses which fail to identify the petty bourgeoisie as a local manifestation of imperialism with its own class interests arising from the place it occupies in social production, help to explain why this school is increasingly losing ground among enlightened scholars. Without concrete analysis of the neo-colonies, one ends up exonerating the mushrooming authoritarian regimes in the neo-colonies from blame exactly as the above school does rather than providing a revolutionary guide to action for the working-class movement.

We proceed to argue that with the attainment of political independence in 1961, the state power in Tanganyika was 'captured' by a petty bourgeois class comprising of trade union leaders, small businesmen, co-operative activists, teachers and other junior civil servants. It was a numerically small class with a peasant class origin but the only one better placed and organised to mobilise the various strata of the population for national self-determination. The wage-earning class was weak and very small given the country's poor industrial base at the material time and the peasantry, though large in number, did not constitute an organised political force under the colonial conditions.

When independence came, the petty bourgeois class in power, bereft of any feasible philosophy or strategy of advancing and consolidating people's political gains, proved a failure on both the political and economic fronts. On the political front, the petty bourgeoisie could not dismantle the colonial state and restructure it to meet the aspirations of the broad masses of the people. Instead, they inherited an oppressive state machine designed to serve colonial interests and became preoccupied with structural reforms which as, Hugh Stevens puts it, "were no more than minor adjustments in the colonial system".[78]

On the economic front, they failed to break up the exploitative production relations and backward forms of social and economic organisation. In other words they retained the colonial economic structure in the country. The furthest they could go was to install a few import-substitution and export industries, carry on with outward looking agricultural policies and adopt a permanent foreign-aid-mobilising strategy. Tanganyika, already an economically wretched country with the bulk of the population dependent on subsistence agriculture and living close to the hunger line, was integrated deeper into the world capitalist system which was responsible for its wretchedness in the first place.

The workers' and peasants' expectations were shattered as they saw no real improvement in their lot. They lost confidence in the leadership which resided in erstwhile European mansions, drove expensive cars and enjoyed all the privileges of the former colonial bosses while their welfare was neglected. Realising that independence was not for them, they lost enthusiasm to respond to campaigns for hard work under the independence government's slogan—"Uhuru ni Kazi" i.e. Freedom Means Work. A clear gulf between the people and leadership emerged which haunted the latter in no small way.

At the same time, a cleavage was emerging within the petty-bourgeois class on the question of the affluent minorities who continued to occupy senior posts in the government and enjoy a dominant position in the commercial sector. A good portion of the petty bourgeoisie, such as the African traders, professionals and civil servants whose main aspiration was to step into the shoes of non-Africans after independence, became vocal on the issue of Africanisation of the civil service and the economy and blamed the government for being inactive. Some trade union leaders, members of parliament and even journalists became the key spokesmen of the Africanisation campaign. Leys reports that several "crudely racialistic" editorials started appearing in the TANU-owned newspaper *UHURU*, some of which echoed controversial speeches made in the House smacking of anti-minority sentiments.[79]

When the government tabled the Citizenship Bill to the House in 1961 which sought to extend automatic citizenship to people of any race but born in Tanganyika and having one parent born in the country as well as previous immigrants into Tanganyika, a number of MPs vigorously opposed it. They proposed that citizenship be based on race. ". . . the white population has been dominating us, both economically and politically, and their neighbours, the Asians, have been economically dominating us, we Africans . . . Do you think the individual African . . . will agree to have equal rights with Europeans and Asians? My answer is no . . . ",[80] John Mwakangale, the Southern Highlands representative told the House.

European administrators and technicians feeling apprehensive for their safety, started resigning from government service. It is estimated that towards the end of 1961, resignations had risen from 20 to 50% and some government services were visibly running down.[81] This was another headache for the government. Nyerere however, could not accept divorcing citizenship from loyalty and marry it to colour. He was also not prepared to embark on the Africanisation programme just for the sake of it. He only accepted in principle the demand for Africanisation in the public service but not at the speed and extent which was being suggested. Nyerere's position widened the area of disagreements between the government and some trade union leaders who apart from differing with the government on the questions of citizenship and Africanisation, were demanding increased autonomy for the trade unions. The differences led to a series of strikes in

1962.[82] The government reacted by passing two pieces of legislation, one which virtually outlawed strikes without permission of the Minister of Labour[83] and other which facilitated official supervision by requiring all unions to affiliate with TFL to retain legal standing.[84]

An outbreak of illegal strikes on the sisal plantations during the latter part of 1962 which saw TFL Secretary General, Victor Mkello deported to a remote part of the Western Region for three months, led to the dissolution of TFL and the requirement on all workers to belong to a single organisation—the National Union of Tanganyika Workers (NUTA).[85] The TANU government became uneasy with other segments of Africans in the economy such as the agricultural marketing co-operatives which appeared to be enjoying a wide autonomy. In 1962, the 34 co-operative unions and 850 primary societies producing about one-fourth of the country's exports, were brought together in the government-sponsored Co-operative Union of Tanganyika (C.U.T.).

During the same period, a crisis was brewing within the ruling Party itself and its popularity was waning fast as a result of the NEC called on January 16, 1962 by pressure of some up-country members, Nyerere was confronted with a sustained criticism, calling for more rapid development, the establishment of a republic (under which they thought their lot would improve), the end of reserved seats for minority races in the Assembly and more rapid Africanisation of government service. Nyerere, who did not expect such strident complaints from his supporters, realised the gravity of the political situation in the country which was bound to worsen. Shortly thereafter, Nyerere resigned as Prime Minister. Although his resignation from premiership is often attributed to his "strong desire" to "reorganise, reshape and recharge" TANU, we believe that it was in response to the growing political tension in the country which shook the foundations of the independence government. His temporary absence from the high office helped in avoiding an imminent split with the radicals in the Party and the government and provided him with ample opportunity to ponder over the next move.

Several factors point to the fact that the ruling section of the petty bourgeoisie, conscious of its weakness numerically an economically, saw its salvation in the establishment of a strong executive power was carried into the parliament. The principal target of the ruling petty bourgeoisie was the Westminster type of constitution of 1961. This had to be dismantled as a first step towards strong executive power. Thus the 1962 constitutional debate saw Nyerere and other ruling petty bourgeoisie seated in the House as back-benchers, campaigning vigourously for the introduction of sweeping changes in the 1961 Constitution. They out smarted their opponents in the House by invoking nationalistic sentiments that the 1961 Constitution was a British piece of legislation which was unsuited to local circumstances. They underscored the need for strong executive government if the country's social and economic problems were to be dealt with effectively. At the end of the day, they emerged the victors with the passing of the 1962 Republican Constitution which dismantled the Westminster Model. Several democratic rights incorporated in the previous constitution were nullified and the National Assembly which was increasingly proving to be obstinate to the government, thus unreliable, was 'castrated'. Armed with enormous powers flowing from the constitution and other representative legislation, the ruling class embarked on a systematic programme to reorganise the state and establish its political and economic hegemony in the country.

The one-party parliament

The movement towards one-party system of government in Tanganyika was part and parcel of the response of the petty bourgeois class in power to consolidate itself and stifle political opposition in face of sharpening contradictions in the country resulting from its failure to deliver the goods of independence to the people. Its response included the dissolution of the militant trade union movement, curtailment of the autonomy of the giant co-operative movement, nullification of democratic rights incorporated in the constitution, vesting of enormous constitutional powers in the president, deprivation of parliament of the prerogative of the supreme organ of power and control over the policy of the state and enactment of legislation conferring on the chief executive wide discretionary powers over life and property.

To prevent the formation of local opposition and improve the responsiveness of government machinery, the government replaced British personnel in all important regional administration posts with staunch TANU members.[87] Stephens says TANU's presence was also extended to the local level when chiefs and their appointed native authority councils were removed and replaced by elected district councils wherever possible. These councils were chaired by local TANU leaders with Area Commissioners as secretaries.[88] This was during the first three years of sovereignty when the nationalist leadership acted for the most part in response to implicit or explicit challenges to its authority.[89]

The strong-power strategy however, could neither bail the country out of economic stagnation nor resolve the contradictions in the country. In January 1964, soldiers of the Tanganyika Rifles at Colito Barracks outside Dar es Salaam mutinied against the government for higher salaries and Africanisation of the officer corps. The mutiny which spread to another barracks in Tabora, was crushed by British Royal Marines at Nyerere's request. The government reacted further by disbanding the army and reconstituted a new one renamed the Tanzania People's Defence Forces (TPDF) which drew its recruits from the ranks of the TANU Youth League and the National Youth Service. Apart from ensuring that TPDF recruits were TANU members, the government gave permission to all civil servants to join the party. The move was to guarantee party loyalty in every branch of government.

It is interesting to note that just after the mutiny, President Nyerere appointed a Presidential Commission to consider and make recommendations on the one-party system in Tanzania. In fact as early as 1962, Nyerere was already underscoring the importance of one-party democracy, albeit indirectly, and by January 1963, TANU's NEC had already decided in principle to abolish opposition parties in the country and establish a one-party state. What we are saying however is that the move was born out of the post-independence challenges against the TANU government. The 1964 mutiny worked as a catalyst which accelerated the process.[90]

The main reasons advanced by the TANU government for the move, were that apart from the colonial government's open opposition to TANU, the political movement managed to snatch 'landslide' victory in both the first and second pre-independence general elections. Thus even to Msekwa, "Tanganyikans had become by the choice of the people themselves, a one-party state",[91] and that TANU represented the interests of the bulk of Tanganyikans. Secondly, a multi-party system of government gives rise to unnecessary factions and internal divisions. We maintain that every political party whether it receives or does not receive enough votes in a general election, is an organised expression of the will of a particular class. TANU which was under the leadership of reactionary petty bourgeois elements, was and remained a vehicle for attaining petty bourgeois class interests. After all, the first and second pre-independence general elections proudly referred to by TANU notables cannot be taken to have reflected an objective picture because of the literacy, income and employment requirements for one to be eligible to vote. Since the bulk of the population was still wallowing in abject poverty and ignorance, only a few Tanganyikans (mostly businessmen, petty traders, kulaks and the urban elite) could meet the tough franchise conditions. In the 1958/59 general elections for instance, only 59,291 people were registered to vote out of an estimated population of 8.8 million. Likewise in the 1960 elections, only 885,000 people out of an estimated population of 8.9 million were registered as voters.[92]

It is apparent therefore that only a small segment of the people of Tanganyika took part in the two elections, a fact which counters TANU's reasoning. Furthermore, apart from the UTP and ANC, there were several other live political parties before 1965 which were gaining increasing support and popularity in the country such as: the All Muslim National Union of Tanganyika (AMNUT), the People's Democratic Party (PDP) led by Kasanga Tumbo, the People's Convention Party (PCP) formed by one Samson Mshala in Mwanza, and the Nationalist Enterprise Party (NEP) established by Yahya Hussein. CPC and NEP were later merged to form the African Independence Movement (AIM).[93] The existence of these parties alongside TANU up to 1965, further disproves the assertion that TANU enjoyed virtually uncontested political support and influence in the country before and after independence. The fact is that TANU was but one political party among several effective parties none of which commanded a monopoly of political support in the country. This is why as early as 1962, TANU—feeling threatened by the growing opposition parties—embarked on a systematic campaign to stifle the entire opposition. According to Pratt, "the several tiny parties ... were harassed out of existence, their leaders deported or detained and their right to register and hold meetings severely restricted".[94] Looking at these post-colonial developments critically, we fail to see, unlike Msekwa, how the people of Tanganyika had become by *their own choice* members of a single party—TANU—and thus in favour of a one-party system of government.

With regard to the second reason advanced by the TANU government to justify the single-party system, we submit that factions and internal divisions are not products of multi-party systems of government but are permanent features in any class structured society. Today, almost two decades after the establishment of a one-party system than trebled principally because the 1965 swing to one-party system neither altered the relations of production in the country nor created favourable conditions towards the achievement of fundamental democratic rights. In any event, the new constitution—the Interim Constitution of the United Republic of Tanzania hereinafter referred to as the Interim Constitution,[95] making Tanzania a formal one-party republic—was approved by the National Assembly on July 5, 1965.[96]

Introduction of the New Electoral System
Five days later, the National Assembly was dissolved to allow the holding of fresh elections under a novel electoral system the legal and administrative framework of which was set out in the Interim Constitution, the National Assembly (Elections) Act of 1964[97] and its Amendment Act of 1965 and the Report of the Election Rules Committee. In brief, the Assembly or the Union Parliament was to consist

of 107 elected representatives plus Regional Commissioners as *ex officio* members. 15 national members who would be chosen by the elected MPs, and up to 10 members nominated by the President, with additional nominated and *ex-officio* members representing Zanzibar.

Unlike the previous elections, there were no service, income or literacy qualifications for one to be eligible to vote or stand for election. The only qualifications for voters were 21 years of age or above and Tanzanian citizenship. Aspiring candidates, apart from the age and citizenship qualifications, were required to be faithful TANU or ASP members, persons of sound mind, not under sentence of death or of imprisonment or under deportation order, and persons nominated by not less than 25 eligible voters and not registered for election in more than one constituency. The electoral process was divided into two separate parts: the selection of candidates which became the special responsibility of party organs, and general elections based on universal suffrage. This was a new development which placed the country's electoral process firmly under the party's control as will be shown in due course.

From June 1965, the constitution of the party had become an integral part of the Interim Constitution and the party became, what Msekwa terms, a Constitutional category not common in the legal theory of parliamentary systems of government.[98] Among the party's new roles was the preliminary and final selection of candidates for election to the National Assembly.[99] The Interim Constitution had therefore elevated the normal role of a political party in the electoral process into a constitutional role which broke down into three stages: primaries, final nomination and running the campaigns.

Under the new electoral system, the primary nomination takes place at district level. The Party Annual District Conference (ADC) interviews all the aspiring candidates and records preference votes. The list of preferences is sent by the returning officer to the NEC, which holds a special meeting to consider all the candidates from the preference lists drawn up by the ADCs. The NEC meeting nominates only two candidates to contest the election in each constituency and is not bound by the order of preferences expressed at the ADC.

Its other function is to give special symbols to the two nominated candidates—the hoe or the house. These symbols had a devastating effect in the 1965 elections for in most constituencies there was a general feeling that the hoe was more important than the house and the voters became more concerned with the symbols rather than the candidates. Even the candidates themselves exploited this confusion to the maximum. In Karagwe, for instance, Gressim Kazimoto (a hoe candidate) was so sure of the value of his symbol that he quite often opened his campaign speeches by saying: ''I think it is enough for me just to stand here and show you my symbol; it is quite enough to win your support . . ."[100]

Researchers into these symbols indicate that hoe candidates were more successful in the elections because the hoe to the electorate, was not only more unequivocal and more universally accepted but also dynamic, linked with positive traditional (agriculture) and modern (development) activities and ideas.[101]

The new electoral system placed the party in a position of ensuring victory to the candidate it preferred by simply giving him a weak opponent and the hoe symbol. For instance, in the 1980 general elections all cabinet ministers with the exception of one, were given the hoe symbol and out of 109 elected MPs, 74 were "hoe candidates."

The third stage is the campaign which is required to be conducted under the auspices of the Party. Candidates are required to share a common platform of campaign meetings and electoral activities organised by the TANU District Executive Committees (DECs). The Party's central role in the electoral process was also extended to the non-competitive Presidential election. A single candidate is nominated by the party (i.e. the joint meetings of the Annual Conferences of TANU and ASP). The voting procedure provided for a direct affirmative vote for the single candidate, who had to receive more than 50% "yes" votes to be returned.

Towards Party Supremacy

The strengthening of TANU's control of the electoral process went hand in hand with the elevation of the ruling party into a supreme organ of power and control over the policies of the state. This was seen as in conformity with Articles 3(1) and 3(3) of the Interim Constitution which provided that, "there shall be one political party in Tanzania" and "all political activities in Tanzania . . . shall be conducted by or under the auspices of the party". On October 30, 1965, the Assembly committed further suicide by passing an Act to confer on the NEC like privileges relating to the summoning of witnesses, the taking of evidence and production of documents as were enjoyed by the Assembly. The Act prescribed suitable penalties for disobeying any order of the NEC for attendance, for refusing to be examined before or answer questions put by the NEC and for presenting false information or fabricated documents to the NEC with intent to deceive it.[102] We see thereafter the country's ruling class increasingly using the Party as the forum for deliberating all important policies and measures in the country. In 1967 for instance, the NEC discussed at length the question of building Ujamaa and Self-Reliance in the country and adopted the Arusha Declaration, an authoritative policy decision which the government and other public institutions including the National Assembly, were simply required to endorse and implement and not to discuss. Msekwa rightly observes that, "it is the Arusha meeting of the NEC which brought that institution (NEC) firmly in the limelight as an important and powerful policy making organ. Thereafter its meetings were given close attention by the public and mass media".[103]

We also note that the Arusha meeting not only brought the NEC in the limelight, but also asserted the Party's *de facto* supremacy over other public institutions. And it is this meeting which sparked off the controversial debate in the country on the position of the NEC and the National Assembly in the hierarchy of authority. In the June/July 1967 Budget session, a question by parliamentarian P.T. Ndobho (Musoma North) appeared on the Order Paper calling upon the government to clear the dust over the supremacy issue between the party and the National Assembly.[104] Although this question was played down by the government, it resurfaced in the next Budget session through the MP for Iringa South, M. Chogga who was taking part in a debate on the Interim Constitution of Tanzania Amendment Bill.

Chogga proposed that Article 6(2) of the Constitution be amended to make provision for the National Assembly to be "constitutionally the adviser of the President" of Tanzania.[105] The amendment, he said, was to make it obligatory on the Preisdent to act only on the advice of the National Assembly which was "supreme". "Any matter which may be initially considered by any other organ, such as TANU or the Cabinet, should ultimately be submitted to the National Assembly for final approval or other action. That is the right kind of democracy for Tanzania and I don't accept any other arrangement as being democratic", said Chogga. This caused a sharp reaction from the then second Vice-President Kawawa who said TANU and ASP were supreme and all MPs disagreeing with the arrangement had to quit. Chogga however went further to attack the requirement for MPs to be TANU members. He argued that while TANU had only a quarter of the population as its members, it had power to strip off membership of TANU from an MP who was elected by three quarters of the population not having TANU membership.[106] Chogga had kindled the fire of war over the supremacy issue.

The issue was raised again in the October session by Chogga when taking part in a debate on the National Assembly (Alteration of the Number of Constituency Members) Bill of 1968. He began by expressing serious concern over the composition of the 204-member Assembly. The composition was 107 elected constituency members, 10 national members appointed by the President from the Mainland and the Isles, 15 members elected by the Assembly out of "mass organisations",[107] 20 Regional Commissioners (*ex-officio* members),

32 members of the Zanzibar Revolutionary Council and 20 members from the Isles appointed by the President in consultation with the First Vice-President who was also the ASP President. Chogga suggested that the National Assembly should have a big majority of elected members and elections should also be held in Zanzibar where since the 1964 Revolution no elections had taken place. He went further to suggest that three quarters of the President's powers be vested in the Assembly, Tanzania be a multi-party state and that there be more than one candidate for the presidency. He concluded by underscoring that it was parliament which was supreme and not TANU.[108]

National MP, W. Mwakitwange called on the government to clarify whether it was TANU which was leading the government or vice-versa.[109] A Junior Minister in the Second Vice-President's Office, Wambura said, "I want to make it clear that it is the party which is supreme and all MPs are expected to work under the leadership of the party. The party picked you in nominations and the party has the right to discipline you and dictate our tasks. It is high time the MPs should know where they come from and it is beyond any doubt that *this parliament belongs to TANU*",[110] (emphasis added). Mwakitwange retorted that while the party had the role to discipline MPs, who would discipline the party? Kawawa took the floor and hammered the point home that the party was supreme and constituted the "vanguard for the revolution. This must be understood once and for all".[111]

The final answer to this controversy which saw MPs like Chogga almost shedding tears by insisting on the supremacy of the *Bunge* and warning that "by trying to make TANU supreme we have been made to suffer many disadvantages",[112] was given by the NEC at its meeting in Tanga in the middle of October 1968. The NEC expelled seven MPs from the party "for having grossly violated the party creed both in their attitude and actions, and for showing clear opposition to the party and its politics and policies".[113] Kjekshus notes that the decision "confirmed the party as the sole policy maker and indicated parliament's subordinate and technical role as a legislature".[114] Two other prominent figures in the country were also expelled from the party. These were: Oscar Kambona (former Cabinet Minister and MP for Morogoro East and now in exile in Britain) and E. Anangisye (former Secretary General of TANU Youth League and MP for Rungwe North, detained and later released).[115]

The expulsion of the seven MPs in particular, meant that they had lost parliamentary seats. Articles 27, 30, 32 and 33 of the Interim Constitution when read together, require a person to be *inter alia* a party member in order to become an MP. By Article 35(1), if a sitting MP loses any of the qualifications, his seat is automatically vacated.

With the key trouble-makers in the House out of the way, the ruling class continued to use the party as the principal decision making organ of all important national policy matters. Among the key decisions made by the party after 1968 were the decentralisation of government machinery in 1972 and the transfer of the capital from Dar es Salaam to Dodoma in 1973. The Assembly's role was simply to rubber-stamp party decisions and directives.

We have already seen that following the 1965 constitutional changes, the 204-member Assembly has 107 elected members and the rest simply appointed or elected through indirect method. After the 1970 general elections, the Assembly opened with an enlarged composition of 220 members. 120 were elected through indirect method. Looking at the composition of the Independence and the Republican parliaments, there were 71 elected members and only 10 nominated members.

The wide margin between the two categories of MPs was narrowed down with the 1965 constitutional changed as shown above, washing away the representative character of parliament. A critical look at the composition of the 1965 and 1970 Assemblies, reveals that even what one sees as a narrow margin was virtually not there. For a good number of ministers and junior ministers are always appointed from the elected MPs, thus drastically reducing the voice of elected MPs in the House. For instance, the 1978 cabinet of 40 ministers consisted of 19 elected members and the 1980 39-member cabinet consisted of 18 elected members. In the final analysis, the number of nominated members has either been on par or exceeded that of elected MPs in the House. The dangers of having a House dominated by nominated MPs were well summarised by expelled MP for Iringa South, Chogga in 1968 when he told parliament that, "in many cases, Mr. Deputy Speaker, I don't believe in nominations. If a person nominates another, the nominee is and must follow and agree with the one who nominated him".[116] For, as the saying goes, he who pays the piper dictates the tunes.

Apart form this element, one notes that although legislative power was formally vested in the parliament by the Interim Constitution, the power was neither absolute nor exclusive. By Article 52 of the Interim Constitution, the Assembly was barred from proceeding with money bills without the President's permission. While on the one hand the government ensured that none of the key national issues were debated in the Assembly but only endorsed, on the other hand it made certain that parliament ceased to be a critic of the executive and a watchdog on government activity through various methods. One of the methods was to deal sternly with vocal MPs as was the case in 1968. The other method was to use state instruments such as the mass media to attack outspoken MPs.[117] What was expected from the post-1965 Assembly was simply to applaud proposed policies and not to criticise or oppose them. A wise parliamentarian was one who kept mum or waited to applaud government proposals, or in a conducive mood, asked inconsequential questions. In 1966 for instance, an MP squandered parliamentary time by demanding explanation as to why soldiers failed to salute MPs. In 1968 another MP is remembered to have suggested that incumbent MPs be honoured by having new streets in Dar es Salaam named after them![118]

The campaign to kill the effective role of parliament indeed paid off. For we see MPs already frightened into submission, supporting the government campaign to relegate Parliament to the sidelines. One parliamentarian, Mrs. Baraka, suggested in the House that if the government had no confidence in an MP, it should sack him and another MP, Ali Migeyo, "called upon the party to wipe out counter-revolutionary elements".[119] MP Crisant Mzindakaya argued that the party had the right to dismiss its members who turned out to be "unfit".[120] Kjekshus, describing the post 1965 parliament, says disagreements were muffled, criticism softened and the parliament arena was made open for compromise and accommodation.[121]

In 1973 however, a majority of MPs opposed the Income Tax Bill which proposed to increase income tax and to do away with children and marriage allowances on pretext that the allowances benefitted a small portion of the population. The next day Nyerere, disturbed by the MPs' stand,[122] threatened to dissolve parliament and ordered the House to meet the following month to reconsider the Bill. When the Assembly met again, it passed the Bill quietly and without any alteration for Nyerere's threat was still fresh in their minds.

The executive during this time continued to amass more powers. It became next to NEC in the country's hierarchy of power notwithstanding the fact that the same faces in the executive constituted the NEC. None of the enormous powers of the chief executive were altered by the 1965 constitutional changes. In fact, with the elevation of the party's authority, the chief executive who was at the same time the chief of the sole ruling political party, gained even more powers. The union between Tanganyika and Zanzibar extended his muscles to the isles. In fact, Nyerere himself admitted in an interview with BBC television in London that, "I have sufficient powers under the Constitution to be a dictator".[123]

The Post-1977 Parliament

The National Assembly received a further blow to its questionable authority with the coming into force of the Constitution of the United Republic of Tanzania of 1977 under which it constitutionally lost its supremacy to the party. The 1977 constitutional changes came as a result of the merger of TANU and ASP to form Chama cha Mapinduzi (CCM). Under Article 54(1) of the Constitution, the National Assembly became a committee of the National Conference of the party. S. 59(ii) of the CCM Constitution of 1977 underscored the point that all MPs were a committee of the National Conference whose function was to ensure implementation of party policies. With the 1977 Constitution therefore, the parliament remained without any significant role. Its function was simply to act as a sounding board and a forum for applauding and legitimising new party policies.

A good example is provided by President Nyerere's New Year message broadcast live by Radio Tanzania on December 31, 1982 (and reproduced in the government newspaper—the *Daily News* of January 1, 1983) in which he announced new tax measures: "You will already have heard of the new taxes which come into force tomorrow, the first of January 1983. *These tax measures will be debated in parliament in its next sitting, but in the meantime they have to be paid by everyone"*, (emphasis added). The President was sure that the Assembly would by any means endorse the measure. Democracy is indeed endangered when such an institution ceases to exercise effective control over legislation.

A unique practice of appointing MPs to hold key executive posts in public institutions is also growing roots in the country. The practice runs counter to the constitution itself which requires the National Assembly to play a supervisory role over the government in implementing party policies.[124] For how can an MP who at the same time holds a key executive position in a public institution effectively take to task an institution he heads? Today, almost all MPs from the mainland have been incorporated into the management of the numerous public institutions in the country. Some of them are directors in three to four different institutions.

With the 1977 constitutional changes, the Assembly's composition also left much to be desired. A breakdown of the members reveals the following structure:

- the Vice-President of the Union (*ex officio*)	1
- constituency members (directly elected)	111
- national members elected indirectly by the Assembly from amongst candidates nominated by mass organisations	15
- national members from regions elected indirectly by the Assembly	25
- Regional Commissioners (*ex officio*)	25

- National members elected indirectly by the Zanzibar House of Representatives	32
- national members from Zanzibar appointed by the President	20
- national members appointed by the President from the Mainland	10
TOTAL	239

Therefore MPs who were not directly elected by the people were 127, constituting the majority in the House. The preponderance of unelected MPs in the House, the relegation of the Assembly to a simple committee of the ruling Party and its deprivation of powers of control over the policies of the state, made the Tanzania parliament resemble a toothless bull-dog. It was no longer the parliament which in the early 1960s could bite; which constitutionally had direct control over legislation and indirect control over the executive's actions. It became after 1977 a passive legitimiser of party and executive decisions. This explains why several harsh and oppressive laws have over the past few years managed to get through the Assembly without any hindrance such as the now repealed Economic Sabotage (Special Provisions) Act of 1983. This Act established tribunals each manned by three people one of whom was a High Court Judge and the rest laymen. Furthermore, some members of the tribunals were MPs who took part in enacting the law in the House. Such a composition clearly disregarded the principle of separation of powers and the rule of natural justice against bias.

The Act also gave the police unlimited powers of search, arrest and detention of individuals on mere grounds of suspicion. It denied individuals suspected of having committed certain specified offences of the right of legal representation and upon conviction the right of appeal. The Act, which had no provision for bail to the accused persons, was made retrospective by the legislature. The Act was replaced in 1984 by the Economic and Organised Crime Control Act which in place of tribunals creates special courts within the ordinary court system, called the Economic Crimes Courts.[125] The special courts' composition remains one High Court Judge and two lay members.[126] It is the majority decision which is the decision of these courts.[127]

The 1977 constitutional changes did not alter the party's heavy hand in the country's electoral process. The National Executive Committee's power of selecting candidates to the National Assembly was retained.[128] S. 6 of the 1977 Constitution also vested powers in the NEC to propose one candidate to contest the seat of President of the United Republic of Tanzania. S. 22 of the Constitution makes the

President an integral part of the Tanzania Parliament.

There are virtually no set rules to follow in proposing the sole Presidential candidate by the NEC. But the practice has been for a party notable to take the floor and propose the name of the candidate who usually happens to be the incumbent chief of the executive. The proposal is followed by a "unanimous show of hands coupled with clappings, stamping and ululations".[129] Since the introduction of this electoral system, no one has ever dared to show their opposition. The proposed candidate's name is thereafter submitted to the Party National Conference for endorsement.

The Party later embarks on a vigorous campaign for the candidate who is normally presented as a "gift from God" standing above class interests. One can easily remember the campaign posters during the 1975 and 1980 Presidential Elections which bore bold letters stating that *"NYERERE NI MWENZETU"* (literally: Nyerere is Our Friend) accompanied by a series of high-sounding attributes of the candidate. The electorate is then called upon to cast a "YES" or "NO" vote. If the sole candidate wins more than 50% of the vote, he is declared to have won the Presidential seat. His victory cannot be questioned in any court and there are no provisions for his removal if he proves unfit or incompetent to lead the country during his 5 year term of office. Mlawa calls the sole candidate system in Tanzania a presidential referendum and not an election. "Election", he says, "presupposes choice between more than one candidate".[130] The undemocratic character of Tanzania's electoral process stemmed from the same reasons we saw earlier which actuated the ruling petty bourgeoisie as early as 1962 to reorganise the state and concentrate power in their hands to sustain their class rule. The process involved the creation of a single-party system of government, curtailment of parliamentary authority, creation of large, politicised armed forces and secret police, enactment of a series of oppressive laws, exclusion of fundamental rights and freedoms in the country's constitution, and the outlawing of independent mass organisations. This process moved the country away from fair government to authoritarianism.

Burlatsky argues that authoritarianism designates the establishment of a regime of personal power[131] and its principal characteristics are: an abrupt increase in the power of the head of state, deprivation of parliament of the prerogative of the supreme organ of power and control over the policy of the state, a weakening of the institutions of social struggle and pressure on government policy, and adaptation of electoral system to the needs for personal regime of personal power and especially the use of referendums to create the illusion that the people and the head of state are one.[132] All these characteristics fit the Tanzanian situation like a glove.

The 1984 Constitutional Changes

Tanzanians have at various stages in the country's constitutional history, come out boldly against the trend of authoritarianism. Their principal demands which grew louder in the 1970s and 1980s with the worsening economic conditions in the country have been for greater democratisation of the system of government, respect for rule of law and human rights.

In 1983, an important constitutional debate initiated by the ruling party took place in the country which saw the ruling class subjected to intense criticism for its undemocratic and authoritarian character. Between February and September 1983, over 9,335 proposals from various parts of the country were received by the Party headquarters in Dodoma calling for sweeping changes in the 1977 Constitution.[133]

One of the key proposals which featured prominently in the debate was for the restoration of parliament's authority as a supreme organ of power and control over the policies of the state. A truly representative parliament, it was argued, must have a big majority of elected members. We note that in 1959, TANU had forcefully made a similar demand to the Ramage Committee that LEGCO be composed of an elected majority! The other demand which was made frequently during the debate was for the introduction of a Bill of Rights in the Constitution which would guarantee the people's right to organise and associate freely without state intervention. The inclusion of a Bill of Rights in the Constitution, it was argued, should go along with the annulment of repressive instruments such as the Preventive Detention Act.

Another key proposal was for the introduction of a multi-party democracy on the grounds that a single-party democracy which had become the norm in Africa today, served no other purpose than stifling political opposition. It was also argued that party supremacy or the vesting of supreme powers of control over all national issues in the ruling party, had denied a majority of Tanzanians, who happened to be non-CCM members, a say in the day to day running of the country's affairs. It is estimated that hardly 3 million people are CCM members out of the country's population of over 18 million. Finally, the introduction of a competitive electoral system and removal of the wide discretionary powers vested in the President, were also among the common demands during the debate.

CCM's National Executive Committee (NEC) met in Dar es Salaam early June 1984 to consider the proposals with a view to effecting amendments to the 1977 Constitution. Apart from recommending the reduction of non-elected members in parliament by a half and the inclusion of a Bill of Rights in the Constitution, the rest of the proposals were considered by the NEC as inconsistent with the country's political aspirations. The two recommendations were reflected in the fourth Constitutional Amendment Bill passed by the National Assembly.

A critical look at the amendments forces us to conclude that they are of little consequence, if any. For to start with, the mere reduction of nominated members would not in any way change the Assembly from its rubber-stamping role. Without restoring its authority as a supreme organ of power and control over the policies of the state, any changes in its composition would carry no substantial effect.

Secondly, the amendments are so well "punctured" with numerous saving and exemptions that the Bill of Rights has been rendered an empty shell. For instance the substance of some of the rights and freedoms (such as the right to freedom of movement) has been closely and carefully qualified "in the interest of public safety, public order," and so on to the extent that little of the substance is left.[134] The Bill also has provisions enumerating the citizens' duties to the community. The most controversial of them all is the duty to take part in the defence of the country. According to clause 28(2) of the Amendment Bill, the National Assembly can make appropriate laws for conscripting civilians into the armed forces. This provision waters down considerably the spirit of the Bill of Rights itself. For conscription or drafting is an exercise of compulsion which disregards an individual's interests and his right to choose and decide as a human being.

Furthermore, clauses 30 and 31 seriously erode all the rights and freedoms entrenched in the Bill of Rights by validating all the notorious laws in the country which are inconsistent or in contravention of the spirit of the Bill. What then, one wonders, is the need for providing in the constitution for the right to a fair hearing and the right to be presumed innocent until proved guilty when the Prevention Detention Act empowers the President to detain any person without trial? What then is the use of guaranteeing in the constitution the right to appeal when such a right has been displaced in other laws of the country such as the Expulsion of Undesirables Ordinance, the Deportation Ordinance, the Preventive Detention Act or the Collective Punishment Ordinance?[135] How can there be freedom of movement when one cannot move freely without carrying a bundle of identity cards?[136]

Another disturbing thing is that the state, having mutilated the Bill of Rights, has gone further to suspend its effective operation. By S. 5 (2) of the Constitution (Consequential, Transitional and Temporary Provisions) Act of 1984, the justiciability of the provisions relating to the Bill of Rights has been suspended for three years from the date of commencement of the constitutional amendments.

With the foregoing observations, we conclude that the 1984

constitutional amendment has not in any way altered the authoritarian character of the state in Tanzania. Parliament remains a bogus institution the only duty of which is to legitimise the excesses of the ruling class. The electoral system remains undemocratic for it is a device of the bourgeoisie in power to perpetuate their class rule.

The 1984 constitutional amendment also bears ample testimony that the ruling class in Tanzania is conceding to people's struggles for democracy half-heartedly. The lesson which the ruling class appears to have not grasped is that democracy is a *sine qua non* for development and that no amount of bullying can bail Tanzania out of its present severe economic crisis. For development is not brought about by state apparatuses, but by the people who can only be effective if they are made part of the political processes and not mere spectators.

The ruling class in Tanzania however, divorced from the masses and increasingly dependent on finance capital, is not able to survive politically through fair government. It is, as a result, on the defensive, relying on political gimmicks (e.g. maintaining an ineffective parliament and a crooked electoral system) to stay in power. It is for this reason that Tanzania continues to suffer from severe economic crisis because the agents for development, the masses, have been deprived of all power to decide and increasingly feel outsiders in the country's political processes.

NOTES

1. S.I. 1961 No. 2274. The Order in Council was assented to by the Queen in Parliament at the Court of St. James in London on the 27th of November 1961.
2. Msekwa, P., *Towards Party Supremacy,* (Dar es Salaam: Eastern African Publications, 1977), p.6.
3. Dicey, A., *The Law of the Constitution,* (London: Macmillan and Co., 10th Ed., 1960), p.40.
4. Harvey, J. and Bather, L., *The British Constitution,* (London: Macmillan, 1968), p.327.
5. See Montesquieu, *The Spirit of the Laws,* (London: Hafner Publications Co., Book XI, 1949), Ch. VI.
6. For instance see Maitland-Jones, J.F., *Politics in Ex-British Africa,* (London: Weidenfeld & Nicolson, 1973), pp.15-17.
7. See Babu, A.R.M., "A More Sinister Form of Colonisation", *Africa Now* (London: Pan-African Publishers Ltd.), November, 1983, p.30.
8. See Woddis, J., *Introduction to Neo-Colonialism,* (New York: International Publishers, 1976), p.15.
9. Lenin, V.I., *Collected Works,* (Moscow: Progress Publishers, Vol. 23), p.43.
10. S.R. & O. 1926. No.991.
11. In practice, politics were divided into two distinct spheres, territorial and local. Participation in the two spheres was based on racial lines. LEGCO comprised

the Governor (as President), 13 official members and not more than 10 unofficial members, all hand-picked by the Governor from among the Asian and European Communities.

12. See Woddis, J., *op. cit.*, p.30.

13. Nabudere, D.W., *Imperialism and Revolution in Uganda*, (London: Onyx Press, 1980), pp.133-144.

14. Patel, L., *Trade Unions, State & Party*, Dar es Salaam, 1972 (unpublished).

15. They were Chief Abdiel Shangali and Chief Kidaha Mwakwaia sworn in by the Governor William D. Battershill on December 3, 1945. The categories of officials and unofficials in LEGCO respectively referred to colonial civil servants and persons who by reasons of their position and occupation the Governor wished to associate with the business of the colonial government.

16. In addition to Chiefs Shangali and Makwala, there was Chief Adam Sapi Mkwawa nominated on June 3, 1947 and Juma Mwindadi (school-teacher) nominated on April 1, 1948.

17. Cap. 388.

18. See S.I. 1959 No. 1048 which effected the changes. The composition of the Council was re-constituted as follows:
    (a) The Speaker, (b) such number (later directed to be seven) of *ex officio* members as Her Majesty might from time to time direct, (c) such nominated members (not being of a number which if added to the number of *ex officio* members would exceed 34) as might be appointed, (d) 30 representatives (10 Africans, 10 Asians and 10 Europeans) representative of 10 constituencies, (e) not more than three representative members appointed by the Governor to represent such interests as he might think fit, (f) temporary members, if any.

19. The franchise was still restricted just as it was for the first general elections, except that the criterion to be eligible to vote was now: ability to read and write English or Swahili (instead of eight years of education); or an annual income of shs. 1,500 (instead of shs. 3,000); or service in any of a number of designated public offices.

20. Lenin, V.I., *Critical Remarks on the National Question*, (Moscow: Progress Publishers, 1974), pp.99-100.

21. Rule 93 of the *Standing Rules and Orders of the National Assembly of Tanganyika*, 1961 provided that, "in all cases not herein provided for (i.e. those rules), resort shall be had to the usage and practice of the Commons House of Parliament of Great Britain and Ireland". The rule stated further that, "in cases of doubt, the standing Rules and Orders of this Assembly shall be interpreted in the light of the relevant usage and practice of the House of Commons".

22. The Legislative Council constituted after the 1960 General Elections became the National Assembly (or *Bunge* in Kiswahili) at Independence.

23. See Article 14, Tanganyika (Constitution) Order in Council, 1961. The Governor-General was Sir Richard Turnbull, the last Governor in Tanganyika who was retained after independence on Nyerere's specific request.

24. McAuslan, J., "The Republican Constitution of Tanganyika", *International and Comparative Law Quarterly*, Vol. 13, 1964.

25. *Hansard*, February 18, 1962, col. 167.

26. *Idem*, June 28, 1962, col. 1085.

27. According to this model, a political party is primarily an electoral organisation. Its functions are said to be to encourage popular interest and participation in politics; to select candidates for political office, and campaign on their behalf; to reflect the interests and views of diverse groups within society; and to provide both organised support for the government of the day as well as organised

opposition for it. Therefore it is inconceivable under the liberal democratic theory of government for a political party to over-ride the powers of the parliament. For a detailed discussion see Msekwa, P., *Towards Party Supremacy, op. cit.*, pp.11-13.

28. Msekwa, P., *ibid.*, p.19.

29. *Ibid.*, at p. 15 Government ministers for instance took great care and attention in the preparation of answers to parliamentary questions and in the majority of cases, an administrative officer of Assistant Secretary level was appointed to handle this schedule.

30. Pratt, C., "The Cabinet and Presidential Leadership in Tanzania", in Cliffe, L., & Saul, J., (eds), *Socialism in Tanzania,* (Nairobi: East African Publishing House, Vol. 1, 1972), p.226. Also see the Independence Constitution, Article 43.

31. *Ibid.*, Article 46(1).

32. *Ibid.*, Article 40. For a detailed discussion see Cole, J. & Denison, W., *Tanganyika: The Development of Its Laws and Constitution,* (London: Stevens & Sons, 1964) pp. 17-22.

33. For instance see the debates on the Citizenship Bill and the issue of Africanisation quoted in Leys, C., "Tanganyika The Realities of Independence", in Cliffe, L. & Saul, J. (eds)., *op. cit.,* pp.191-192; Shivji, I.G., *Class Struggles in Tanzania,* (Dar es Salaam: Tanzania Publishing House, 1976) pp.66-70; *Hansard,* February 13, 1962, Col. 42.

34. *Hansard,* December 11, 1961—February 17, 1962, p.77.

35. *Idem,* February 15, 1962, col. 174.

36. *Ibid.*

37. *Ibid.*

38. *Ibid.*

39. *Ibid.*, cols. 180 & 183.

40. *Ibid.* col. 178.

41. *Hansard,* June 28, 1962, col. 1101.

42. *Ibid.* Col. 1105-1106.

43. Constituent Assembly Act. No. 1 of 1962 (Cap. 499)

44. The Nationalist Assembly adopted the procedure earlier resorted to in Ghana in 1960 and other places of investing itself with power to resolve itself from time to time into, and constitute, a Constituent Assembly for enactment of provisions for the establishment of a Republic and for a Constitution therefor.

45. As a result of the colonial government's attempts to suppress and impede the growth of TANU and the administration's resistance to alter the racial parity concept started in 1954 (under which an equal number of representatives of each race was nominated into LEGCO as unofficial members) and the voter qualifications for the first grade elections, Nyerere was under pressure from within TANU to adopt a more radical course of action against the colonial administration such as boycotting the 1958/59 elections and calling a general strike. At the fourth Annual Conference of TANU at Tabora in January 1958, Nyerere refused to yield to the persistence of radical pressure. To him, TANU's participation in the elections was the only wise course. It was at this point that Mtemvu and other radicals broke away.

46. Ending with the first dissolution of parliament after December 9, 1962, which by virtue of the Independence Constitution was to take place not later than October 11, 1964: See Republic of Tanganyika (Consequential, Provisions) Act (C.A. Act No. 2), s.19.

47. Except that "reserved" seats became "open" seats and that non-citizens of Tanganyika vacated their seats.

48. Government Paper No. 1 of 1962.
49. He had powers to institute and confer honours, dignities and awards. (Presidential Affairs Act, 1962 (C.A. Act. No. 4), s.4). He also wielded whatever power may be conferred, from time to time on a Head of State by International Law, e.g. the power to declare war, or to make treaties, whether subject to ratification by the legislature or not.
50. He had powers to order the armed forces to defend Tanganyika and to take part in any other operations, within or out of Tanganyika, as he might have thought expedient. His powers as Commander-in-Chief however did not permit him to raise or maintain any armed forces without the authority of parliament in accordance with Articles 64 and 65 of the Constitution.
51. Republican Constitution, Article 3.
52. *Ibid.*, Article 44(2).
53. Independence Constitution, Article 40(3).
54. *Ibid.*, Article 43(2).
55. Republican Constitution, Article 15(2).
56. Compare Article 15(2) of the Republican Constitution with Article 43(2) of the Independence Constitution.
57. *Hansard,* June 28, 1962.
58. Act No. 60 of 1962 (Cap. 490)
59. Hopkins, R., *Political Roles in a New State: Tanzania's First Decade,* (New Haven & London: 1971), p.27.
60. See cap. 490, ss. 2,3 & 7.
61. See Cap. 38 of 1921, s.2.
62. See Cap. 39 of 1930, s.2.
63. This power was inherited as a prerogative of the Crown by virtue of s. 28 of the Republic of Tanganyika (Consequential Transitional and Temporary Provisions) Act of 1962.
64. See Republican Constitution, Article 36.
65. See McAuslan, J., *op. cit.,* p.533.
66. On January 28, 1964, the President announced the setting up of a Commission which was placed under the chairmanship of the then Vice-President Rashidi Kawawa. The Commission's terms of reference were "to consider what changes were necessary in the Constitution of Tanganyika and the Constitution of TANU, as well as in the practices of government, in order to bring into effect at democratic one-party state", see *General Notice No. 300,* Tanganyika Gazette, February 7, 1964.
67. Formerly Prime Minister. His position was established under the Republican Constitution which under Article 11 established the office of the Vice-President, the principal assistant of the President in the discharge of this executive functions and leader of government business in the Assembly.
68. *Hansard,* February 13, 1963, Cols. 148 & 149.
69. *Ibid.,* Col. 182.
70. Shivji, I.G., "State in the Dominated Social Formations of Africa", in Tandon, Y. (ed)., *Debate on Class, State and Imperialism,* (Dar es Salaam: Tanzania Publishing House, 1982), p.180.
71. *Ibid.*
72. See Nabudere, D.W., "Imperialism, State, Class & Race: A Critique of Shivji's Class Struggles in Tanzania", in Tandon, Y. (ed)., *op. cit.,* p.62.
73. *Ibid.*
74. Lenin, V.I., *Collected Works,* (Moscow: Progress Publishers), Vol. 23, p.52.
75. See Nabudere, D.W., "Imperialism, State, Class & Race . . .", in Tandon, Y.

(ed), *op. cit.*, p.58.

76. Tandon calls the local classes "servicing agents" and Odeke & Co. reduces them to the level of "care-taker committees" of the interests of the financial oligarchy. See Tandon, Y. (ed), *op. cit.*, p.169, and Odeke, A. & Panduka, G., "Can Law Bring Social Change in Africa"? *Dar es Salaam University Law Journal,* (Dar es Salaam: University of Dar Law Society), Vol. 7, April, 1978, p.174.

77. See the Introduction by Babu, A.R.M. in Tandon, Y. (ed)., *op. cit.*

78. Stephens, H.W. *The Political Transformation of Tanganyika: 1920—1967,* (New York: Frederick A. Praeger Publishers, 1968), p.166.

79. Leys, C., *op. cit.*, p.187.

80. Quoted in Shivji, I.G., *Class Struggles in Tanzania, op. cit.*, p.68.

81. Leys, C., *op. cit.*, p.189.

82. Stephens, H.W. *op. cit.*, p.164.

83. Trade Disputes (Settlement) Act, No. 43 of 1962.

84. Trade Union (Amendment) Act, 1962.

85. NUTA established under the National Union of Tanganyika Workers (Establishment) Act No. 18 of 1964, Cap. 555.

86. Subscription to the party from its claimed 1.25 million members in a population of 10 million started drying up, the enrolment of new members ceased and attendance at public meetings was shrinking. See Benett, G., "An Outline History of TANU," *Makerere Journal,* (Kampala: University of Makerere), No. 7, 1963.

87. These were redesignated Regional and Area Commissioners who served concurrently as party secretaries for the same units.

88. Stephens, H.W., *op. cit.*, pp.162-163.

89. *Ibid.*, p. 166.

90. Following the mutiny, according to Cliffe, a number of trade union leaders were detained and released within a matter of days or weeks, although a handful were restricted for a longer time. The last two detainees among the group—Kasanga Tumbo (a former trade unionist) and Victor Mkello (ex-TFL President) were finally freed in July 1966. See Cliffe, L., "The Political System", in Svendsen, K. and Teisen, M., *Self-Reliant Tanzania,* (Dar es Salaam: Tanzania Publishing House, 1969), pp. 135-136.

91. Msekwa, P., "The Decision to Establish a Democratic One Party State in Tanzania: A Case Study", *TAAMULI,* (Dar es Salaam: Department of Political Science, University of Dar es Salaam), Vol. 5, No. 2, December, 1975), p. 39.

92. Halimoja, Y., *Bunge la Tanzania,* (Dar es Salaam: East African Literature Bureau, 1975), pp. 11-17.

93. See Biennen, H., *Tanzania: Party Transformation & Economic Development,* (New Jersey: Princeton University Press, 1970), pp.57-58.

94. Pratt, C., *The Critical Phase in Tanzania 1945—1968,* (London: Cambridge University Press, 1976), p.187.

95. Act No. 43 of 1965 (Cap. 596).

96. Because of the merger of Tanganyika and Zanzibar on April 26, 1964, the single party was designated as "TANU and the Afro-Shirazi Party" (the former on the mainland and the latter on Zanzibar).

97. Act No. 63 of 1964.

98. Msekwa, P., *Towards Party Supremacy, op. cit.*, p.34. For in a parliamentary democracy, parties however dominant they may be in the process of political rule and government, there is usually no legal provision for the position, status and responsibilities of parties.

99. See the Interim Constitution, Article 28.

100. Hyden, G., "Buhaya: Selection and Election Process in Bukoba and Karagwe

Districts'' in Cliffe, L. (ed)., *One Party Democracy*, (Nairobi: East African Publishing House, 1967), p.71.

101. Molnos, A., ''An Attempt at a Psychological Analysis of the Role of Symbols in Districts'', in Cliffe, L. (ed), *ibid.*, pp.410-430.
102. Act No. 49 of 1965.
103. Msekwa, P., *Towards Party Supremacy, op. cit.*, p.40.
104. *Hansard*, 18 July, 1967, Quest. No. 500.
105. *Idem*, 22 July, 1968, Col. 2472.
106. *Ibid.*, Col. 2481.
107. These were ''institutions of national character'' designated by the President, (see the Interim Constitution, Article 30). The following institutions were so designated: The National Union of Tanganyika Workers (NUTA), the Co-operative Union of Tanganyika (CUT), The Tanganyika Association of Chambers of Commerce (TACC), The TANU Youth League (TYL), The Union of Women of Tanzania (UWT), The Tanganyika African Parents' Association (TAPA), and the University College of Dar es Salaam (UCD). The inclusion in the National Assembly of this special category of MPs was proposed by the Presidential Commission on the Establishment of a Democratic One-Party State and incorporated in the Interim Constitution.
108. See *The Standard*, (Dar es Salaam: Tanganyika Newspapers Ltd.), October 2, 1968.
109. *Ibid.*
110. *Hansard*, October 1, 1968, Col. 23.
111. See *The Standard, op. cit.*
112. *Hansard*, October, 1968, Col. 34.
113. Msekwa, P., *Towards Party Supremacy, op. cit.*, p.48. The dismissed MPs were: G. Kaneno (Karagwe); T. Bakampenja (Ihangiro); T. Kasella-Bantu (Nzega East); W. Mwakitwange (National) and S. Kibuga (Mufindi).
114. Kjekshus, H., ''Perspectives on the Second Parliament'', in *Socialism & Participation: Tanzania's 1970 National Elections*, (Dar es Salaam, Tanzania Publishing House, 1974), pp.77-78.
115. The reasons for their expulsion was stated in an editorial of the influential party English daily, *The Nationalist* of October 21, 1968 which said the two ''tried to subvert the TANU government . . . the two . . . had to be expelled because they did not believe in TANU nor its socialist ideology''.
116. *Hansard*, July 12, 1968, Col. 2481.
117. See *The Standard, op. cit. The Nationalist* of July 14, 1967 was unhappy with the MPs' attacks on the executive. It wrote in an editorial that ''MPs should not ask questions which are embarrassing and put the Ministers to the limelight and hence MPs claiming empty victories''.
118. Kjekshus, H., ''The Question-Hour in Tanzania's Bunge'', *The African Review*, Vol. 2, No. 3, 1972, p.365.
119. *The Nationalist*, October 2, 1968.
120. *Hansard*, March 25, 1969, cols. 19-20.
121. Kjekshus, H., ''Parliament in a One-Party State—The Bunge of Tanzania, 1965—70,'' *Journal of Modern African Studies*, Vol. 12, 1974, p.28.
122. See *UHURU* (Dar es Salaam: Mwananchi Publishing Company Ltd.), November 28, 1973.
123. See Hopkins, R., *Political Roles in a New State: Tanzania's First Decade, op. cit.*, p.26.
124. Article 54(1) of the 1977 Constitution.
125. S. 3 of the Act.

126. S. 4(1).
127. S. 16.
128. See Ss. 27 & 28.
129. Mlawa, G., "The Constitution of the United Republic of Tanzania: Proposed Changes", *Eastern Africa Law Review.* (Dar es Salaam: Faculty of Law), Vol. 11-14, 1978—81, p.130.
130. *Ibid.*, p.132.
131. Burlatsky, F., *The Modern State and Politics,* (Moscow: Progress Publishers, 1978), p. 58.
132. *Ibid.*
133. See the *Daily News & Sunday News, Uhuru & Mzalendo* of between February & September, 1983.
134. See, for example, clause 17 of the Constitutional Amendment Bill, 1984.
135. Cap. 74.
136. A person has to carry receipts of the "Development Levy" imposed under the Local Government Finances Act of 1982, an identity card showing that he is engaged in gainful employment and is a bona fide resident of a particular area as required under the Human Resources Deployment Act of 1983.

3. THE STATE AND THE PARTY

A.K.L.J. Mlimuka
P.J.A.M. Kabudi

Introduction

The party and the state in Tanzania are closely related to the extent that one cannot discuss either of the two without referring to the other.

As will be seen in this Chapter, the party is part of the state. The party is not only a special ideological apparatus of the state, but it also uses repressive apparatus to consolidate its hegemonic position. In turn, the state borrows the ideological prestige of the party to legitimize its rule. The party therefore provides the state with a legitimate base for the ruling class in Tanzania.

One can easily see the close relationship between the party and the state when one looks at the structure of the party at the national level.

Before we embark on proving the foregoing assertion, let us first define the two terms, i.e. the party and the state. A political party is a class organisation with definite material and economic interests. The basic criteria for determining the nature of any party is to understand its social and class essence, its ideology, programme and political goals. The ultimate aim of any political party is to capture state power. Marx and Engels in the Communist Manifesto explained that: 'political power, properly so called, is merely the organised power of one class for oppressing the other.'[1]

We should hasten to add here that though a political party is essentially a class organisation, it may attract members from different classes. For example, we may have a party which appeals to the sentiments of peasants and workers but which in fact serves the interests of the bourgeoisie. What is decisive therefore, is the ideology and programme of a particular political party and not the membership.

The state is an organ for maintaining the rule of one class over another. This means that the state exists only in a class society. It exists because class antagonisms cannot be reconciled.[2] Since the state is a class category, every state must have a certain class character. The class character of the state depends on the class which controls it.

The Tanzanian state is a neo-colonial one. This state is under the leadership of the compradorial bourgeoisie which consists of two factions, the state bourgeoisie and the private big bourgeoisie. The state bourgeoisie is in a hegemonic position, and this is clearly reflected in its total control of the party.

Evolution of the Political Party

The two political parties, Tanganyika African National Union (TANU) and Afro Shirazi Party (ASP), predecessors of CCM, were all established during the nationalist struggle against colonialism. They all aimed at removing the colonial state, although the leadership and members of these political parties had no identical views on what was to follow on the morrow of independence. TANU was born on 7th July, 1954. Its birth was a result of intense contradictions which necessitated the former social association Tanganyika African Association (TAA) to turn itself into a political party. TAA drew its members mainly from the civil service and traders. The composition of the leadership of the new political party was entirely dominated by the petty bourgeoisie[3] (these were teachers, traders and kulaks) while the membership was mainly from peasants and workers.

TANU was the only political party in the Mainland up to 1958. Two more political parties were registered in 1958. These were the United Tanganyika Party (UTP) and the African National Congress (ANC). UTP was registered on 27th March, 1958 and ANC on 14th June, 1958. ANC was formed by Zuberi M.M. Mtemvu who broke away from TANU, after the Party had agreed to take part in the 1958 elections. The voters in that election were required to vote for Europeans, Asians and Africans at the same time.

In the Isles, ASP was born on 5th February, 1957 being a merger of the African Association and Shirazi Association. The leadership of the ASP was from the petty bourgeois class but it was mainly a party of workers, landless labourers and small peasants expressing their sentiments on the land question.[4] However, the nationalist politics of Zanzibar from the beginning were dominated by manyna-tionalist parties. There were Zanzibar Nationalist Party (ZNP), Zanzibar and Pemba People's Party (ZPPP) which was a break-away from ASP and latter Umma Party, a break-away from ZNP.

All these political parties were led by the petty bourgeoisie because it was the only class during that time which was in a better position and more enlightened to lead. They were educated and had knowledge of the outside world. They also understood the existing contradictions between the colonial power and the colonised people.[5] It was the only class which was prepared and in a position to lead a constitutional struggle against colonialism. Both parties pursued the peaceful constitutional way of struggle to independence until 1964 when ASP was forced to use arms to overthrow a puppet regime that was installed after the 1963 Lancaster House constitutional conference.

The ideology of these political parties during the independence struggle, and particularly TANU, were mainly hinged on nationalism, populism and economism borrowing much from the Fabian society and the Labour Party of the United Kingdom. The Fabians had close contact with most of the nationalist leaders before and after the birth of TANU.[6] Nationalist and populist ideology was invoked to arouse the sentiments of the peasants and workers to fight against colonialism. This was the major mobilising factor and TANU identified the main enemy to be the foreign rule and rallied all the people to fight it.[7]

Thus during the struggle for independence both TANU and ASP were political parties, which like all political parties, were aspiring to get state power.

1961-1967: Independent Tanganyika and Westminster Democracy

Tanganyika became independent on 9th December, 1961 and was accepted as a member of the Commonwealth under the Tanganyika Act.[8] The attire was essentially that of Westminster.

The Tanganyika (Constitution) Order in Council, 1961[9] which was assented to by the Queen in Parliament at the Court of St. James on November 27th, 1961 proclaimed Tanganyika to be a multiparty parliamentary democratic government. The Governor-General represented the Queen locally. The Parliament consisted of him and the National Assembly. The Government which was constitutionally responsible to the Parliament was headed by the Prime Minister from TANU which had the majority seats in the House.

During this time the parliament remained constitutionally supreme. Both the independence constitution and the republican constitution unequivocally provided in the preamble that the parliament was supreme.[10] This part of the preamble is reproduced wholly even today when party supremacy has constitutionally replaced parliamentary democracy!

The move towards a republican constitution was initiated by TANU. The final decision that Tanganyika should be a republic was taken by the National Executive Committee (NEC) or TANU. In order to implement it the Government produced a Government Paper entitled "Proposals for a Republic".[11] Warioba and Seaton[12] argue that one of the reasons for Tanganyika becoming a Republic was to end the colonial legacy by transferring the sovereignty from the British crown to the Republic and to vest power in the constitutionally elected head of state.

The government paper pointed out that the government had attempted in the proposals to institute a government which could be understood by the people and an executive which would have the necessary power to carry out the functions of a modern state. The speech by the then Prime Minister, Rashidi Kawawa, introducing the proposals and the contributions of Julius Nyerere show that the republican constitution was introduced for two main purposes. One, to create an executive which was strong and capable of acting. Two, to enable the state to intervene fully and effectively in social and economic sectors of the life of the people. In short, therefore, the aim was to have a strong centralised government.

The decision to form a Republic with a strong executive President was speeded up by the bitter opposition the petty bourgeoisie, in the government, faced from those in trade unions, co-operatives and other sectors. These differences were very much pronounced in the parliamentary debates. The parliament played its role as the arena for these intra-class struggles.

There were fierce debates in the parliament on government bills. Among the hotly debated bills was the Citizenship Bill of 1961. While the government advocated citizenship to be open to all races in Tanganyika, those who were outside the government insisted it be confined to Africans only. Tempers flared and Nyerere threatened to resign if the bill was not passed. Athough the bill was passed, it was only after defiant remarks from some members.[13] The government faced further opposition on the question of Africanisation which Nyerere was adamantly opposed to from the beginning.

At the same time the party was facing other strife from within. Soon after independence, TANU leaders in the provinces and districts expected to take over from the colonialist. To their disappointment only a few acquired lucrative and prestigious positions in the government. These were those who were at the top in the party andco-operatives. The majority were disgruntled and dissatisfied.

William Tordoff links with the emphasis on nationality and race in the debate on the Citizenship Bill, the disenchantment of party leaders in the provinces and districts.[14] The upshot was Nyerere's resignation from the Premiership to go and strengthen the Party. When the Republican constitution was passed and presidential elections held, Nyerere was returned with a resounding victory after defeating his opponent Zuberi Mtemvu of the opposition party, African National Congress, and one of the vocal supporters of Africanisation. But that was not the end of the intra-class struggles of the petty bourgeoisie.

The contradictions among them intensified despite a strong executive. It is this which led to a resolve to move to a one party state and away from Westminster democracy.

One Party State
ack in 1961, Nyerere had already advocated for the establishment of a one party state. He argued that Tanzania was a *de facto* one party state. However he assured himself that:

> In future it is possible a second political party will grow in Tanganyika, but in one sense such a growth would represent failure by TANU. The existence of two or more stable parties implies a class structure of society, and we aim at avoiding the growth of different social and economic classes in our country.[15]

These were mere wishes which could not turn back the wheel of history and development of society, for classes were there even before independence. After independence class formation was even faster throwing up numerous contradictions in the struggle for hegemony.

Cliffe says the first proposal to turn Tanganyika into a single one party state was made early in 1963 by Nyerere in his proposals to TANU National Conference.[16] Nyerere then argued:

> Where there is one party, and that party is identified with a nation as a whole, the foundations of democracy are firmer than they can ever be where you have two or more parties, each representing only a section of community.[17]

Before Tanganyika was declared a one party state, many political parties had already mushroomed. Many of these were formed after 1962. There was People's Democratic Party (PDP) led by Kasanga Tumbo. Tumbo was one of the trade union leaders who were arch opponents of the TANU government. In order to silence him he was appointed High Commissioner to the United Kingdom. He resigned, came back and formed a political party.

Another party was People's Convention Party (PCP) which was formed in Mwanza. There also there was the Nationalist Enterprise Party (NEP) which was established by Hussein Yahya. In the same year he joined hands with Samson Mshala who was the President of PCP to form the African Independence Movement (AIM). Another effective party which was formed during the time was the All Muslim Nationalist Union of Tanganyika (AMNUT).

But before formal death certificates to these parties were issued, they were intimidated and suffocated. Pratt recounts that:

> In Tanzania the several tiny parties which appeared in 1962 were
> harassed out of existence, their leadership deported or detained
> and their rights to register and to hold meetings severely
> restricted.[18]

As in the case of the decision to form a Republic, the decision to
establish a one party state was taken by NEC in January 1963. NEC
authorised the President to set up a commission to consider and make
recommendations on the appropriate structure and procedures to be
followed by the Government and the party in order to effectively
implement the proposal. Nyerere formed the commission under the
chairmanship of Rashidi Kawana. One of the terms of reference given
to the Commissioners was:

> In order to avoid misunderstanding, I think I should emphasize
> that it is not the task of the commission to consider whether
> Tanganyika should be a one party state. The decision has already
> been taken. Their task is to say what kind of one Party state
> we should have in the context of our national ethic and in accord-
> ance with the principles I have instructed the commission to
> observe.[19]

It is important to pinpoint here the fact that the Party (TANU) gave
itself the mandate to declare Tanganyika a one party state. We hold
that the Party was incompetent to make such a decision, for not all
Tanganyikans were members of TANU. A few appointed people
therefore could not purport to decide the destiny of the majority. The
party's decision on the establishment of a one party state ought to have
been subjected to a referendum so that all people could have participated.

The commission appointed by the president finalised its report
quickly. The report was submitted to a joint meeting of the NECs
of TANU and ASP held on 3rd May 1956. The decision of this
meeting culminated in the enactment of the 1965 Interim
Constitution[20] declaring Tanzania a *de jure* one party state. TANU
in the Mainland and ASP in the Isles were constitutionally declared
to be the only political parties.

The Party and the Parliament

The formative stage of the one party state carried with it the ambivalence
of what institution should be supreme—the party or the parliament.
The 1965 Interim constitution provided that all political activities in

Tanzania should be conducted under the auspices of the party.[21]

There was already a move towards party supremacy. This was shown in the proposals of the Presidential Commission on the Establishment of the One Party State. The commission proposed three things in this regard: firstly, that the NEC be concerned with laying down broad policy; secondly, because of the higher status of NEC it should have power to summon witnesses and call for papers, which is conferred by Chapter 359 of the Laws of Tanzania on the National Assembly; thirdly, those NEC members who were not Members of Parliament should be paid the same salary as MPs.

The commission drew a distinction between the National Assembly and the NEC, it said:

> ...NEC is concerned with the formulation of the broad lines of policy while Parliament is concerned with giving effect to the government policy through appropriate legislation measures and exercising vigilant control over all aspects of government expenditure.[22]

In practice the NEC became more powerful and decisive as compared to the National Assembly. Matters that formerly were under the National Assembly were now moved to the NEC. The NEC was now the organ of formulating national policy and supervising its implementation.

The NEC exercised power to summon officials for the first time in 1973 when it summoned the General Managers of Tanganyika Packers and the Dar es Salaam Development Corporation to explain the meat shortage. It also summoned the Minister for Water and Energy who was asked to explain the water shortage in Dar es Salaam. Others summoned to explain various problems connected with their Corporations included the General Managers of National Agricultural and Food Corporation (NAFCO), National Development Corporation (NDC) and National Textile Corporation (NATEX).[23]

More important than the status of the NEC is the fact that it is the only body which decides who should be a member of parliament through making final nomination of the two candidates who then face the electorate.

The party was forced by the contradictions and intra-class struggles existing then to legislate on party supremacy. This was done in the 1975 constitutional amendments after the decision of the NEC which met in Shinyanga from 10th to 12th March, 1975. The amendments were passed by the National Assembly on 3rd June, 1975 declaring that the party was supreme in law as well as in practise. This has been firmly retained in the 1977 Constitution which was passed after

the birth of Chama cha Mapinduzi (CCM). The constitution now provides: 'All activity of the organs of the state of the United Republic
shall be conducted under the auspices of the Party'.[24]

The Constitution also declares CCM to be the sole political party
which is supreme.[25] It provides for all political activity to be conducted under CCM.[26] The subordination of the Parliament to the
party is further evinced in the constitution by the fact that the former
is a committee of the party.[27] This means that the National Assembly
is not expected to go against the party, for it is a committee of the
highest policy-making organ of the party. This should be so since every
member of the parliament is expected by the constitution to be a
member of the party who has complied with membership conditions
as provided for in the party constitution.[28] This includes being loyal
to the party, following and implementing various decisions and resolutions of the party. Revocation of party membership has been used
to end tenure of members of parliament. This was used in 1968 to
axe 7 vocal MPs and has been used whenever the need has arisen.

The move to concentrate powers through the party can be explained
by what has been taking place since independence. After independence
in 1961 the call was for a strong executive presidency. In 1965 the
ruling class strived for a one party state so as to thwart opposing
elements and especially those in the parliament. That did not extinguish
the inherent contradictions. The class struggles and the intra-class
struggles intensified even more. For example, in 1968 the issue of
what was supreme, the party or the National Assembly, was
resuscitated. Chogga, an MP for Iringa, led a group of MPs who
bravely led the assault for the establishment of parliamentary
supremacy over the NEC and the party. He moved a formal amendment to the 1965 Interim Constitution intending to amend article 6
(2) aimed at making the parliament supreme.[29]

This was not tolerated. The NEC expelled them from the party
and as a consequence they lost their seats in the National Assembly.
The debates in the National Assembly had proved to the ruling class
that the parliament was no longer a unitary voice and forum for
them.

Suppression of Mass Movements

Among the earliest mass movements to be strangled by the ruling class
were the trade unions. Government policy in regard to the trade unions
evolved in the direction similar to that taken towards political opposition groups and towards the co-operative movement and local governments. The independence of each of these was thoroughly undermined.

After independence, the government encouraged people to
establish co-operatives. The motivation for establishing these co-

operatives was mainly political, i.e. to cut out the middlemen, particularly Asian traders. Thereafter, various moves were made to put the co-operatives under the firm grip of the ruling class. More changes followed the enactment of Co-operatives Societies Act, 1968. This Act increased the powers of the Commissioner for Co-operative Development who was also the Registrar for Co-operatives. Under the Act, the Registrar or his representative in the regions was given ultimate powers to decide on a number of important management issues. Hyden says:

> The extensive powers given to the Commissioner for Co-operative Development reflected a desire by the Party, through the government, to control the co-operative more effectively in accordance with the newly adopted policies after the Arusha Declaration.[30]

He mentions three different measures aimed at breaking the power of the traders and kulaks in the co-operative union leadership. These were: the creation of regional co-operatives union all over the country; increased control over recruitment of union staff; and intervention in the election of the committee men in the unions.[31]

The creation of regional co-operative unions helped the extension of central control to rural areas. These were later to be disbanded in 1975 and have now been reconstituted under the new co-operatives law passed by the parliament in 1982.

Though local governments *strictu sensu* cannot be considered a mass movement, their autonomy means a lot in the democratisation of a political system in a country. In Tanzania one notes that soon after independence there were reforms in local government which paved the way for extensive control by the central government. The Minister responsible for Local Government was empowered to approve by-laws. He also formally appointed all elected members to the council so that he could vet any individual election merely by refusing to make the appointments. Finally the Minister had the authority to issue restrictions to the council concerning many aspects of their responsibilities, while the Regional Commissioners were in a position to influence the development of local governments in many indirect ways such as provision of senior staff to District Councils.[32]

As if the above reform was not enough, the state decided to disband the local governments altogether in 1972 through the policy of decentralism. The policy which followed a consultancy feasibility study made by the Mckinsey Corporation, was rationalised as giving more power to the people. An analysis of this policy however reveals that it was more a deconcentration of administrative powers and procedures to Regional and District Offices of the administration, rather than a devolution of power of actual decision-making to the people. As one writer notes: 'Decentralisation requires effective representative institution at the regional and district levels to which power and authority would be decentralised.'[33]

In 1982, the National Assembly passed a law re-establishing local governments.[34] Though the local governments have been re-established, in no way do they whittle down the powers and authority of central government over them.

The suppression of mass movements and other local autonomous bodies has been fully formalised under the Chama cha Mapinduzi in its 1982 constitution. Now all the five designated mass organisations are under the party. They therefore only exist in name. Under the new party structure all secretary generals of these mass organisations should be NEC members appointed to that post by the NEC of the Party.

During this period, which marked the heyday of the ruling class, the state bourgeoisie favoured the party rather than other forums in the process of creating its hegemony over all other bodies and the other sections of the ruling class. And even in the party it favoured the central committee and the NEC. The NEC usually endorses decisions which have been made by the Central Committee whose composition is more restricted.

The dominating image of the Chairman of the Party who is also the President of the country is even more visible in the party in general and the NEC in particular. Msekwa argues:

NEC decisions are more associated directly with the President himself, because of the fact that he is the Chairman of the NEC. This clearly adds value to the status of the body and the esteem with which it is held, than the National Assembly which is chaired by the speaker.[35]

1967-1975: The Arusha Declaration

The Arusha Declaration was pronounced by the Party in 1967. It outlined two fundamental principles—Socialism and Self-Reliance. Socialism was defined as three things, firstly, absence of exploitation; secondly, people's ownership of the means of production and exchange; and thirdly, existence of democracy. Self-reliance was taken to be development dependent principally upon ourselves and our own resources, that is, land and people.

A leadership code with five leadership conditions was issued. It provided that: (1) every TANU and Government leader must be either a peasant or a worker and should in no way be associated with the practices of capitalism or feudalism; (2) no TANU or Government leader should hold shares in any company; (3) no TANU or Government leader should hold directorships in any privately owned enterprises; (4) no TANU or Government leader should receive two or more salaries; and (5) no TANU or Government leader should own houses which he rents to others.

Several policies followed the promulgation of the Arusha Declaration. On February 7, 1967 the Government nationalised all commercial banks except the Co-operative Bank and the People's Bank of Zanzibar; eight export-import firms including Smith Mackenzie and Co. Ltd.; Delgety (E.A.) Ltd., International Trading and Credit Company of Tanganyika; Co-operative Supply of Tanganyika Ltd., A Bauman and Co. (Tanganyika) Ltd., Twentsche Overseas Trading Co. Ltd., African Mercantile Co. (Overseas) Ltd., and Wigglesworth and Company (Africa) Ltd. and eight milling firms were also nationalised. The National Insurance Corporation was wholly brought under public ownership and was to acquire a monopoly insurance business in the Republic. Nationalisations did not end there. The government went on to make compulsory acquisition of up to 60% of the shares in seven industries. Also 60% of the sisal business was nationalised.

Two policy documents were issued in March and September of the same year i.e. 1967. These were Education for Self-Reliance and Socialism and Rural Development. The policy directives contained in these documents plus the nationalisations have been taken by the leadership to be socialist moves which marked a 'turning point' in Tanzania politics. President Nyerere once remarked:

> The Arusha Declaration marked a turning point in Tanzania politics. The ideology of the country was made explicit by it; also the introduction of leadership qualifications and the measures for public ownership, began a new series of deliberately socialist objectives.[36]

Even the leftists took the Declaration as a step in the correct direction. They saw the Declaration as a beginning in the march towards Socialism:

> ...the Declaration was received with a lot of enthusiam and they accepted its declared policy of socialism and self-reliance as a good start on the long journey to the development of an independent national economy.[37]

The leftists saw the practicability of the implementation of the policy of self-reliance. They gave a much wider application to the meaning of self-reliance, "they received it as a policy of gradual delinking our economies from the pernicious domination by metropolitan markets which we had no control".[38]

It is important at this juncture to ask ourselves if the Arusha Declaration was aimed at directing Tanzania towards socialist development. It is our contention that the Arusha Declaration was promulgated mainly for two reasons. Firstly, the failure to attract foreign capital which had been expected to flow easily, hence the state thought it was being ignored. For example, the First Five Year Development Plan which started in 1964 was shelved in 1966 because the envisaged flow of foreign aid of more than two thirds of the total investment did not pour in. Amir Jamal, one of the longest-serving members of the Cabinet, supports the view that the Arusha Declaration was a result of the failure of the state to attract foreign capital. He was once quoted as saying:

As far as Tanzania is concerned, there is little private foreign investment even interested in Tanzania. *One of the reasons why Julius Nyerere made his Arusha Declaration in February, 1967 was that six years after independence practically no foreign investment for Tanzania had been forthcoming.*[39] (Emphasis ours)

Therefore money was discarded in the Arusha Declaration not because it was bad, but because it was not forthcoming. That is why the policy of self-reliance was thrown overboard when foreign capital began to pour in. Whereas in the six years before the Arusha Declaration, total foreign assistance had amounted to shs. 588 million, the figure trebled to shs. 1,730 million in the six years after the Declaration (the figure exludes the Chinese loan for the Tanzania Zambia Railway Authority—TAZARA). The figure had shot up to shs. 13,000 million by March 1978.[40]

Tanzania gets aid and loans from both bilateral and multilateral sources. These aids and loans have further intensified imperialist exploitation of Tanzania. Finance capital has penetrated up to the door-step of a peasant through different projects financed by foreign capital. The recently introduced Regional Integrated Development Programmes (RIDEPs) help to illustrate this. Under these programmes, the state has assigned the various development plans for the regions to different countries, e.g. Arusha to the United States of America, Kilimanjaro to the Japanese, Dar es Salaam to the Canadians, Coast to the Swedish. One wonders how can socialism be built with the assistance of finance capital, for since when have capitalists been able to build socialism?

The second reason behind the pronouncement of the Arusha

Declaration was the desire on the part of the ruling class to consolidate its economic position through nationalisations. President Nyerere came closer to the reasons underlying the nationalisations in his speech at the opening of the extension of the Tanzania Breweries when he said:

> We decided to secure majority ownership in the industries because they are key points in our econony, and because we believe that they would therefore be under the control of Tanzania. Our purpose was primarily a nationalist purpose; it was an extension of the political control which the Tanzanian people secured in 1961... As I have said *this economic nationalism has nothing to do with the ideologies of socialism, capitalism or communism*[41] (Emphasis ours)

In fact, nationalism has been a worldwide phenomenon which has nothing to do with socialism. For in socialism, what is important is not nationalisation as such, but the character of the state which is directing the nationalisations. If the state is under the control of the exploiting classes, nationalisation will not help the toiling masses for it will not change the production relations. But if the state is under the leadership of the working class, nationalisation will change the relations of production by liquidating exploitation.

It is no wonder, therefore, that the form of nationalisations was not fundamentally opposed to the interests of imperialism. In the final analysis, the state found itself in partnership with multinational corporations (MNCs). This was so because the state promoted joint ventures and signed management agreements with foreign capital.[42] One writer put this trend sarcastically when he said: '...for foreign corporations the situation is one in which, with minimum risks and almost no responsibility, they can get maximum returns.'[43]
We can rightly assert that the post Arusha Declaration policies of paving the way for greater state intervention in the economy helped to open new forms of neo-colonial exploitation. The ruling class found itself being an economic intermediary *vis-a-vis* imperialism.

But the Tanzanian ruling class would like to be seen to be independent. It has a populist ideology which appeals to the common sentiments of the people. Such populist policies as the Arusha Declaration are essentially petit bourgeois socialism like that of Sismond and Russian Norodniks. This ideology which purports to be aimed at building a socialist society does not recognise class struggles. It declares the society of peasants and workers by proclamation. It plucks the principles of socialism out of their class context, a practice which makes them unapplicable and impractical. It talks of public ownership without the dictatorship of the proletariat, hence it finds itself having state capitalism presided over by the state bourgeoisie.

It hates development of productive forces and seeks to control distribution of commodities instead of developing production of commodities, hence it is a 'socialism' always hit by shortages and finds itself daily at war with those who are forced to engage in the blackmarket.

The limitations of the petty bourgeois ideology as contained in the Arusha Declaration are well illustrated in the failure to restructure the economy; failure to speed up industralisation—both heavy and light industries—and failure to mechanise agriculture.

The leadership castigated the ideal of developing Tanzania through large industries arguing that it was unrealistic. It also castigated the idea of mechanising agriculture saying that it was a mistake. In fact it said industralisation and mechanisation, if they were to take place at all, would be exceptions. It thought agriculture would be developed independently of industry. That is why stress was laid on the use of hand hoe until such time that it would be eliminated by the plough which in turn would be eliminated by tractor. It was seen as impossible for the hand hoe to be eliminated by the tractor.[44]

The Position of the Party After the Arusha Declaration

It has been argued that the Party's position with regards to decision-making was enhanced after it promulgated the Arusha Declaration. From then, the Party assumed a greater importance in terms of decision-making. This is exemplified when one looks at a number of decisions and policy directives that were issued by the Party after the Arusha Declaration.

Two years after the promulgation of the Arusha Declaration, the second five year development plan was approved by the Party. The Party asserted more power after it proclaimed its guidelines (Mwongozo) in 1971. The guidelines outlined in clear terms the role of the Party in providing guidance to the Government and its implementing agencies. Clause II read:

> The responsibility of the Party is to lead the masses, and their various institutions, in the effort to safeguard national independence and to advance the liberation of the African. The duty of a socialist party is to guide all activities of the masses. The government, parastatals, national organisations, etc; are instruments for implementing the Party's policies. Our short history of independence reveals problems that may arise when a Party does not guide its instruments. The time has now come for the Party to take the reigns and lead all the people's activities.

According to the TANU guidelines, the major functions of the party fall into four main categories: Firstly, defining the national goals as well as issuing directives and guidelines for implementation; secondly, politicising, organising, and mobilising the people; thirdly, overseeing and supervising the work of all public institutions charged with the task of implementing the policies laid down; lastly, reviewing the record of performance of these institutions.[45]

It has been suggested that it was the TANU guidelines which mentioned Party supremacy for the first time when it said: 'The time has now come for the Party to take the reins and lead all people's activities.'[46] In 1972 the Party issued a policy statement on agriculture known as *Siasa ni Kilimo* (Politics is Agriculture). The policy was aimed at guiding the development of agriculture. The year 1973 witnessed four major decisions which were made by the Party, firstly, the Party approved a directive on small scale industries organisation (SIDO). Secondly, the Party decided to move the capital from Dar es Salaam to Dodoma; thirdly, the Party decided to move peasants to villages by force and 1976 was set as the deadline for the completion of this exercise and fourthly, the Party decided to combine the offices of TANU Branch Secretary and Ward Executive Office (Katibu kata) an arrangement similar to that at the district and regional levels where the commissioners headed both party and government offices.[47]

In 1974 the Party issued a directive on irrigation farming commonly referred to as the Moshi Resolution. The Party also issued another directive on education known as the Musoma Resolution, this directive emphasised that education meant work.

The Party in the same year (1974) formed seven sub-committees in order to increase its capacity for making policies and supervising their implementation. These sub-committees which comprised members of the central committee were: political affairs; economic affairs; social welfare; defence and security; finance and planning; national guidance; and affiliated associations, elders and cultural affairs. Each sub-committee was serviced by a department established for the purpose of ensuring effective functioning of the sub-committees.[48]

Efforts were made to staff these departments with experts by attracting qualified people to join the services of the party through the introduction of a scheme of service and review of the salary structure within the party.

It has been argued that the reason behind the introduction of such massive bureaucracy within the party, like that obtaining in the government, was to equip the party with necessary tools as a main decision and policy maker. The argument proceeds to assert that the aim is

to enable the party to exercise leadership functions more effectively, not to carry out the actual tasks of administration and execution.[49]
It has been emphasised that:

> The purpose of building such a secretariat was not to set up a sort of "shadow government" at the party headquarters, it was rather to have qualified staff members for each sub-committee who can collect relevant data, analyse it as background briefs for the members of the sub-committees.[50]

The question is not whether the secretariat was a shadow government or not, but the changing role of the party. To be precise, the party in fact started to create structures comparable to those in government on the pretext of supervising implementation of its policies. For example, each of the sub-committees was charged with the responsibility of supervising activities of a set of ministries and their parastatals. Let us take the sub-committee for social welfare as an example. This sub-committee supervised the activities of the ministries of National Education; Health, Labour and Social Welfare; Water, Energy and Minerals and Irrigation farming section of the Ministry of Agriculture.[51]
It is important to point out that all these major decisions were made by the party when the concept of party supremacy was only *de facto*. This supremacy was expressed in the following terms:

> ...under our one Party Constitution, TANU is supreme. It is able to give directions to Government about the general policy which must be adopted for national development, and it has power to give specific instructions about priorities of action in any aspect of our national life...[52]

The concept became *de jure* on 3rd June, 1975 after the amendments were made to the interim constitution by the National Assembly after the NEC had decided and directed that the constitution be amended to that effect. This amendment provided that all political activity in Tanzania shall be conducted by or under the auspices of the Party; and that the functions of all organs of the state of the United Republic shall be performed under the auspices of the Party.

The Role of the 'Left' in the Party 1967-1975
In discussing the role of the 'left' in the Party in period under discussion, we take the Arusha Declaration and 1971 Party Guidelines as our case studies.
The 'leftists' received the Arusha Declaration with vigour thinking

that it was only a start on the march to socialism. They therefore started to question the structure of the state that had been inherited from the colonialists. To them the solution lay in the dismantling of the state and creating a people's state in its place. The 'leftists' also advocated the restructuring of the colonial economy and called for the development of an independent self-sustaining national economy in its place.[53]

These proposals were not implemented because the ruling class was not capable of implementing them for they were contrary to what it (ruling class) stood for. In fact the 'leftists' inside the party made a mistake of overestimating the ideological clarity of the petty bourgeoisie. The petty bourgeoisie with its ideological limitations was not capable of executing a socialist revolution. Socialist construction cannot be undertaken by any class except the working class itself.

It is also difficult to see the possibility of creating a people's state or a state of the whole people[54]—is it a state accommodating all the poeple's interest in a particular society? We ask this question because we think the state is a class category i.e. every state has got a certain class character which in turn depends on the class which controls it.

As for the party, the 'leftists' questioned the ability of the Party as a mass party to lead a socialist revolution.

There were two camps in this regard. The first comprising of radicals who advocated for the creation of a vanguard party so as to lead the revolution. The other camp of moderates called for the creation of a vanguard within the mass party. They argued:

> ...the Party needed to cleanse itself of antisocialist elements in its ranks and must have a well-knit clear headed group at its centre, at the same time retaining its mass character, and it must put forward a clear socialist ideology. That is to say, a vanguard party can exist within the broad national liberation movement that TANU is.[55]

They went on to argue that:

> ...only such a party, then, would be able to destroy this colonially inherited state and its institutions, and build on their ruins a new state, one that would be able to address itself fully to the phase of our development, namely the national democratic revolution.[56]

The above argument overlooked the fact that the party which was being called upon to purge itself was a class party—a party of the petty bourgeoisie. The question then was who was going to purge whom.

It has often been suggested that the 'leftists' within the Party played a leading role in formulating the TANU guidelines (*Mwongozo*) of 1971. *Mwongozo* has been taken by many to be more radical the the Arusha Declaration.

The promulgation of *Mwongozo* witnessed a number of strikes at a number of work places. This is not to suggest that *Mwongozo* was the cause but rather the occasion for the workers to air their grievances. The workers used the often quoted clause 15 to press for their demands. The clause reads:

There must be a deliberate effort to build equality between the leaders and those they lead. For a Tanzanian leader it must be forbidden to be arrogant, extravagant, contemptuous and oppressive. The Tanzanian leader has to be a person who respects people, scorns ostentation and who is not a tyrant. He should epitomise heroism, bravery, and be a champion of justice and equality.

It was the *Mwongozo* which established the people's militia. It is said that the creation of a people's militia was a long cherished demand of the 'leftists' in the Party. But it would be incorrect to hold that the people's militia was created because the party accepted the leftist demand, but rather the events that took place in Uganda and Guinea which precipitated this move.

Once again the limitations of the petty bourgeois ideology were exposed in the response of the state to events which took place after the proclamation of *Mwongozo*. Using *Mwongozo*, the workers waged an onslaught on arrogant, extravagant, contemptuous and oppressive leaders at places of work. Their aim was to change the production relations at their working places. To their dismay they were suppressed by the ruling class which wanted to maintain the status quo.

As we shall see in the next section, the 'leftists' in the Party have been used whenever the regime has felt it was in crisis. We can therefore assert that the Party 'leftists' in Tanzania have sustained and maintained the ruling class for all this time. This has been possible because of the method of work which these 'leftists' have adopted. They have decided to work from within, thinking that they would be able to influence changes from within or 'seize' an opportunity, when it comes, of capturing the state power. They have therefore ended in opportunism.

1976 to the Present
This period is important in the analysis of the politics and the development of the party in Tanzania. It significantly and clearly shows the beginning of the end of the ideological and political heyday of the

ruling class and its legitimacy in the country. It has now become evident event to the party itself that it has lost its popularity and acceptance among the people notwithstanding the politicking that has continued all along.

As it has already been discussed in this book, during this period the state has found itself in deep economic crisis with no hope of immediate recovery. This economic crisis traces its visible appearance back to 1973/74 but growing more acute in 1977. This was more compounded by the intra-class contradictions at the East Africa region level leading to the collapse of the East African Community (EAC). Ideologically the collapse of E.A.C. was exploited by the ruling class to show the devilish and callous nature of capitalism that was being pursued by the "Nyang'au" in Kenya (the ruling class with capitalist policies) and the superior humane nature of socialism—"Ujamaa".

During the same period TANU and ASP merged to form one political party—Chama cha Mapinduzi. This was a major landmark event in the development of the political party and its relationship with the state in Zanzibar. The birth of CCM was popularly and enthusiastically received by the people in Zanzibar where ASP's popularity had ebbed. ASP was associated with the Revolutionary Council which was unpopular.

These economic crisis which have squeezed the people of Tanzania, have gone hand in hand with the enactment of more oppressive laws implementing party policies. This growing authoritarianism of the state has forced it to use the historical legitimacy of the party to justify its actions. On the other hand, the party has extensively used the state apparatus to entrench itself more in the civil society.

Reasons which were and are given by the ruling class and their apologetic sympathisers as the cause of the economic problems and the current political situation are ridiculous and populist. They justify the present economic situation to be externally caused and out of their control and consequently the present political situation as inevitable. With this the ruling class has used its tussle with the IMF to impress the people and harp on their sentiments. This rhetorical war against the IMF forced the ruling class to sacrifice some of its members who defended IMF policies openly. In times of peace, but especially in difficulty, the ruling class in Tanzania has favoured a populist line and pursued a petty bourgeois ideology. Under the disguise of being independent, it was intolerable for it to show the the public that it was openly supporting the IMF conditions. It organised mammoth rallies in support of the party decision to refuse to bow to the IMF. However, before the enthusiasm of the people had waned, the ruling class began to concede to IMF conditions silently. A good example was the devaluation of the currency.

Further populist steps were taken by the ruling class during this time. It sacrificed some of its members so as to boost its image among the people. Economic problems aggravated more problems inherent in it. Embezzlement, corruption and graft became the norm. This not only caught the eye of the public but aroused complaints which were openly raised as in the case of one Regional Commissioner. The President had to dismiss him after the residents openly raised complaints against him alleging corruption.

Due to complaints and cynicism in the streets, the ruling class was forced to take steps that were aimed at bolstering its image and raising its popularity. These steps were also aimed at appeasing the masses and the petty bourgeoisie who form the majority of the middle leadership of the party. This hook was swallowed by the radicals in the party leadership who have all along been advocating the transformation of the party into a vanguard party, a party that is led by committed leaders and cadres. To them this was to be preceded by purging all uncommitted and anti-socialist leaders. Hence when the party announced a special campaign to purge these "corrupt" elements within the ruling class, it was taken to be a progressive step.

This campaign started after the special meeting of NEC which was called by the President. The purposes of the meeting as given in the government statement were:

(1) To consider failures in the implementation of that government policy which is directed at securing the fair distribution of goods throughout the country together with the associated problem of *magendo* and blackmarket.
(2) To consider the manner in which certain operations of government and parastatals institutions have been carried on with particular reference to some action which have led to great losses of public money or foreign exchange.[57]

The statement went on to say that at the end of the meeting NEC reiterated the party's commitment to a distribution based on the principle of fair share for all. It (NEC) also instructed the Central Committee (CC) to carry out further investigations into certain other matters and afterwards make recommendations for action.

The CC had a series of meetings. It had begun its work with a consideration of a number of public contracts involving millions of shillings in Tanzanian currency and foreign exchange. The Committee interviewed a number of government and parastatal leaders, and received written documents. The government statement emphasised that:

In every public corporation there are individuals who have been entrusted with the responsibility for carrying on the people's business in the public interest; these individuals are accountable to the people and have to accept responsibility for the failures it was to their jobs.[58]

It was due to that reasoning that a number of leaders were dismissed. We shall deal with the leaders of three parastatals who were dismissed, Air Tanzania Corporation (ATC), Tanzania Investment Bank (TIB) and Tanzania Elimu Supplies (TES).

In relation to ATC, it was due to the contract between ATC and George Hallack, a Beirut-based owner of the Caledonian Airline. The CC was satisfied that there had been at the very least a massive mishandling of an international business arrangement, which had resulted in loss of much public money and had damaged the reputation of ATC as a reliable carrier. The statement issued by the CC said that some aspects of the contract had shown a lack of elementary business prudence and competence. It also said that no consultation was carried with other organs of the government which might have led to the early correction of the fault. As a result of this, the President removed Augustine Mwingira from Minister and Chairman of ATC Board of Directors and Lawrence Mmasi as ATC General Manager.

The TIB scandal involved the selling of its ship mv. *Jitegemee* to a private company, Tanzania Colt Motors (TCM) for shs. 39 million. The company was owned by A.M. Rajpar. TCM only paid shs. 14 million and then christened the ship Lord Rajpar. This resulted in the sacking of the Chairman and Managing Director, G. Mbowe and the General Manager, Tibesigwa. The buyer was also detained together with Abdul Haji, under presidential orders because of their suspected connection with economic actions prejudicial to the security and well-being of the state. The government statement issued on 23rd January, 1981 said that the two were detained on 10th January, 1981. It said that certain actions by each of these two had undermined or endangered the good repute of Tanzania in its foreign transactions and called into question the integrity of certain public institutions.

The ship later reverted to TIB after a consent judgement given in early March, 1982[59] by the High Court. This judgement was given after the parties, i.e. TIB and TCM, had agreed that the ship should be delivered to the Bank upon repayment of shs. 14 million to Colt Motors. In the case the Attorney General had filed a suit on behalf of the government against TCM on grounds that the ship was irregularly sold to TCM by TIB.

The *Daily News* of 27th February, 1981 carried a banner headline "TES FRAUD UNEARTHED". The CC said that greedy individuals within the TES had taken advantage of the current acute shortage of stationery and school equipment to enrich themselves in collaboration with capitalist businessmen. As a result, retail stationery shops owned by the TES had empty shelves purportedly as a result of the non-availability of items while shops belonging to individual businessmen were fully stocked with the same items selling at higher prices. CC cited Family Stationeries and Sherali as examples of such capitalist firms that had collaborated with TES in exploiting a purported shortage of school equipment and stationery supplies. It said that some people in TES had used the company to enrich themselves under various pretences including non-availability of material. This led to mushrooming of lucrative business in printing, stationery and school equipment while TES shelves remained empty, the excuse being shortage due to economic hardships.

It was no wonder therefore that on 12th March, 1981 President Nyerere dismissed the TES General Manager, Gervas Chilipweli.[60] He also directed the Ministry of National Education, which happens to be the parent ministry, to take appropriate actions against some TES workers found to have acted contrary to national interests. The sacking was therefore seen as a punishment following the unearthing of the business scandal by the CC.

It should be pointed out that the cleansing exercise which was carried out by the CC was under the Chairmanship of the Vice Chairman of the Party, Aboud Jumbe. This exercise did not last long. The Chairman of the Party in an address to the nation indicated that in the exercise some innocent people may have been punished and therefore they should not be surprised if some of them were re-appointed to take other posts.[61] Indeed, that is what happened. No sooner had these people been dismissed and settled down than they were given other posts, for example Augustine Mwingira (who was sacked as Minister of Communications and Transport) was appointed Regional Commissioner which post carries the status of a ministerial position.

The government during this time took some emergency measures to try to solve the economic problems. The earlier liberalisation policy which was intiated by the de-confinement policy in the earlier period was abandoned. Instead new steps were taken. These were outlined in the National Economic Survival Programme (NESP) and Structural Adjustment Plan (SAP). All these documents were prepared by the Tanzania Advisory Group which was formed by the World Bank and Tanzania. Interestingly even the NEC was informed on NESP after the government had already begun implementing it. It was during the discussion on NESP in the NEC that finally the 'leftists' in the party were able to moot the need for the party having its programme instead of always taking ad hoc measures. A special committee of NEC was formed to work out a programme. The committee included both the 'leftist' and the rightists. The programme was later approved by NEC and it was decided to call it "The CCM Guidelines 1981". Definitely the programme in its final version has a lot of ideological overtones found in similar documents of socialist countries. This was even clear in the party structure proposed and later fully adopted in the party constitution.

The adoption of the 1981 Guidelines was crucial and important to the ruling class in Tanzania. It hoped to invoke the historical legitimacy of the 1971 TANU Guidelines and of the Arusha Declaration. Thus in the 1981 CCM guidelines the Party itself says as much: 'Inspite of the historical legitimacy, which is very much based on heritage, CCM must establish its own legitimacy.'[62] However, this time unlike in 1967 when the Arusha Declaration was promulgated, people did not flock into the streets. Also it did not receive the same response as that of 1971 Guidelines which stands out till today as a monumental work of the 'leftists' in the party.

It is evident that when the ruling class has been rocked by crisis, it has utilised the services of the 'leftists' in the party to salvage it. The 'leftists' using their populist and progressive rhetoric that appeals to the sentiments of the people have temporarily made it popular. But after the ruling class has weathered the storms and securely consolidated its position it has unceremoniously discarded the 'leftists'.

It is clear that in the 1981 CCM Guidelines the state bourgeoisie envisaged the use of the Party to further consolidate its hegemonic position in the ruling class. This time not only ideologically but even organisationally. The party has been restructured in order to assume that leading role. A strong secretariat headed by a strong secretary general who is number 3 in the state hierachy has been created. In it various departments headed by members of Central Committee of the NEC have been formed. The party now has every bureaucracy that competes with that of the government to oversee the day to day activities of the state. It has even a full time secretary to the secretariat who is also the chief of service in the party. This is equivalent to the Head of Civil Service who is also Principal Secretary to the President's Office.

Organisationally the state bourgeoisie has consolidated its hegemonic position after the 1982 party elections. For example, now the membership of the Central Committee has been trimmed down from 40 to 18. If one looks at the individuals in the Central Committee it is crystal clear that all of them are either top or former top members of the government and especially the Cabinet. The Central Committee comprises of the Chairman of the Party who is also the head of the executive as the President, the Vice Chairman of the Party who is also the head of the executive in Zanzibar, the Secretary General of the Party who is also a Cabinet Minister and not more than 15 members elected by NEC from among its members.[63]

There is an overlapping of functions between top government and party posts. For example 11 members of CC of NEC are also in the Cabinet[64] and the remaining are former cabinet members who have a big likelihood of being re-appointed. In the list of Regional Commissioners who were appointed soon after the Party elections, among the 19 on the Mainland 10 were NEC members and among the 5 in Zanzibar 1 was a NEC member.[65] Living and Van Donge have correctly concluded that:

> Those who dominate the government machinery appear to be in the leadership position of CCM. CCM does not open its leadership position to those directly engaged in production.[66]

This means that the state bourgeoisie has ensured and secured that it is only a small number in the ruling class in general which is in important political decision-making positions in the highest organs of the party. In addition, deliberations of both the Central Committee and the NEC are held in camera denying the public any information of what is happening especially at the NEC level which is supposed to be representative.

Some writers like Pratt[67] have portrayed the NEC to be a place where deliberations are more frank and lively than the Parliament. But an analysis of the National Conference of the party done by Mfupe shows that usually there is little diversity of ideas at that level.[68] We submit that the same is reflected at the NEC level. This is proved by the fact that although constitutionally the Central Committee is a subordinate body to the NEC, in actual practice it is the Central Committee which decides most of the issues and NEC endorses them. And in the party structure the position of the chairman is dominant and central. He appoints the Secretary-General and heads of departments in the Secretariat. His influence is more proved by the fact that two members of the Central Committee who are also cabinet ministers entered the NEC from the list of members nominated by the chairman.[69]

Also so long as the discussions are not made in the glare of the public that in itself makes the body lack one of the important attributes of democracy.

Recently party decisions have led to enactment of very harsh and oppressive and draconian pieces of legislation. These are the Human Resources Deployment Act[70] and the Economic Sabotage (Special Provisions) Act.[71] The CCM Guidelines 1981 had made an analysis of the economic crimes in Tanzania and suggested enactment of aspecial legislation to deal with the problem. This was done after the crackdown on the alleged economic saboteurs had already begun. Initally when the campaign began it was received with enthusiasm and processions were staged. But it did not take long before the masses discovered that the whole campaign was a mere hullabaloo. Cynically the masses began to say openly that *vigogo* (the big fish) had been left untouched.

The enactment of the two legislations clearly shows that once the ruling class is facing a major crisis and it can no longer bury itself in its populist ideological cocoon, it will resort to the only alternative—the use of the repressive state apparatus. Thus it will use the logic of force rather than the force of logic.

This has happened hand in hand with another interesting trend in the party, the militarisation of the party. Soon after the 1964 Army mutiny, the trend which was taken by the ruling class as regards the army was that of politicising it. An entirely new army was formed with recruits mainly from the TANU Youth League who were throughly screened by the Party. The army mutiny taught the ruling class in the country that it no longer needed an apolitical army. That was impossible when the material conditions necessitated it not to be apolitical but mutinous. Thus politicisation of the army was aimed at creating a loyal army. The task of politicisation of the army was handled by loyal and trusted politicans who were transferred to the army and commissioned as officers.

However this trend was somehow reversed after 1971. In response to the mercenary invasion of Guinea and a coup d'etat in Uganda, the 1971 TANU Guidelines recommended the formation of a people's militia. This was an emulation of the principle of people's defence which had shown success when Guinea was invaded. With it the trend was reversed to that of militarisation of the party. Most of the party leaders and functionaries had to attend officers cadets courses at the Tanzanian Military Academy at Monduli, Arusha. After the course they were commissioned and most of them remained in the party service while others remained in the army on special assignment. The Party also has a system of party structure in the Army. However, unlike in ordinary working places, the army has a special system. Under that system it is laid down categorically that the chairman of a party branch at company level is the company commander. This affects all the other party organs at other levels. At the level of a battalion it is the Battalion Commander, at the brigade level the Brigade Commander, at the Division level the Division Commander and at the national level the Chief of Defence Forces. The rationale given on this peculiar party leadership system was the need to maintain discipline by having one source of command.

In the last party elections a new quota system was introduced in order to ensure that there was group representation of some sectors. Among them was the armed forces or to be precise the repressive apparatus of the state, the army, police and prisons. However the results showed that it was mainly those from the army and not police or prisons who were elected. In that list, the total number of candidates from the repressive apparatus of the state was 20. Out of these 11 were from the army and 9 from the police and prisons. Out of 20 only 10 were to be elected and 8 out of the list of the army were elected. This amounts to 73%, and only 2 from the list of police and prison were elected amounting to only 22%.

This is an indication of the development of militarisation of the party at the organisational level. The same is reflected in the bio-data of contestants who mentioned *mgambo* or their participation in the war against Idi Amin regime in Uganda as a qualifying item for party leadership.[72] But the new *mgambo* which was regarded as a people's force and therefore under the party when it began in 1971 has now become totally part of the regular army. *Mgambo* now forms a whole division of the army under a Major General. During times of peace the *mgambo* plays the role of police or a para-military force.

After the 1982 party elections, under a new party structure, a new post of Regional Party Secretary was established. All the Party Regional Secretaries were appointed from the NEC. Of all appointed 32% were from the armed forces and two of them popular senior army officers who were division commanders of the army.

The militarisation of the Party at the organisational level cannot be properly explained without taking account of the economic crisis which now persists in Tanzania. The economic crisis which has continued unabated has made the ideology of the ruling class hollow; hence its resort to militarisation.

Conclusion

In conclusion, we would like to summarise the important propositions of this Chapter as follows:

1. The Party and the State in Tanzania are closely related organisationally to the extent that it is very difficult to make a distinction between them.
2. There has been a trend of concentrating important powers in the Party rather than other state organs.
   (a) The Party (TANU) gave itself mandate to declare Tanzania a one Party State. We think it was incompetent to do so, for

not all Tanzanians are Party members.

(b) The several mass organisations have been heavily suppressed and they only exist in name.

(c) The Party assumed a greater role in terms of decision-making after the promulgation of the Arusha Declaration.

3. The supremacy of the Party has weakened the role of the Parliament which has now been turned into a mere committee of the National Conference of the Party.

4. The 'leftists' in the party have all along been used to bail the regime out of crisis by producing 'revolutionary' documents such as the TANU guidelines of 1971 and the CCM guidelines of 1981.

5. The crisis which has ridden the country has made the ideology of the ruling class hollow, hence there has been a tendency towards militarisation of the Party at the organisational level.

NOTES

1. Marx, K. & Engels, F., *Selected Works*, (Moscow: Progress Publishers), p.127.
2. Lenin, V., *State and Revolution*, (Moscow: Progress Publishers, 1977), pp.10-11.
3. Iliffe, J., *A Modern History of Tanganyika*, (Cambridge: Cambridge University Press, 1979), pp.512-513.
4. See Bhagat and Othman, "Colonialism and Class Formation in Zanzibar", *Utafiti*, Vol.3, No.7 (1978), p.209.
5. Shivji, I., *Class Struggles in Tanzania*, (Dar es Salaam: Tanzania Publishing House, 1975).
6. Illiffe, J., *op. cit.* p.508.
7. Nyerere, J., *Freedom and Socialism*, (Dar es Salaam: Oxford University Press, 1968), p.28.
8. *10 Ely 2.*
9. S. 1 1961 No.2274 (EA).
10. The Preamble read in Part: "And Whereas such rights are best maintained and protected in a democratic society where the government is responsible to a freely elected Parliament representative of the people and where the courts of law are free and impartial".
11. Government Paper No.1 of 1962, (Dar es Salaam: Government Printers, 1962).
12. Warioba, E., & Seaton, E., "The Constitution of Tanzania: An Overview", in *E.A. Law Review*, Vols.11-14 (Faculty of Law, University of Dar es Salaam).
13. Wambura said: "We are also members representing the people just as the members of the Cabinet do. Now when certain matters are brought before this House, we have an equal right to discuss it without fear".
    See *Tanganyika, National Assembly Official Reports* 36th session, Vol.V. Column 33, 18 October 1961, p.6.
14. Tordoff, W., *Tanzania: Government & Politics*, (Nairobi: East African Publishing House, 1967), p.6.
15. Nyerere, J., *Freedom and Unity*, (Dar es Salaam: Oxford University Press, 1966), p.134.
16. Cliffe, L. "Democracy in a One Party State: The Tanzanian Experience", in Cliffe, L., & Saul, J., *Socialism in Tanzania* Vol.I (Nairobi: East African Publishing

House, 1972), p.242.
17. Nyerere, J., *Freedom and Unity, op. cit.* p.196.
18. Pratt, C., *The Critical Phase in Tanzania, 1945-1966, Nyerere and the Emergence of Socialist Strategy*, (Cambridge: University Press, 1974) p.187.
19. *Report of the Presidential Commission on the Establishment of a Democratic One Party State*, (Dar es Salaam: Government Printer, 1968), p.2, paragraph 8 (hereinafter cited as Commission on 'One Party State).
20. Act No.43 of 1965.
21. Article 3 (3) .
22. *Commission on One Party State*, p.16 paragraph 40 (a).
23. Barkan, J., & Okumu, J., (eds.) *Politics and Public Policy in Kenya and Tanzania*, (New York: Praeger Publishers, 1971), p.52.
24. Article 3 (3).
25. Article 3 (1).
26. Article 3 (2).
27. Article 54 (1).
28. Article 26 (1) (b).
29. *Parliamentary Debates (Hansard)* of 22nd July, 1968 Column 2478.
30. Hyden, G. (ed.), *Co-operatives in Tanzania: Problem of Organisation Building* (Dar es Salaam: Tanzania Publishing House, 1976), p.13.
31. *Ibid.*, p.13.
32. Pratt, C., *op. cit.* pp.194-195.
33. Rweyemamu, A. & Mwansasu, B., (eds.), *Planning in Tanzania*, (Nairobi: East African Literature Bureau, 1977), p.125.
34. Local Government (District Authorities) Act, 1982.
35. Msekwa, P., *Towards Party Supremacy*, (Arusha: Eastern African Publications, 1976), p.62.
36. Nyerere, J., *Freedom and Socialism, op. cit.*, p.231.
37. Babu, A.M., ''The Tanzania that might have been'', *Africa Now* (London: Pan-African Publishers Ltd., December, 1981).
38. *Ibid.*
39. *New Africa*, June 1980, p.69.
40. *Ibid.*, p.71.
41. Nyerere, J., *Freedom and Socialism, op. cit.*
42. See Shivji, I., ''Capitalism Unlimited: Public Corporation in Partnership with Multinational Corporations'' in Mapolu, H. (ed.) *Workers and Management*, (Dar es Salaam: Tanzania Publishing House, 1976), pp.40-70.
43. Salim, S., ''The Tanzanian State: A Critique'', *Monthly Review*, (New York) Vol.28, January, 1977 pp.51-57.
44. Babu, A., *Africa Now, op. cit.*
45. Clause 13.
46. Clause 22.
47. Mwansasu, B., ''The Changing Role of the TANU'', in Mwansasu, B. & Pratt, C. (eds.), *Towards Socialism in Tanzania*, (Dar es Salaam: Tanzania Publishing House, 1979), p.181.
48. Kapinga, D., *Party Supremacy and Economic Enterprise: A Case Study of the Practice of the Concept in Tanzania with Special Reference to Tanzania Tobacco Processing Plant Party Branch*, M.A. (DS) Dissertation, University of Dar es Salaam, pp.112-117.
49. Mwansasu, B., *Towards Socialism in Tanzania, op. cit.*, p.187.
50. *Ibid.*, p.185.
51. Kapinga, *op. cit.* p.116.

52. *Ibid.*
53. Babu, A., *Africa Now*, *op. cit.*
54. Refer to the great Debate between the Communist Party of the Union of Soviet Socialist Republic (USSR) and the Chinese Communist Party on whether there can be a state of the whole people. In this debate CPC held that there can be no state of the whole people, for the state is an instrument of the ruling class; on the other hand the CPC-USSR held that during socialism the state belongs to the whole people.
55. Othman, H., (ed.) *The State in Tanzania*, (Dar es Salaam: Dar es Salaam University Press, 1980), p.12.
56. *Ibid.*
57. *Daily News*, 24 January 1981.
58. *Ibid.*
59. *Daily News*, March 15, 1982.
60. *Daily News*, March 13, 1981.
61. *Daily News*,
62. Chama cha Mapinduzi (CCM) Guidelines of 1982.
63. Article 70 (2) of the CCM Constitution, 1982.
64. Authors' Observation.
65. *Ibid.*
66. Liviga, A. & Van Donge, J., "The 1982 Elections of the National Executive Committee of CCM—A Case Study of Political Recruitment in Tanzania", *Seminar Paper Presented to Department of Political Science Seminars*, p.27 (mimeo).
67. Pratt, C. *The Critical Phase in Tanzania...*, *op. cit.*
68. Mfupe, D., *Party Democracy and Ideological Orientation—An Inquiry into the Extent of Democratic Participation and Ideological Struggle in TANU's Post-Arusha Declaration National Conference*, M.A. (Political Science Dissertation, University of Dar es Salaam, 1976), p.106.
69. Those elected were Cleopa Msuya and Salim Ahmed Salim.
70. Act No.6 of 1983.
71. Act No.6 of 1983.
72. Liviga, A. & Van Donge, J., *op. cit.* p.7.

4. STATE CONTROL OF THE WORKING CLASS THROUGH LABOUR LEGISLATION

Wilbert B. L. Kapinga

Introduction

Quite a few accounts of the character of the Tanzanian state have identified its growing authoritarian tendencies. The term 'authoritarian' is used in the relative sense, for while all political systems maintain repressive state apparatuses there is no doubt that some states are more authoritarian than others in that they rely more often on coercion against recalcitrants.[1] The authoritarian nature of the colonial state finds substantial continuity in the post-colonial Tanzanian state.

As regards the existing labour regime, the state has characteristically suppressed almost all forms of labour resistance and created a stringent legal machinery for the control of wage-labour. The legal control of labour has assumed two forms. Firstly the control of unionized labour action under a system of compulsory arbitration in labour disputes. This has virtually abolished strikes, the most important weapon of workers in collective bargaining. Secondly, the rigorous disciplining of individual labour action under a system of individual labour grievance settlement. In both cases state officials occupy predominant positions in decision-making.

Tanzania experienced a British colonial legal system whose labour legislation was predominantly punitive.[2] With the development of the country's political economy the last years of the colonial era saw the gradual reduction and eventual abolition of penal sanctions in labour laws. However, the ensuing neo-colonial system methodically embarked on employing penal sanctions to deal with any semblance of autonomous organised action of the growing working class in Tanzania.

The vagaries of Tanzania's dependent economic formation have compelled the state to enact a law which appears to be a reversion to the colonial labour utilisation system. The legislation is aimed at deploying labour with a view to compelling all able-bodied persons to engage in productive work in the so-called economic interests of the nation.[3] For the better operation of the Human Resources Deployment Act of 1983, the notorious vagrancy provisions of the penal law[4] have been amended to enlarge the category of the so-called 'idle and disorderly persons' who are now liable to be deployed. The state has also recently introduced personal tax dubbed 'development levy' on all adult citizens.[5] Not unlike the colonial 'poll-tax', this levy is presumably calculated to compel the unemployed to offer their labour to capitalist farming concerns whose development is clearly being encouraged by the state.[6]

This Chapter seeks to illustrate that the authoritarian stance of the colonial era with regard to the labour regime has now been augmented under the existing dependent economic formation of post-colonial Tanzania. The use of law in controlling wage-labour is one of the peculiar manifestations of the authoritarian legal system in Tanzania. This Chapter will only be concerned with the post-colonial state control of the working class through labour legislation.

Legal Control of Organised Labour
The attitude of the early post-colonial Tanzanian state towards labour reveals some interesting contradictory features. On the one hand, the state appeared to have consciously given concessions in the form of social security and other protective labour legislation; these concessions being held up as evidence of the state's progressive and sympathetic attitude to workers.[7] On the other hand, during the same period a host of laws were enacted completely throttling all forms of working-class organisations. Workers' organisations were by legislative fiat placed under the firm control of the government. In view of this, it may be argued that the purported social security and other concessions by the state were at best half-hearted and at worst political and ideological control mechanisms over the working class.

The first thing that the independent government did in an effort to place working-class organisations under its control was to curb what it thought was the obstinacy of the Tanganyika Federation of Labour (TFL). TFL had run into disfavour with the government for attempting, among other things,[8] to assert the autonomy of the trade union movement. The government resorted to the same authoritarian methods of the colonial state to ensure that trade unions were under the firm grip of the state. Four pieces of legislation which had significant impact on the trade unions were passed by the Parliament. The first enactment was the Trade Disputes (Settlement) Act, 1962[9] which virtually abolished strikes by setting up a complex procedure for compulsory arbitration and settlement of labour disputes. The procedure for arbitration was made even more elaborate by later legislation, discussed later in the Chapter.

The second enactment was the Trade Union Ordinance (Amendment) Act, 1962.[10] This legislation made the continued registration of any trade union subject to its being affiliated to federation of labour so designated by the state. The TFL was so designated. The law empowered the Registrar of Trade Unions to cancel the registration of any trade union which, within three months of its registration, failed to become a member of the designated federation. A trade union's registration could also be cancelled if the Registrar was satisfied that having become a member of the designated federation, the union had ceased to be a member thereof. TFL itself was placed under the supervision and control of the state through the Minister responsible for labour matters and the Registrar of Trade Unions. For example, the Minister had powers to direct the designated federation as to the purposes to which any money received as union dues were to be applied. The federation was obligated to give effect to such directions.[11] Furthermore, the Registrar was empowered to suspend officers of the federation if he was satisfied that the funds of the trade unions had been or were being used in an unlawful manner or on unlawful objects or on matters not authorized by the law.[12] It may be recalled that during the colonial era the scrutiny of trade union finances by the colonial government was intended to ensure that trade union funds were not used for political purposes. The reasons for government control of trade union funds in the post-colonial period were similar.

The 1962 amendment to the Trade Union Ordinance was followed during the same parliamentary sitting by the enactment of the Civil Service (Negotiating Machinery) Act, 1962.[13] The Act excluded all civil servants earning more than £702 per annum from becoming members of any trade union. This law was in essence aimed at undermining the leadership of the trade unions, for it was from the civil service that the movement's literate and articulate leadership came.

And finally on the heel of this legislation came the Preventative Detention Act, 1962[14] which empowered the President of the country to order the detention of any person who in his opinion was conducting himself in a manner prejudicial to the state. The first victims of the detention law were the so-called stubborn leaders of TFL, Victor Mkello, then its President, and Magongo, another leading TFL official. The detention of these trade union leaders came after their brief banishment to a remote up-country region of Sumbawanga. It was clear that the government was looking for an opportunity to snuff out the trade union movement. The late Sheikh Amri Abeid, the then

Minister of Justice, in 1962 urged the government to get rid of the trade unions and was not pleased with the 'leniency' with which the government treated trade union leaders who were stubborn.[15] Through legislative measures the state assumed increasing control over the trade union movement and the so-called obstinate opposition was eventually abolished. In the wake of the army mutiny of 1964, which was subsequently suppressed by British troops, the state was given a pretext to kill whatever autonomy was left in the trade union movement. TFL was banned and its leaders were placed in detention. The National Union of Tanganyika Workers (Establishment) Act, 1964[16] formally abolished TFL and created in its place one workers' union, NUTA.

NUTA was made an affiliated organisation of the ruling political party, the Tanganyika African National Union (TANU).[17] Top leaders of the new union were Presidential appointees. Throughout its life, the General Secretary of the Union was also a Cabinet Minister responsible for labour matters. The President was empowered by the law establishing the union to dissolve the union if in his view it did not serve the purpose it was established for.[18] Union members themselves were deprived of legal power to dissolve the union or to make provision for its dissolution.[19]

With regard to union democracy at grassroots level, the power of selection of union leaders and their subsequent removal left much to be desired. The state played a crucial role. Only at branch level were there direct elections to elect committee members. The General Secretary of the Union and his Deputy were appointed by the President of the United Republic and were to hold office for five years unless they died sooner, resigned or were removed by the appointing authority. The financial secretary, nine assistant secretaries for the various industrial sections of the Union, Directors of Organisation and of Economics and Research were all appointed by the General Secretary after consultation with voting members of the General Council. All those officers held office at the pleasure of the General Secretary. The lower ranks of the leadership, that is to say Union Branch secretaries, Branch Treasurers and Sectional secretaries were appointed and could be removed by the Executive Council.

At the level of collective bargaining, the rules of the Union, which incidentally wholly undermined the traditional trade union role in this area, provided for the manner in which trade disputes had to be handled. In the event of a dispute at the place of work union members had to report the matter to the Branch Secretary who subsequently had to submit the full facts and issues involved in the dispute to the Executive Council through the office of the General Secretary of the Union. The Union rules made it categorical that in no case was the cessation of work to take place or be threatened without the prior sanction of the General Council. The General Council itself was barred from sanctioning or proposing strike action in respect of any trade dispute without exhausting the procedures provided for under the Trade Disputes (Settlement) Act, 1962.

The so-called workers' union was virtually a department of the government and was under complete control of the ruling political party. The legal restriction imposed in 1962, prohibiting of senior cadres of the civil service from joining trade unions, was eventually removed at the end of 1964.[20] Obviously such restraint was no longer necessary because the so-called stubborn trade union movement had already been eliminated and the new Union, NUTA, to quote Rashid Mfaume Kawawa, the then Second Vice-President of the United Republic of Tanzania, "was quite cooperative with the Government."[21]

Collective Labour Action
Although NUTA was more or less a department of the state, the Union continued with the old tradition of demanding higher wages and better terms of service for its members. In 1967, the state reacted against that tradition and tightened its control over NUTA. The state enacted the Permanent Labour Tribunal Act, 1967[22] which set up a machinery for controlling wage increases and provided for arbitration of industrial disputes. The Permanent Labour Tribunal (PLT), a kind of industrial court established under the law, was made the final arbitrator and adjudicator over all collective disputes. PLT was empowered to register all wage agreements and other incentive agreements if they conformed to specified guidelines for wage increases and those not registered by it had no legal effect.

The principles[23] guiding the PLT included such general matters as the need to maintain a high level of domestic capital accumulation; expand employment opportunities; preserve the competitive position of local products in the domestic and overseas markets; provide incentives for increasing productivity through such measures as payment-by-result scheme and the need to maintain a fair relation between the incomes of different sectors of the community and reasonable differentials in rewards between different categories of skills and level of responsibility. In addition, before reaching its decisions, the PLT was also to be guided by the impact its awards would have on the balance of payments and on government's ability to finance development programmes and recurrent expenditure in the public sector.

To gauge the import of the system of compulsory arbitration and the extent to which the traditional working-class weapon of strike has been undermined in Tanzania it may be illustrative to examine the statutory process of collective bargaining. Successful negotiations between workers and their employer in respect of, say, wage increases may be embodied in what is called a voluntary agreement. The law requires that the details of the voluntary agreement should be sent to the Ministry of Labour which subsequently submits it with the Ministry's comments to PLT for consideration. If the agreement conforms to the guidelines outlined above, the PLT would register the agreement as an award. The award would be final and binding on the parties until varied by a subsequent award. Such an award is an implied term in the contract between the employer and the employees to whom the award relates.[24] Where the PLT refuses to register a voluntary agreement as an award, then the wage negotiations have to start afresh and a previously registered wage agreement, if any, remains in force.

On the other hand where wage negotiations end up in a dispute, the law disallows strike action on the part of workers or lock-outs by employers. The dispute, whether actual or apprehended, is supposed to be reported to the Labour Commissioner in writing by the General Secretary of the Union on behalf of its members involved in the dispute. In case of employees who are not union members, they may request the Labour Commissioner to act on their behalf without going through the trade union. After the Labour Commissioner has been appraised of the full facts and issues involved in the trade dispute a conciliator from the Ministry of Labour is appointed to attempt to conciliate. If the conciliation succeeds a negotiated agreement ensues. The same is then sent to PLT for consideration and registration as an award. If conciliation fails, the law requires that the matter be referred to PLT for hearing and determination. As in other cases, the award becomes final and binding on the parties unless varied by a subsequent award. Awards and decisions of the PLT are final and not subject to challenge, review, nor called in to question in any court of law except on the ground of lack of jurisdiction.[25]

During proceedings before the PLT the Chairman, or in his absence the Deputy Chairman, sits with the assessors. The Chairman and his deputies are appointees of the President and hold office at his pleasure. The assessors are selected by the Minister of Labour. One of the assessors must be from a panel of assessors submitted to the Minister by the Workers' Union or from among the members of the Union. The other assessor should be selected by the Minister from a panel of assessors submitted to him by the Association of Tanzania Employers or any other body which, in the opinion of the Minister, represents the interests of the employers in Tanzania.[26] The proceedings of the PLT may continue regardless of the absence of either one or both of the assessors who were present at the commencement of the proceedings. The opinion of the assessors is not binding on the chairman who has the final say. The Chairman is only bound to record the opinion of the assessors and the reasons for his disagreement. Thus the process of arbitration is greatly dominated by the state appointees.

As can be seen from the foregoing, the system of compulsory arbitration of trade disputes is quite complex. And while conciliation at the Ministry of Labour or an enquiry or hearing before the PLT are going on, undertaking a strike or lock-out is against the law. Engaging in or inciting people to take part in a strike or lock-out in contravention of the provisions of the Permanent Labour Tribunal Act, 1967 is an offence which on conviction may result in a fine not exceeding three thousand shillings or imprisonment for a term not exceeding fifteen months or both fine and imprisonment. The police in Tanzania are empowered to arrest without warrant any person whom they reasonably suspect of having engaged in or incited a strike or lock-out.[27]

The Demise of Trade Unionism

It has been argued that the rationale behind the Parliament Labour Tribunal Act, 1967 was to control the haphazard rise in wages, which according to Professor Turner, was responsible for inflation and the lowering of the income of peasants.[28] The establishment of the PLT deprived NUTA in a subtle way of its last important role as a trade union in collective bargaining in respect of wage increases and better employment conditions. In 1977 following the merger of TANU and Afro-Shiraz Party (ASP) to form 'Chama cha Mapinduzi' (CCM), the only political trade union. It was then made a mere 'mass organisation' of the ruling political party under the name of 'Jumuiya ya Wafanyakazi wa Tanzania' (JUWATA) i.e. a workers' mass organisation affiliated to CCM.

The consequences of the collapse of genuine and independent trade unions in Tanzania have been epitomized by Shivji in the following words: "As a result the gains that the (working class) had made in terms of increased wages during the late '50s and early '60s, were swiftly eroded over the next ten years resulting in the real wages in the '70s being lower than those of the early '60s. Since the loss of trade union autonomy wages have failed to keep pace with the galloping inflation".[29] In 1976 when the minimum wage was shs. 380 per month, the real wage was sh. 130, being about 30% below the 1963 level.[30]

JUWATA was established by the CCM constitution. By virtue of Article 70 of the said constitution JUWATA was designated the so-called workers' mass organisation and it began to operate on the

5 February 1978. It had lived for a year before it was accorded statutory effect to operate as a trade union. It has been argued that the delay was deliberate for a debate was going on as to the need to have an Act of Parliament to make a mass organisation of the party a trade union. When tabling the Bill to enact legislation to give JUWATA the legal status of a trade union, the then Minister for Labour and Social Welfare, Crispin Tungaraza said: "Since NUTA was established by an Act of Parliament NUTA still exists in law and JUWATA has no legal status. The principal object of the Bill is to accord legal existence to JUWATA and to dissolve NUTA by repealing the law which established the union in 1964". The JUWATA Act, 1979,[31] was introduce retrospectively. The Act was deemed to have come into effect on the 5 February 1978.[32] JUWATA was made the sole body representative of all employees in Tanzania.[33]

Thus Tanzania by law has only one employees' trade union in clear contravention of the traditional principle of free trade unions voluntarily formed, a principle which was enshrined even in the colonial trade union legislation.[34] The freedom of JUWATA members, whose membership was made automatic any way upon dissolution of NUTA, is completely curtailed by section 7 (4) of the JUWATA Act which prohibits the making of rules empowering the union to provide for its dissolution. The selection of the 'Union's leaders' is done from outside the Union. The Secretary General and his two deputies occupying executive positions in the union are appointees of the Chairman of CCM, who is also the President of the Tanzanian state. The Registrar of Trade Unions, who is also the Principal Secretary of the Ministry of Labour and Social Welfare (an appointee of the President), is placed in a rather awkward position. He is unlikely to effect control on the top trade union leadership, which until 1982 included the Minister of his own ministry, for he was also the Secretary General of the Union. This state of affairs, where the trade union is virtually a government department, probably contributed to the 'oversight' on the part of the Union leadership in not registering the union for nearly four years until it was brought to its senses by a law suit in which the union's legality was questioned.[35]

The President of the United Republic of Tanzania has enormous powers over JUWATA. He may order its cancellation in the register of trade unions if, in his opinion, it was no longer serving the interests of the public, and may establish some other body which would be representative of the employees and which would then be deemed to be a trade union.[36] One can clearly see that what the colonial state did with a somewhat shy face in passing legislation which completely placed trade unions under the thumb of the state, the neo-colonial state has done it with a straight face.

Control of Individual Labour Action

Having passed the law to place collective labour action under firm state control, the government proceeded to create a legal machinery for the disciplining of individual labour action. This was provided for by the Security of Employment Act[37], which was passed in December, 1964 and became operative on the 1 May, 1965. Its enactment was necessitated by the nature of industry and labour regime of the post-colonial era. It may be noted that import-substitution industrialisation developed a somewhat permanent labour force. But indigenous labour force with its peasant hangovers lacked the long tradition of industrial discipline of the West European type. Thus the emergent state attempted to grapple with this problem by the enactment of the Security of Employment Act.

The Security of Employment Act legislates on individual labour grievance settlement procedure which restricts the powers of the employer to dismiss summarily or take any disciplinary action against an employee. Thus one gets the impression that the security of tenure of employees is specifically provided for by legislation. One legal commentator even went to the extent of applauding the Tanzanian legislature for filling a gap in her heritage of English industrial law which provided no legal protection against arbitrary dismissals of employees.[38]

But it is submitted that the Security of Employment Act is singularly deceptive. Until 1975 even the employer's right to 'hire and fire', that is to say to terminate the service of his employee, had not been encumbered in any way. As it will be shown later, although a legislative amendment in 1975 restricted termination by making it subject to appeal by the employee, the amending law in practice has been circumvented. Additionally, of particular significance are the powers of the President of the United Republic to dismiss, remove from office or terminate the appointment of any person holding office in the service of the Republic, which have been specifically saved by section 3 of the Security of Employment Act.

The Security of Employment Act provides, among other things, an elaborate procedure for the imposition of disciplinary action against employees. The administration of the Act is placed solely in the executive arm of the state, in particular the Labour Department of the state. The law requires that disciplinary questions should be resolved in *camera*[39], that is to say away from public glare. Furthermore, the Act has ousted the jurisdiction of courts of law in respect of labour disciplinary matters.[40]

The ouster of the jurisdiction of courts has been justified by the state on two main grounds. Firstly, that unlike the breaches under section 37 of the Employment Ordinance, 1955, cap. 366 of the laws of Tanzania, the Disciplinary Code under the Security of Employment Act has short and clear explanations in respect of every breach and its corresponding penalty. Thus such ease of explanation or interpretation, it has been argued, should hardly necessitate institution of proceedings in court. Secondly, the elaborate internal labour grievance settlement system facilitates quicker communication between the parties and a consequent speedy determination of the disputes.[41]

It can be argued, on the other hand, that the fact that labour disputes are kept away from judicial enquiry and the public in general is a matter which has significant politico-economic implications. To be sure, the system effectively individualizes the workers and labour grievance. The other workers or the public in general are denied the opportunity of the first hand story of the labour grievances dealt with in private. This is undoubtedly an effective method of thwarting working-class consciousness and solidarity. At another level, the individualisation of labour grievances, minimizes the effect of such grievances on productivity or efficiency in the particular business. The powers-that-be clearly appreciated the economic implications of this system of disciplining labour. It was made clear that the system was intended to attract investment capital and to ensure that production in industries was not hampered by prolonged labour disciplinary proceedings.[42]

The Disciplinary Code
The Disciplinary Code, which is the second schedule to the Security of Employment Act, tabulates nineteen offences and their corresponding penalties. The Disciplinary Code can be conveniently likened to the Penal Code. The disciplinary offences are fairly wide extending over matters of indiscipline, dishonesty, attendance at work, insubordination, safety of persons and property and even immorality. The penalties in their order of ascending severity are written warning, reprimand, severe reprimand, fine (not exceeding one day's pay) and summary dismissal. It has been argued that the Code attempts to make the punishment appear appropriate to the offence committed. For example, lateness for work or unauthorized absence from the workplace attracts a written warning for the first breach; subsequent breaches ascend the scale of severity and for the fifth breach summary dismissal is imposed. It appears these two offences can be fairly tolerated before summary dismissal can be imposed.

Absence from work without reasonable cause was originally enacted as a four step breach beginning with reprimand. That is to say an employee would be served with a reprimand on the first breach, the second breach would invite a severe reprimand, a fine for the third breach and the fourth breach would attract summary dismissal. That position has now been altered and the severity of the penalty enhanced by section 21 of the Labour Laws (Miscellaneous Amendments) Act, 1975,[43] which amended item (c) of the Disciplinary Code (which relates to absence from work without reasonable cause). The penalties of reprimand and severe reprimand for the first and second breach respectively have been deleted and in each case substituted by a fine of an amount not exceeding the employee's pay for the number of days during which he remained absent from work without reasonable cause.

When an employee fails to complete his task, a written warning and reprimand constitute the penalty for the first and second breach respectively. A fine is imposed on the third breach and the fourth breach invites summary dismissal. Neglect of duties (but not endangering property) and failure to comply with the employer's instructions are the only disciplinary faults which are four step breaches beginning with the penalty of reprimand. The remaining thirteen offences, about 70% of all the scheduled offences, carry summary dismissal on the first breach. A close study of the disciplinary offences and their corresponding penalties reveals a close relation between the severity of punishment and the possible effects of the offence on efficiency and/or productivity at the place of business. That is to say offences which are likely to disrupt industrial harmony such as brawling at the place of work or insubordination, or offences which may cause loss to the employer's property such as dishonesty, misappropriation or wilful destruction of the employer's property attract the most severe punishment, namely, summary dismissal.

The Administration of the Security of Employment Act

It has been shown that the Security of Employment Act has created an elaborate and, undoubtedly, a stringent disciplinary code. The Chapter will now examine the code's administrative machinery. It has been argued that such a machinery was designed to serve a double purpose. Firstly, to forestall the resistance of employees to such rigorous discipline. Secondly, to assist the employer in the administration of the code. To facilitate this, two important organs were set up —the Workers' Committees (which were later abolished and field branches substituted in their place) and the conciliation boards.

Originally the Act required the establishment of Workers' Committee in every enterprise employing more than ten union members. Membership to the committee was elective, the only qualification being that the candidate had to be a union member. Union members themselves elected the committee.[44] The constitution of the committee was determined by the number of the union members employed at the business at the time of election. Where the number of union members was between ten and twenty, the committee had to be made up of three members; where it was between twenty one and one hundred, the committee had to be made up of five members; where it was over one hundred union members, the committee had to be made up of five members plus one additional member for every additional five hundred union members.[45]

The functions of the committee were two-fold. Firstly, it was supposed to advise the employer on such matters as efficiency, safety and welfare arrangements, work rules, redundancies and the furtherance of good employee-employer relations.[46] It can be seen that this limb of functions was purely advisory and consultative and it conferred no executive powers upon the workers' committee. Secondly, and this was presumably the most important function, the committee had to be consulted by the employer before he imposed any punishment on a worker for a breach of the disciplinary code.[47] The committee thus helped to administer the disciplinary code. However, its opinion was not binding on the employer.

The Tanzanian government had hoped that close cooperation and frequent consultation between employers and workers' committees would lead to positive advantages in promoting sound industrial relations at places of work resulting in real progress for industry and the nation.[48] Although in their essential aspects the workers' committees, having no executive powers, were ineffective, they became important instruments in the struggles of the workers in the early 1970s against representatives of foreign capital.[49] Soon there were suggestions that workers' committees were the cause of indiscipline in factories. This was attributed to the committees' grassroot character and relative autonomy from the trade union structures.[50] It was then proposed that workers committtees should be abolished and replaced by union branches. The proposals received a legislative blessing in 1975 by virtue of Act No. 1 of 1975. Under section 11 of the Act a new section 7A was added to the Security of Employment Act. Workers' committees were abolished and their functions were vested in field branches which were then established. Not unlike the workers' committees, the field branches have no executive powers and their opinions have no binding effect on the employers.

Besides the Workers' Committees (and later the field branches), as noted above, the other important organ set up to administer the Security of Employment Act, were the Conciliation Boards. Conciliation Boards were established in every district of Tanzania by the Minister for Labour vide Government Notice No. 155 of 26 March 1965. The compostion of the Board is provided for under section 11 of the Act. The Board is supposed to consist of a permanent chairman appointed by the Minister from among labour officers and for each reference, two members are selected by the chairman, one from each of the lists of nominees submitted by the workers union and by the appropriate employer group. The Conciliation Board is thus tripartite—representing the state, the employers' association's interests and the workers' union's interests.

The powers and functions of Conciliation Boards are provided for under section 24 of the Security of Employment Act. Contrary to what its name may suggest, the Conciliation Board is empowered to decide (actually to adjudicate) whether the disciplinary penalty which is the subject of the reference before it was justified or appropriate. The Board is empowered to reverse, confirm or modify the penalty including ordering re-engagement or re-instatement of the dismissed or terminated employee. The order of re-engagement or re-instatement shall have effect for the purpose of payment of wages and other employment benefits from the date of the employee's summary dismissal or suspension as the case may be.[51] Where the Board substitutes termination for summary dismissal, the termination of employment would be deemed to have taken effect on the day on which the employer informed the employee that he desired to dismiss him summarily. The employee's terminal benefits would thus be computed with reference to that date. An order for refund of any deductions from the wages of the employee, would require the employer to make the refund accordingly.

The law allows the party who may be aggrieved by the decision of the Conciliation Board to appeal to the Minister of Labour within twenty eight days of the decision of the Board. The Minister may exercise upon such an appeal the same powers as those conferred upon the Board. The parties to a reference to the Minister have no right to appear in person or by advocate or by any other representative before him. However, they are entitled to submit memoranda in support of their respective cases. The decision of the Minister or that of the Board where it has not been appealed against, is final and conclusive and binding on the parties to the reference, and such a decision may be enforced in any court of competent jurisdiction.

Disciplinary Proceedings and References

The power of the employer to impose a disciplinary penalty upon the employee is provided for under sections 19 and 20 of the Security of Employment Act. Section 19 restricts the employer from dismissing summarily his employee or from deducting his wages as a punishment. He may only do so if the employee has breached the provisions of the disciplinary code which permit such penalty. Clearly as it was noted earlier in this chapter, the employer's power to impose a disciplinary penalty upon a worker has not been entirely abrogated;

it has only been restricted. It should also be noted that subsection (3) of section 20 of the Act gives the employer an unrestricted power to withhold any increase in or increment to wages for what he might consider to be an unsatisfactory performance of work, inefficiency or inability. It is submitted that this discretion is ill-placed and punitive and may allow unscrupulous employers to frustrate their employees without being restrained by law. It also appears that the employee has no legal forum to complain or make any representation in respect of the employer's act of withholding an increase in or an increment to his wages.

When the employer wishes to impose a penalty upon the employee for an alleged breach of the Disciplinary Code the law requires him to observe a specific procedure. The precise procedure to be adopted will basically depend on the type of disciplinary penalty which may be imposed, and also whether or not a Union field branch operates in the particular place of work. Section 21 of the Security of Employment prescribes the procedure for imposition of disciplinary penalties including summary dismissal in an establishment where a union branch functions; and section 22 provides for those where none has been established.

The following is the procedure which the employer must comply with in imposing a penalty upon an employee in an establishment where a union field branch exists. The employer has to complete an information form or charge sheet. The form is supposed to be addressed to the chairman of the field branch, and therein the employer's intention to impose a penalty is made and details of the breach given. The employer must also appraise the field branch of any prior breaches of the disciplinary code by the same employee. Those prior breaches must, however, have been recorded in accordance with the law. The field branch is then supposed to communicate the matter to the concerned employee immediately.

The employer must afford the field branch an opportunity to make such representations as it may consider appropriate in relation to the proposed penalty. It may be noted that the representations to be made by the field branch may not necessarily be in defence of the charged employee. The employer is precluded from proceeding with the implementation of the proposed penalty except in the following cases:

(a)   If three days elapse without receiving a written representation, then the employer may impose the proposed penalty or any lesser disciplinary penalty.

(b)   If the employer receives a protest representation, he must discuss the matter with the field branch. After the discussion and regardless of its outcome (which must be recorded in the prescribed form and submitted to the employer) the employer may impose the proposed penalty or a lesser one. But he cannot then summarily dismiss the employee unless the field branch agrees.

As it can be noted that opinions or representations of the field branch in respect of the employer's proposal to impose a written warning, reprimand, severe reprimand or fine upon any employee have no binding effect on the employer. Thus the consultative or advisory role of the field branch, by and large, become cosmetic.

The employer is entitled to impose summary dismissal on an employee if he has informed the field branch of his proposal and the same has agreed upon within three days of the proposal. Where there is no agreement with the field branch, the employer may summarily dismiss the employee if the employee informs him that he has no intention of making a reference to the Conciliation Board. Alternatively, if fourteen days have expired after the employee has been appraised of the proposed penalty and has not both formally informed the employer that he intends to make a reference to the Board and made the reference accordingly. If the employee abandons the reference within the limitation period the employer is entitled to dismiss him in accordance with his earlier proposal.[52]

The employer may also summarily dismiss the employee, if the proposed penalty is confirmed by the Board or, if the same is not confirmed by the Board, then if it is confirmed by the Minister. During the time of reference, that is any time after the employer has discussed its proposal with the field branch, he may suspend the employee on half pay. Although no employee shall be entitled to be suspended, the employer's discretion as to suspension is restricted to either suspend on not less than half pay or not to suspend at all, that is to leave the employee in employment with full pay.

With regard to establishments where no union field branch operates, the disciplinary procedure, as it was noted earlier, is provided for under section 22 of the Security of Employment Act. Before the discussion of procedure may be embarked upon, it is worth noting that field branches may only be established in businesses where ten or more union members, being employees within the meaning of the Act, are employed. There can thus be an establishment without a union field branch either because of the foregoing reason or neglect to establish the same; in which case the disciplinary procedure under section 22 of the Act will apply.

The procedure is less cumbersome here. The employer is entitled to impose any penalty, except summary dismissal, upon an employee provided he explains to the employee the reasons for such a penalty and has reported the matter to the labour officer. Where the employer proposes to impose summary dismissal on the employee he must notify the employee and the labour officer giving his reasons for such a proposal. The employer is precluded from proceeding with the implementation of the proposed summary dismissal unless:

(i)   a period of three days has expired after making the report to the Labour officer;

(ii)   where no reference has been made to the Board within fourteen days after an intention to file the same has been made or the reference has been abandoned within that period.[53]

In the past the employee had to get the assistance of the local representative of the workers' union to make a reference to the Board. Now the practice is that District Union offices invariably assist aggrieved employees who are covered by section 22 to make references to Conciliation Boards. As it has been observed above representations made by the field branch in respect of an employee who has been aggrieved by a disciplinary penalty against him need not be in his support. More often than not aggrieved employees have been barred by limitation of time because of delays in getting prescribed forms completed by the field branch for the purpose of instituting references to the Conciliation Board. It appears where the field branch does not support the aggrieved employee it tends to be un-cooperative resulting in delay in making the reference within the prescribed time.

It will be recalled that Part III of the Security of Employment Act provides for three situations each of which may be the subject of a reference to the Board by an aggrieved employee. These situations are where the employee has been summarily dismissed or has been informed of the employer's proposal to dismiss him summarily, or has suffered a deduction by way of a disciplinary penalty from the wages due to him from his employer.[54] A fourth situation has been provided by virtue of Act No. 1 of 1975. A new section 40A was added to the Security of Employment Act which enables an aggrieved employee to make a reference to the Board in respect of termination.

The amendment introduced by Section 40A of the Security of Employment has enlarged the scope of protection of workers in their employment by enabling them to appeal against unreasonable and unconscionable termination of employment in certain circumstances. But section 40A (5) of the same Act gives the employer considerable leeway to refuse to re-instate or re-engage an 'unwanted' employee in defiance of the Board's order to re-instate or re-engage him. The only obligation of the employer when he fails or refuses to comply with the Board's or the Minister's order (upon further references to him) to re-instate or re-engage an employee is to pay the employee some compensation.

Thus the Security of Employment Act is clearly a misnomer. The

Act is unique in its deception of purporting to protect workers. In its operation this law affords security of labour for the employer through workers themselves who sit in the union field branches and enforce the Disciplinary Code at the instance of the employer.[55] In pointing out the absence of protection and security of workers it may be of great significance to note that when the Security of Employment Act was tabled for amendment in 1969 with a view to enlarging the category of persons covered by the Act, the wage criterion of shs. 700 was removed and only the managerial cadres were exempt. During the parliamentary debate on the amendment proposal, A.S. Kwilasa, a Member of Parliament, questioned why persons engaged in the management of the business of the employer should not enjoy the security afforded by the Act. The short answer by the Minister who tabled the Bill was to advise the Member of Parliament to make a distinction between those who discipline and those who are to be disciplined.[56] The deception of the Security of Employment Act was being unveiled by the law-makers themselves.

Some Concluding Remarks

The Chapter set out to discuss the authoritarian state control of the working class in Tanzania through labour legislation. Substantial continuity of the repressive character of the colonial state has been found with regard to the labour regime. The state has completely strangled collective labour action and a stringent individual labour discipline has been imposed by legislative fiat.

It would seem ironic that while the independent state continued to be authoritarian, legislative business was overtly pre-occupied with promulgating laws which were apparently protecting the welfare of the workers. Apart from numerous legislation concerned with the social security of workers, such as the protection of wages, the provision of retirement benefits, leave and the provision of rest-days, the most controversial piece of legislation purporting to be protective of labour is the Security of Employment Act of 1964. It should be asserted that this Act is singularly deceptive. The employer's powers to impose disciplinary penalties, as has been illustrated in this Chapter, seem to outweigh the purported security of tenure.

The neo-colonial state is thus enmeshed in an irreconcilable contradiction between the interests of labour and capital. On the one hand the state has to don a welfare garb so as to win the support of the working masses in bolstering the post-colonial economy. On the other hand the economic policies of the emergent state have to conform with the interests of foreign and local capital; consequently a compulsory arbitration of labour disputes and rigorous discipline in creating "industrial harmony" is inevitable.

NOTES

1. Williams, D.V., "State Coercion against Peasant Farmers: The Tanzanian Case", *Journal of Legal Pluralism and Unofficial Law* No. 20 (1982), at p.95
2. For a detailed analysis of this aspect see Shivji, I.G., "Semi-proletarian Labour and the use of Penal Sanctions in the Labour Law of Colonial Tanganyika (1920-1938)," in Sumner, C., (ed.) *Crime, Justice and Underdevlopment* (London: Heinemann, 1982).
3. The Human Resources Deployment Act, No. 6 of 1983 has unique parallels with the colonial Labour Utilisation Ordinance, 1947, cap. 243. The 1983 legislation repeals the 1947 Ordinance but declares all the regulations made under the Ordinance to continue in force as if they were made under the present law. The 1947 Ordinance was passed at the height of labour crisis which continued after the second imperialist world war of 1939-1945. The Ordinance set up labour utilisation boards in an effort to secure the employment of available resources of native labour in the interest of colonial enterprises.
4. The Written Laws (Miscellaneous Amendments) Act, No. 11 of 1983 has amended section 176 of the Penal Code, cap. 16 which relates to idle and disorderly persons by adding paragraph (8) which states: "any able-bodied person who is not engaged in any productive work and has no visible means of subsistence", and paragraph (9) which reads: "any person employed under lawful employment of any description who is without any lawful excuse, found engaged on a frolic of his own at a time he is supposed to be engaged in activities connected or related to the business of his employment". Persons caught by these provisions are criminally chargeable as vagabonds under the Penal Code.
5. The Local Government Finance Act, No. 9 of 1982 under section 13 empowers local government authorities to make by-laws imposing the so-called 'rate' on all adult citizens. The law does not exempt women from paying tax. It will be recalled that the colonial tax law only imposed tax on male adults.
6. See "The Tanzania National Agricultural Policy (Final Report)" by the Ministry of Agriculture, United Republic of Tanzania (Dar es Salaam: Government Printer, 1982).
7. See *Tanganyika Parliamentary Debates* (Hansard), National Assembly Official Report, 1st Session, 3rd Meeting, Sitting from 25th September to 27th September, 1962 (Dar es Salaam: Government Printer, 1962) Columns 104-105.
8. There were two other issues of divergence. Firstly the trade union movement demanded the break-up of the East African High Commission for its disregard and insensitivity to the union's demands. Secondly, militant white collar unions demanded rapid Africanisation while the Government appeared somewhat slow on the matter. There is some more detail on this aspect in Shivji, I.G., "Working Class Struggles and Organisation in Tanzania, 1939-1975", *Mawazo,* (A Journal of the Faculties of Arts and Social Sciences, Makerere University, Kampala) Vol. 5 No. 2, December, 1983.
9. No. 43 of 1962.
10. No. 51 of 1962.
11. Section 41 (B (1), Act No. 51 of 1962.
12. Section 47 A, *ibid*
13. No. 52 of 1962.
14. No. 60 of 1962.
15. See *Tanganyika Parliamentary Debates* (Hansard) National Assembly Official Report, 1st Session, February 1962 (Dar es Salaam: Government Printer, 1962), Col. 120.

16. No. 18 of 1964.
17. See Article 3(2) of the NUTA Constitution which was made a schedule (and therefore part of the substantive law) to the National Union of Tanganyika Workers (Establishment) Act, 1964.
18. Section 5(1), Act No. 18 of 1964.
19. Section 5(2), *ibid.*
20. See Trade Unions and Trade Disputes (Miscellaneous Amendments) Act, No. 64 of 1964.
21. See Parliamentary Debates (Hansard) National Assembly Official Report 15th Meeting, Sitting from 1st December, 1964 to 3rd December, 1964, (Dar es Salaam: Government Printer, 1964), Col. 64.
22. No. 41 of 1967.
23. Section 22(e), Act No. 41 of 1967.
24. Section 27(2), *ibid.*
25. Section 27(1), *ibid.*
26. Section 19(1), *ibid.*
27. Section 13, *ibid.*
28. See the *Turner Report* (International Labour Organisation, Report to the Government of Tanzania on the Past, Present and Future of Incomes Policy in Tanzania printed as Government Paper No. 3 of 1967 (Dar es Salaam: Government Printer, 1967).
29. Shivji, I.G., "The State of the Constitution and the Constitution of the State in Tanzania", *Eastern Africa Law Review* (Faculty of Law, University of Dar es Salaam) Vols. 11-14, 1983.
30. *Ibid.*
31. No. 24 of 1979.
32. Section 2, *ibid.*
33. Section 4(1), *ibid.*
34. See the Trade Union Ordinance, 1956 (now cap. 381 of the Revised Laws of Tanzania).
35. See *Pallangyo v. Zambia Tanzania Road Services Ltd.* H.C. DSM Civil Appeal No. 9 of 1982. (unreported).
36. See Section 8(1) of Act No. 24 of 1979.
37. No. 62 of 1964.
38. Stoll, G., "The Tanzanian Security of Employment Act", 1 *East African Law Journal* (No. 4) (Nairobi: Oceana Publications, 1965) p.192.
39. Section 13 of Act. No. 62 of 1964.
40. Section 28, *ibid.*
41. See speech by M.M. Kamaliza, then the Minister for Labour, in Parliamentary Debates (Hansard) 3rd December, 1964 (Dar es Salaam: Government Printer, 1965) Columns 146-160.
42. *Ibid.*
43. No. 1 of 1975 which came into force on 1.5. 1975.
44. Section 5 and 1st Schedule to Act No. 62 of 1964.
45. *Ibid.*
46. Section 6(1) (b)—(h), *ibid.*
47. Section 6(1) (a), *ibid.*
48. Kamaliza, M.M., "The Security of Employment Act, No. 62 of 1964: A Guide to the Disciplinary Code" (Mimeo), (Dar es Salaam: Ministry of Labour, 1965).
49. See Shivji's paper referred to in footnote. 8 above and his Ph.D. Thesis, *Development of Wage-Labour and Labour Laws in Tanzania:* 1920-1964 (University of Dar es Salaam, 1982).

50. Shivji, I.G., *Class Struggles in Tanzania,* (Dar es Salaam: Tanzania Publishing House, 1975) p.130.
51. Section 25(1) (a), Act no. 62 of 1964.
52. Section 21(3) (b) (i) of the Security of Employment Act, as amended by section 15 of Act No. 1 of 1975.
53. Section 22(3), Act No. 62 of 1964.
54. Section 23(1), *ibid.*
55. For an analysis of this aspect and other related matters see Mihyo, P.B., "Labour unrest and the Quest for Worker's Control in Tanzania", *Eastern Africa Law Review,* Vol. 7 No. 1 (1974); and Shivji, I.G. *Class Struggles in Tanzania* (Dar es Salaam: Tanzania Publishing House, 1975), pp. 128-131.
56. See Parliamentary Speech by Mr. Wambura, then the Junior Minister for Communications, Transport and Works in *"Majadiliano ya Bunge"* (Hansard), "Taarifa Rasmi, Mkutano wa Kumi na Nane, tarehe 21 Oktoba, 1969" (Dar es Salaam: Government Printer, 1971), Col. 230.

5. THE STATE AND THE PEASANTRY

Henry Mapolu

Introduction

Tremendous changes have taken place in rural Tanzania in the two decades or so during which the country has been independent. After experimenting with a variety of "rural development" policies in the first ten years of independence, the authorities in 1973/74 launched a gigantic "villagisation" programme for the entire mainland country-side. Basically, the programme consisted of abolishing the traditional system of rural settlements by which households are located in small isolated pockets and its replacement by the creation of large villages. Millions of people were thus moved into new areas in a relatively short period.

There has been considerable debate on the merits and demerits of the programme, and particularly on the forceful manner in which it was implemented.[1] The stated purpose of the programme was to facilitate the provision by government of essential social infra-structure to the rural areas, particularly water, medical/health services, and primary education. Whether large settlements are a necessary pre-requisite for the provision of these facilities, and whether Tanzania had the resources to provide them any way, are obviously different and debatable questions.

But at least there has not been much disagreement on the performance of rural production ever since "villagisation". In many cases agricultural output has been declining over time and only in a few cases has output shown some minor increase. For this poor performance, of course there are many causes: the weather, world commodity prices, and so on, being some of them. We would argue, however, that too much blame has often been put on weather conditions. As Coulson has indicated, shortages of food, for instance, cannot really be ascribed to drought conditions as rainfall figures for the decade do not bear this out.[2] In any case, Tanzania—by African standards—is a vast territory with diverse ecological zones capable of complimenting each other in terms of variety of output.

> Virtually every crop known to agriculturalists will grow in one or more of these (ecological) areas. Wheat, coffee, tea, potatoes, and pyrethrum grow in the cool mountains. On the inland plateau grow maize, rice, sorghum, varieties of millet, cotton, and tobacco, as well as sisal . . . Coconuts, cashew-nuts, rubber, cocoa, cloves, and a wide variety of spices grow on the coastal strip or on Zanzibar and Pemba. Each ecological unit produces its own fruits and vegetables.[3]

In such a situation, one cannot but expect abundance as far as agricultural output is concerned. Yet not only have food imports been rising, but even production for export—on which emphasis by the authorities is usually heaviest—has also been declining over the years, (See Table X below). In the years 1972-1980, over-all growth of food crops was at the rate of 5% per annum, that of export crops was a negative 3% per annum.[4] When related to rural population, both food and export crops have been on a steady decline over the years (see Table IX) below).

We wish to argue that the root causes of this poor performance lie not in natural conditions but rather in the very social and economic policies pursued by the authorities. The strategies intended to raise the agricultural production proved to be the very fetters of this development. Nearly all countries in independent Africa have elaborated policies for bringing about change in the rural areas. Tanzania is however exceptional in that it has done so with considerable eloquence and consistency—bringing out a number of political statements that have given rise to considerable debate both within Tanzania and outside. We wish to argue, on the contrary, that in substance these policies have not differed much from those attempted elsewhere in Africa nor from those attempted earlier on by the British in the then colonial Tanganyika and elsewhere.

Imperialism and Rural Africa

With the coming of colonialism to Africa towards the end of the nineteenth century, the continent was set on a road of dramatic economic changes. The primary task of the colonial powers was to integrate the African people into the world-wide capitalist economic system. Since initially most of the African colonies were considered essentially as sources of agricultural raw materials, in concrete terms this task consisted basically of compelling the population to produce those products required by European industry: sisal, cotton, tea, rubber, and so on. Different colonial powers used different methods in different colonies to attain this objective. Yet in nearly every instance the initial method used was one of naked force. Hand in hand with the violent oppression of the people euphemistically referred to in colonial history as "pacification", colonial powers everywhere initially used force to make people cultivate the crops that European industry needed.[5] In quite a few instances, such force gave rise to armed resistance on the part of the people. In then German East Africa, for instance, German endeavours to compel people to grow cotton led to the celebrated Maji-Maji war of 1905-1907.[6] In practically every colony this resistance against colonialist exploitation continued for a long time despite the brutal methods used to stamp out rebellion.[7]

Naturally, force was not the only form of resistance resorted to by the people in their struggle against domination and exploitation. Depending on local conditions and historical experience, the people devised all sorts of tricks to sabotage colonial efforts to make them produce raw materials for export. In colonial Tanganyika, for example, people learned a long time ago to boil cotton seeds prior to planting them so as to ensure they did not germinate.[8] In all countries there are numerous such historical stories.

This resistance was the specific form of class struggle at the time. Each side, in the last instance, had material interests to defend and in so far as such interests were objectively contradictory, struggle was the permanent feature of the relationship between the people and the colonial rulers throughout the colonial period. Such struggle took ever varying forms as the process of integration into the world economic system grew in both scope and intensity. With the expansion and intensification of commodity production in society, social differentiation inevitably took place and a divergence of vested interests began to emerge. For this reason, different segments of the rural people resorted to different forms of struggle, and of course various segments soon acquired vested interests in the new system of commodity production and exchange.

It must be noted that it is the colonial state that in each particular colony played the key role in these endeavours to subjugate local inhabitants under the world capitalist system. While different monopoly companies stood to benefit directly from the introduction and generalisation of, say, cotton production in a particular colony, it is the state that played the direct and leading role in this exercise. Laws were enacted to compel villagers to cultivate various crops, the state formulated policies for all sectors of the economy, and so on.

Apart from direct violent repression, this task in fact constituted the primary function of the colonial state.

This campaign continued throughout the colonial period. By the time of independence this task of integrating the rural people into the capitalist market had by and large been accomplished. Socio-economic structures had been built to ensure a more or less permanent flow of agricultural raw materials from Africa to the advanced countries of Western Europe and North America and firm dependence of the economies on the world market ensued.

Yet a number of problems still remained unsolved at the end of the colonial period. First, nowhere was integration of rural dwellers into the market economy fully accomplished. To begin with, everywhere one found pockets of rural communities subsisting outside the cash economy. Often residing in inaccessible areas, or simply engaged in productive activities not easily penetrable by the cash nexus, such communities continued for long to lead traditional communal forms of life more or less free of commodity production and exchange. In Tanzania, for instance, it was only in the mid-sixties that government authorities "discovered" the Hadzabe in the Singida region, and began to "pacify" them and put them in government-supervised villages so that they could engage in commercial production. Constant attempts by colonial rulers to break up such communities often failed as the communities receded further and further, or resorted to violent means of resistance. This part of the task was therefore somehow unaccomplished by the end of the colonial period, and it was left to the new independence governments to complete it. Of course on this issue one is really talking in relative terms for practically every community felt somehow the pressure of the capitalist economy.

But more critical is the fact that even those people who, by the end of the colonial period, had by and large become used to commodity production and exchange frequently went back to subsistence economy whenever it suited them. This feature is in the nature of peasant economy itself. The peasant generally produces his subsistence outside the process of producing commodities, and once production of cash crops proves dangerous to subsistence then he shifts more and more resources to subsistence production. In particular, price incentives play a key role in the ebb and flow of cash crop production. Thus the colonial rulers could not easily solve the problem of keeping raw materials as cheap as possible while at the same time ensuring their maximum production. This again is a problem with which independence governments in Africa have had to wrestle constantly.

Thirdly, the colonial rulers everywhere faced the problem of

raising productivity in the rural areas. Various strategies and tech-
niques were used to try and increase rural output *vis a vis* resources
used—ranging from ambitious schemes in which peasants were
resettled and managed directly by appointed officials to more modest
efforts to provide technical advice and assistance to villagers on a
small scale. The literature on these policies and the results thereof
is enormous,[9] and we have no intention of reviewing it here. It has
been shown abundantly that through ignoring the people's wishes,
experience, and above all interests, often these policies bore little fruit
in terms of bringing out fundamental change in the level of productivity in rural Africa. Specifically, the special schemes for resettled
villagers ended in a fiasco practically everywhere.[10]

The fundamental problem with these policies of the colonial times
is political. The policies envisaged the achievement of socio-economic
development within the structure of colonialism. In essence, colonialism is a politico-economic system which stifles the productive forces
in the colonised society. In Cabral's words, colonialism is "the
negation of the historical process of the dominated people by means
of violent usurpation of the freedom of development of the national
productive forces".[11] Besides violent repression, colonialism always
comes with the economic plunder and social and political repression
of the colonised people, thus choking and hindering their creative
energies. Hence, the wish to rapidly increase productivity of the
African people while shackling them to the colonial post was indeed
a contradiction in terms. Throughout the colonial period, the colonial
governments tried vainly to resolve this contradiction; the more they
tried through politico-economic measures, the more they intensified it.

The subsequent independence governments inherited this contradiction. As soon as independence had been attained, practically
every African government found itself formulating some policy or
other toward the rural areas. There are a number of reasons why this
has been considered important. Africa is overwhelmingly rural, it is
difficult even for those regimes least inclined to interest themselves
with the affairs of their own people to completely ignore more than
90% of their population. At least some lip-service has to be paid to
the rural dwellers. Secondly, Western aid donors on whom Africa
is dependent to an ever increasing extent have constantly pushed
African governments to adopt some strategies that can increase
agricultural exports. Naturally, this is in the interest of those donor
countries themselves. As a result, therefore, despite differences in
ideological nuances, all governments have had to put forward some
policy or other for "rural development". That there has not been much
"development" is of course another matter altogether. Finally,
however, African governments themselves feel the need to raise

agricultural output, particularly in the export sector. It is only in agriculture that most governments can expect to extract sizeable amounts of financial resources for running the very expensive state apparatus.

For all these reasons, numerous policies have been experimented upon the African peasantry since independence. As can easily be seen, these policies in substance have been a mere continuation of the colonial ones. Their basic orientation has been to try to achieve greater integration of the peasantry into the world-wide capitalist system. Hence the need to repeat what the colonial rulers had tried to do. As for results, experience shows that with a few exceptions the African governments have not done much better than their predecessors. In some cases, they have repeated the same mistakes and blunders committed during the colonial times. But more important, in so far as African independence has not really altered fundamentally the economic relationships between the continent and imperialism, the development of the productive forces is still as stifled as ever. Neocolonialism, as with colonialism, is a socio-economic system that fetters the development of the productive forces.[12] Thus whatever energies are spent in trying to increase agricultural output in the rural areas they hardly bear any meaningful results. As a consequence, Africa is in fact becoming more and more dependent on food imports, for instance.

Pressured to show results by both internal and external factors, some governments have had to constantly change their policies. One of these is the Tanzanian government, and it is to its rural development policies that we now turn.

Contradictions in the Rural Policies in Tanzania

Soon after independence in 1961, the new government of then Tanganyika emphasised the importance of rural areas in its development efforts. Emphasis was to be placed on increasing production and generally the living standards in the countryside where more than 95% of the population lived. The specific programme adopted for this purpose was actually inherited from the colonial government. As a result of recommendations by a World Bank team, two "approaches" were adopted: the "improvement" and the "transformation" approaches. While the former basically consisted of attempts to gradually raise output within existing rural households through extension services, the latter sought to radically transform agriculture through the resettlement in special schemes of pre-selected villagers who would then engage in "modern" farming under the supervision and direction of officials. By the end of 1965 there were 23 such schemes with some 15,000 acres of crops and about 3,400 farming families.[13]

Regarding these early policies, we can observe two important features. First, it is a matter of significance that there was an obvious bias towards export crops in this two-pronged programme for rural development. As far as the "improvement" approach was concerned, concentration was almost entirely on the improvement of cash crops that had by then become traditional—cotton, coffee, and so on. In the settlement schemes, also, emphasis was put on those crops that needed greater technical supervision, especially tobacco, and of course here there was greater official control of what to plant as everything in the schemes was planned and dictated by government agencies appointed for the purpose. With hindsight, we can easily see that de-emphasis on the production of foodstuffs started then as a result of both these approaches; greater and greater attention came to be placed on export crops until the country became a net food importing country. Grain imports have been increasing over the years, and now stand at about half a million tons per year.

Second, the basic orientation of "development" as such was always the resettlement of the peasants in new and larger villages. It was felt that without "villagisation" there could not be much progress in the long run. We would argue, however, that the substance of the "villagisation" idea is control.

Tanzania is one of those countries in Africa whose population density is relatively low. According to the 1978 population census, there are some 2.82 hectares per capita in the country—and if we take only the rural economically capable population then we have an average of 7.27 hectares per capita or 16.97 hectares per household.

From Table II it can clearly be seen that there is a great variation of density between the regions. Yet the vast majority of the people live in areas with relatively low density: 30% live in areas with less than 15 persons per square kilometre, and half of the entire population live in areas with less than 20 persons per square kilometre. This is not to say that there is no population pressure on the land as yet. Despite the relatively vast landmass, only a small proportion is at the moment habitable. Presently the entire small-holder cultivation is carried out on only 5% of the landmass, for instance. What this means is that the peasant population is concentrated in small pockets yet possessing considerable leeway for manoeuvre. Peasants can and do move a great deal, opening up uninhabited areas for cultivation. For many decades during the colonial period many rural areas continued to use the shifting method of cultivation despite government attempts to stamp it out. Both colonial and post-colonial governments have laid emphasis on containing the peasantry into designated settlements so as to be able to enforce agricultural policies.

Thus the first phase in the formulation of rural development

TABLE I

IMPORT AND EXPORT OF MAJOR FOOD GRAINS IN TANZANIA ('000 TONS)

Year	Maize	Wheat	Rice
1970/71	(53.4)	11.6	-
1971/72	92.3	49.5	(4.2)
1972/73	78.9	8.2	(10.2)
1973/74	183.6	35.8	23.0
1974/75	317.2	109.6	63.0
1975/76	42.3	31.2	20.5
1976/77	48.0	34.0	5.0
1977/78	34.0	45.0	61.0
1978/79	-	60.0	41.0
1979/80	29.0	33.0	43.0
1980/81	249.0	43.0	78.0

(N.B. Brackets denote exports)

Source: Government of Tanzania, *Annual Trade Reports*.

TABLE II

DISTRIBUTION OF POPULATION IN REGIONS

No. of Persons Per Sq. Km.	No. of Regions	Total Population (Thousands)	%
Less than 10	3	1,544	9.5
10 — 19	8	6,469	39.9
20 — 29	2	2,295	14.2
30 — 39	3	2,771	17.1
40 — 49	1	772	4.8
50 — 59	-	-	-
60 — 69	1	902	5.6
70 — 79	1	1,443	8.9
TOTAL	19	16,196	100

Source: 1978 Population Census Reports
(Dar es Salaam: Government Printer)

policies in Tanzania was a very logical continuation of the colonial efforts to integrate to the furthest extent possible the peasantry into the world capitalist market. And this could be done only through assembling the peasantry into sufficiently large settlements to facilitate government supervision and control. Through greater involvement in the cash economy and greater dependence on the foreign market both for marketing their produce and for essential inputs, rural dwellers in Tanganyika came to be part and parcel of the world-wide economic system. The initial manifestation of this external integration was the growth of social differentiation in the rural areas. The "transformation" approach was explicitly intended to give birth to a Kulak class with vested interests in the employment of labour. But even the "improvement" approach ultimately was bound to bring about class differentiation in the rural areas through its emphasis on the "progressive" farmer in the provision of extension services. In other words, the end result of this "rural development" policy was the formation of classes that would be the social basis of imperialism in the country.

It did not take long for this policy to be abandoned. By 1966 it had become clear that the "improvement" approach was not really bringing about improvement in the countryside. Although the area under cash crops had tended to increase over the years, output continued to fluctuate more as a result of weather conditions than as a result of the extension services provided by government agencies. As to the "transformation" approach, government soon realised it was incurring enormous expenses in establishing and running the settlement schemes whose production continued to be minimal. One of the things found out then was that the resettled peasants tended to see themselves as government employees rather than independent farmers receiving government technical assistance, hence they tended to put in minimal initiative and creativity.[14] But this was by no means a question of mere appearance, in fact there was a real change in social relations. As a smallholder on his own farm, the peasant has relative control over resources: land, tools, seeds, and above all his own labour. In the settlement scheme, however, all these resources are under the control of the government agency which is responsible for the scheme. What is more, while in his own small farm the peasant generally made the decision regarding disposal of the output of his family labour, in the scheme officials disposed of the harvest and paid the settler peasant whatever remained after deducting costs for all inputs used—social infrastructure, administration, seeds, chemicals, and so on.

Thus the settler peasant was more or less a semi-worker. No wonder he often resorted to withdrawal of labour-power as the main form of protest against exploitation. Whenever he felt that he was not paid enough for his toil, he often deserted the settlement, and such desertion often brought about some changes in the deductions made prior to paying the settlers. As was bound to happen in such a situation, some sections of the settlers soon made a break-through and came to accumulate substantial resources in the countryside and employed seasonal labour to a greater and greater extent. The bulk of the settlers, however, stagnated and remained small-holder cultivators dependent on family labour.

In general, then, the initial attempts to radically change the rural scene in Tanzania were largely a failure. It is true that in the sixties agricultural output generally did register some growth, but as we have seen such growth could not easily be ascribed to the specific policies or programmes pursued then.

It must be further noted that as a result of many changes in the country as a whole, changes in policies were becoming inevitable towards the end of the decade. At independence, those who took the reins of government in the country largely came from the petty bourgeoisie: the intelligentsia, bureaucrats, traders and rich peasants. The aftermath of independence saw ever increasing struggles between these elements on the one hand and the predominantly Asian commercial bourgeoisie that controlled the wholesale and import-export trade on the other. The petty bourgeoisie had to find a foothold in the economy if its political position was to be consolidated. Steps taken by the petty bourgeoisie soon after independence included the replacement of private buyers of agricultural produce by government organs and government-controlled co-operative institutions, launching of state trading and transport corporations, and so on. The culmination of all these endeavours was the proclamation in 1967 of the Arusha Declaration on socialism and self-reliance. The declaration led to the nationalisation by the state of all the "commanding heights" of the economy: wholesale trade, import and export businesses, plantations, banking and insurance institutions, major factories, and so on. Thus by the end of the decade one could rightly talk of the existence of a state bourgeoisie in Tanzania, a class which—by virtue of its position in the state apparatus—controlled the major means of production in the country.[15] Needless to say, because of the nature of the economy itself and its relation to the world capitalist system, this bourgeoisie was—and continues to be—a dependent bourgeosie.

As far as the rural areas were concerned, the efforts of the state bourgeoisie to consolidate its position in the economy as we have seen began with the taking over of the middleman's role: the purchase and sale of agricultural produce. But this could not end at that level—if actual control of the agricultural sector was to be attained obviously this had ultimately to be at the level of production. Thus with the demise of the "improvement" and "transformation" approaches, new stategies had to be formulated by the end of the decade: the policies of "state farms" and "ujamaa villages". For lack of resources by the government, "state farms" were bound to be limited. As for "ujamaa villages", these were conceived as the basis upon which the entire countryside would ultimately change dramatically from the situation of low level production and poverty to one of high level production and prosperity. Basically, the ujamaa village was conceived as an agricultural producer co-operative unit, managed by its members with state institutions playing a catalytic role: providing technical advice, assistance, and so on.

The policy of ujamaa villages appeared novel at the time, and a great deal of resources were put at the disposal of the ujamaa villages programme. The political campaign to implement this particular programme was much more far-reaching than any previous exercise for the rural areas, and a substantial number of ujamaa villages were launched in each region in the late sixties. The party and government machinery were resolutely mobilised towards "ujamaa" and the President personally spent weeks in villages. By 1974, according to official reports, there were more than 5,000 such villages with 2½ million people.

While there was considerable enthusiam regarding this policy initially, after some five years there were not many convincing signs that soon a break-through would take place in the rural scene as a result of the ujamaa villages. To begin with, the growth of these villages left much to be desired; while some showed signs of economic growth and expansion, others were completely mismanaged and it was clear that in time they would collapse.[16] In any case, the ujamaa sector constituted a very small proportion of the total rural economy, and there was not much indication that this would in due course change since the more new villages were started a considerable number of the old ones died. The villages themselves differed a great deal in organisation, leadership, and degree of communality. In some cases ujamaa villages were mere front organizations for kulak operations.[17]

Co-operatives in themselves cannot guarantee rapid socio-economic development in the rural areas. Unless they are part of a larger strategy of both rural transformation and industrialisation, producer co-operatives in underdeveloped countries simply become another instrument for the continued domination of the country by imperialism. Thus by 1973/74 interest in the ujamaa programme began to waver not only among the people but even in official circles. While the earlier policy of "improvement" and "transformation" was officially and publicly withdrawn in 1966, the ujamaa villages policy is officially still in force. Yet since 1974 emphasis has radically changed from communal production to village settlement. In 1974 the Tanzania Government launched the most ambitious and gigantic programme for rural mobilisation ever undertaken in the country. Its impact has been greater and more far-reaching than any other previous programme.

TABLE III
LAND USE IN TANZANIA

	Square Kilometres	Percentage
A. Agricultural Use:		
1. Rough grazing	442,450	50.1
2. Smallholder cultivation	46,733	5.3
3. Large scale cultivation	5,850	.7
4. Total non-agricultural use	495,033	56.1
B. Non-Agricultural Use:		
1. Common Woods/Forests	369,054	41.7
2. High altitude forests	3,900	.4
3. Other (urban, rocky, etc.)	16,000	1.8
4. Total non-agricultural use	388,954	43.9
C. Total Land Use:	883,989	100.

SOURCE: D. McHenry, *Tanzania's Ujamaa Villages*, (Berkeley: Institute of International Studies, 1979), p.52.

TABLE IV
DEVELOPMENT OF UJAMAA VILLAGES

Year	Number of Villages	Total Population (millions)	Average Membership
1969	809	n.a.	n.a.
1970	1,956	.53	272
1971	4,484	1.55	345
1972	5,556	1.98	357
1973	5,628	2.02	360
1974	5,008	2.56	511

SOURCE: I.L.O., *Towards Self-Reliance*, (Addis Ababa: 1978) p.43.

TABLE V

VILLAGISATION PROGRAMME

Year	Number of Villages	Total Population
1973	5,628	2,028,164
1974	5,008	2,560,472
1975	6,944	9,140,229
1976	7,684	13,087,220

SOURCE: R.M. Mayaya, *Public Policy Implementation in Tanzania*, M.A. Dissertation, University of Dar es Salaam, p. 90.

The villagisation programme was aimed at re-settling the entire rural population into large and "planned" settlements. Instead of the traditional practice whereby peasant households lived in scattered and at times isolated pockets—frequently shifting from area to area in order to balance resources and requirements—the aim was now to create fairly large settlements of at least some 250 families each. Between 1973 and 1975 as many as 9 million rural inhabitants were shifted and by 1976 it was declared that practically all rural Tanzanians were living in these new "development" villages.

This does not mean, however, that every single villager was affected. Those peasant areas in which large settlement was already a way of life, and those areas in which there was already a land shortage and thus no available place to which to move people were unaffected by this exercise. But as we have already seen, because of the settlement pattern in the country such areas were few and far between. When therefore the tally of "registered villages"—encompassing new as well as old but newly designated settlements—was done in June 1979, there were 8,299 villages with a total population of 14.9 million, i.e. 87% of the country's population.[18]

The manner in which the programme was implemented left a lot to be desired. In some cases, violence was unduly used, in other cases the sites chosen for settlement were most unsuitable, in still other cases the planning process was most deficient.[19] Above all, the whole exercise was done most hurriedly. All the above factors brought about widespread resentment among the rural population, and in a few cases open opposition to the party and government.[20] Still the over-all result was that tremendous changes occurred in the rural areas: millions of people had to be re-settled, old homes were destroyed and new ones built, people used to living in isolated homesteads now found themselves in mini-towns with—in many cases—houses built in straight lines and close to each other. All this meant a great deal of change in rural life; whether the change was for the better or worse is of course a different question.

The costs of the operation, however, were undoubtedly very high. Apart from the social dislocation that resulted, the effect of the exercise on rural production was very big—there was a decline in rural output in practically all areas. Thus although there had been disagreements as to the merits and demerits of the programme, its costs are beyond doubt. In Coulson's words:

> ... what is not in dispute is that marketed production of almost all crops fell, leading to a deficit of over a million tons of cereals spread over the four years 1974-77 ... The cotton crop also declined, from 77,000 tons in 1972/73 to 42,500 in 1975/76. Cashew nut production fell by a third. These declines were associated with the villagisation, although other factors (such as a low price for cashew nuts) were also involved. The total costs of the villagisation, including the value of property destroyed, the direct costs of the 'operations', and the value of crops that were not planted or harvested, were evidently very great indeed.[21]

The Dynamics of Class Structure and Class Struggle

The significant question of this entire programme, however, is its class character. Villagisation marked the apex of the state bourgeoisie's efforts to put rural production under its hegemony. If the "commanding heights" of the economy had been "won" by the end of the sixties, clearly smallholder production in which close to 90% of the population participated had to be tackled sooner or later. But smallholder production could not be tackled by "nationalisation" measures; resettlement of peasants in chosen localities to facilitate state supervision and control was the logical strategy to be adopted.

We therefore see villagisation as the culmination of efforts that started way back in the colonial days to restructure rural economic life so as to facilitate exploitation of the rural masses by international capitalism. Petty commodity production being what it is cannot be dominated, and thus the producers exploited, without the existence of centralised institutions that directly control the peasants. The attempts to create settlement schemes during the colonial period and also during the early days of independence were in substance attempts to create such institutional structures for in the schemes the settlers would be directly controlled by government agencies and still remain outside wage employment. It is in this way that capitalism, in this particular context of underdevelopment, exerts its domination over petty commodity production.

The "tobacco villages" are perhaps an extreme form of this state control over the peasantry, but they very much exemplify the general trends in the relationship between the state and the peasantry. In these villages, because of the numerous technicalities involved in the proper husbandry of tobacco, officials of government and of companies with interest in the tobacco industry decide every little detail for the peasant. The role of the peasant in fact resembles that of a worker to a striking extent. It is the officials who decide how much of the land should be under tobacco, when and how to plant, weed, harvest, and cure the tobacco leaf, they supply the seeds, fertilisers, and insecticides as a matter of course, they grade the tobacco and of course market it. The villager actually supplies only the labour power. At the end of it all, the officials decide what proportion of the turnover should be paid back to the peasant. Needless to say, the bulk goes to those who supplied the various technical inputs, those who provided the administrative services, and those who actually marketed the crop. The peasant inevitably ends up the loser, he has practically no control over the production process nor over the product of his labour.

But even in non-tobacco growing areas, we can see the same trends whereby the state directly exerts pressures on the peasants to concentrate on those economic activities that are of interest to the state bourgeoisie. At times such pressure takes ridiculous proportions. The government newspaper, *Daily News,* for instance carried these two items in 1979:

> Bariadi: All traditional *ngomas* (dances) have been suspended during week days in the district to allow peasants to harvest cotton. This was resolved at a week-long seminar for Party and Government leaders last Friday. (29th May).

> Rufiji District has banned petty business which makes it difficult for peasants to concentrate on working on cashew farms. The ban prohibits burning and selling of charcoal, fishing and transporting of fish outside the district. (June 15th).

One could easily argue that "ngomas" as cultural activities are as important as picking cotton, and hence should not be interfered with by government—particularly a government which has spoken so much on the importance of "traditional culture". Yet we know that the material interests of the state bourgeosie do not lie in the people's culture but in their cotton, and precisely for that reason culture must be sacrificed at the altar of cotton. Similarly, one might argue that fishing and the making of charcoal are just as important productive activities as the farming of cashew nuts. Yet we that the products of such activities as fishing and the making of charcoal could easily end up serving only the peasant's subsistence or be marketed outside the state structure, in either case it would be to the advantage of the peasant but definitely not to that of the state bourgeoisie. Cashew-nuts, on the contrary, are export crops and their production and sale necessarily come to benefit the state bourgeoisie.

State direction and control over the peasants are therefore very key issues in the question of the relation between the bourgeoisie and the rural producers in countries like Tanzania. It is perhaps important to recall that apart from the villagisation drive, the government in the seventies introduced a number of other fundamental changes as regards existing rural institutions. Along with the resettlement of the peasants, practically all the local institutions that had grassroot level participation were overhauled and new bureaucratic ones directly controlled from the centre were established in their place. In 1972, to begin with, in accordance with the recommendations of an American consultancy firm, district and town councils were abolished and the central administration was devolved into the regions and districts to assume all the roles formerly played by these local government bodies. These councils had a significant democractic feature in that they were directly elective and had certain autonomy from the central government. With the "decentralisation" measures all powers until then vested in these institutions were transferred to central government civil servants who were sent to the regions and districts but who were not answerable to the people of those regions and districts.

Then in 1975 the marketing co-operative movement—then one of the most advanced in Africa—was demolished by the state. Peasants used to market their crops to co-operative organisations which were answerable to their members, i.e. the peasants themselves. True, the institutions were marked by considerable mismanagement, but at any rate they tried to and had to be responsive to the interests of their members. With the abolition of the co-operative societies, government agencies which formerly were responsible only for export trade were empowered to buy produce directly from the peasants. But the peasants themselves had no say over these bodies. Not only did these bodies prove to be even more inefficient and mismanaged, but they also turned out to be extremely corrupt. What is more, the peasants then began to suffer from yet another form of exploitation: actual non-payment for crops collected. For various reasons, practically all the government bodies involved in the purchase of agricultural produce are unable to pay cash to the peasants and instead offer promissory notes for produce collected. As is bound to happen in such situations, actual payment is very much delayed and in some cases the peasant is not paid at all or paid only in part.

By the beginning of the eighties it had become absolutely clear that the abolition of the local government authorities and the co-operative movement had not at all served the interests of the state bourgeoisie. The central government failed dismally to perform some of the essential functions formerly played by town councils, for instance; and the ''Authorities'' charged with collecting agricultural produce failed to reach some villages for years thus leaving export crops to rot at a time when the state needed to export as much as possible. Thus a decision was made to re-introduce both institutions and one can only wait to see the exact form the re-introduced institutions will take.

We can therefore see that drastic changes have taken place in the Tanzanian countryside over the last twenty years or so. The process of integration and control of the peasantry has to a large extent been accomplished as a result of the numerous policies tried on the peasantry subsequently. Export crops have become predominant in the countryside. Cotton for instance was by 1971 grown as a main crop by 12% of all households in the country, coffee by 10.3%, and cashew nuts by 8.1%.[22] One of the areas that has undergone dramatic changes in this regard is the so-called ''Western Cotton Zone''—covering Tabora, Mwanza, Shinyanga, and Mara regions. Table VI shows that while the average farm size in the area has grown by 173% between 1949 and 1978, the proportion of the farm under cotton has risen from 13% to 39%, i.e. an increase of 300%—making for an absolute increase of more than 520% of the total area under cotton.

As we have already seen, the peasants have first had to be regrouped to facilitate control, and second political and administrative organs have had to be reorganised to ensure that the state apparatus reaches down to the level of the peasant. In the final analysis this control and domination over the peasant is most advantageous to the international division of labour that characterises world capitalism: it ensures that peasants cannot resort to their traditional tactic of withdrawing from market forces into subsistence.

The changes that have occurred in the rural areas not only have brought about greater integration of the peasantry into the world market, but have also intensified the exploitation of the peasantry. It goes without saying that prices of primary products from underdeveloped countries have no relations whatsoever with their values—the socially necessary labour-time spent on their production. Multinational companies continue to rip off huge profits from the trade of raw materials from underdeveloped countries. Within the country, however, this exploitation is magnified even more. In the specific situation of Tanzania, a greater and greater proportion of the peasant produce is siphoned off by the state bourgeosie. Indeed, the abolition of both local government and co-operative institutions was objectively a means for ensuring this increased exploitation.

If we take cotton, for instance, we see that the return that goes back to the grower as proportion of what the state receives from the world market has been declining steadily over the years. Despite occasional improvements in the price of cotton in the world market, the actual grower in the country has not fared any better, instead those playing the role of middleman are the ones who seem to benefit more and more.

TABLE VI

AREA UNDER VARIOUS CROPS IN WESTERN COTTON ZONE
(Hectares)

	1945	1962	1978
Cotton	0.34(12.98%)	1.18(40.97%)	1.77(38.90%)
Paddy	0.21(8.02%)	0.32(11.11%)	0.15(3.30%)
Maize	0.32(12.21%)	0.75(26.04%)	1.62(35.60%)
Sorghum	1.19(45.42%)	0.04(1.39%)	0.57(12.53%)
Cassava	0.56(21.37%)	0.59(20.49%)	0.44(9.67%)
Average farm Size:	2.62(100%)	2.88(100%)	4.55(100%)

SOURCE: U.R. of Tanzania, *Agricultural Census Report,*
Dar es Salaam: Government Printer, 1971.

TABLE VII

COTTON PRICE STRUCTURE
(Percentages)

	1970/71	1971/72	1972/73	1973/74	1974/75
Sales Price:	100	100	100	100	100
Export Tax:	4.2	3.5	3.5	2.3	7.1
Parastatal Margin:	15.2	28.7	28.2	50.6	40.5
Co-op. Margin:	16.5	13.9	13.5	11.4	11.9
Producer Return:	64.1	53.9	54.8	35.7	40.5

SOURCE: *Quarterly Economic Review of Tanzania
and Mozambique* (London), various issues.

But perhaps a much more graphic picture can be discerned from the examination of the maize business. It must be borne in mind that maize is by far the leading staple food in the country, and that the National Milling Corporation (N.M.C.)—a state parastatal—has the legal monopoly for the 'purchase of maize and other grains in the country. The N.M.C. purchases the maize, stores it, mills it, and distributes the flour through wholesalers and retailers. As can easily be seen in Table VIII below, even when both the producer and the consumer of the product in which a state organ deals are next to each other—or indeed are one and the same client as in the case of maize (many villages have to buy back after some months the maize they sell to N.M.C.)—the state as middleman siphons off a great proportion of the ultimate selling price. The producer is paid only about 37% of what the consumer ultimately pays for the product, or in other words the purchaser has to pay some 266% of what he paid for as seller.

It can clearly be seen that the relation between the state bourgeoisie and the peasantry is one of exploitation. Since the peasant is not paid a wage, however, this exploitation is facilitated through politico-economic structures that regulate the activities of the peasantry and the most important activity is of course production. Villagisation has created such structures. It would of course be misleading to imply that in all these developments the state has all the time had the upper hand. Needless to say, there has been intense opposition on the part of the peasantry. We noted earlier on the constant resort by the peasantry to withdraw physically from establishment settlements, to sabotage official regulations, and so on. What took place during the colonial period has undoubtedly continued to this day although in ever changing forms. It is well-known that in coffee growing regions, for instance, peasants have been uprooting coffee trees in order to plant food crops, in cashew nut growing areas peasants have stopped weeding cashew farms and instead have resorted to burning them, in nearly all the areas peasants have been selling food crops on the black market, and so on.

The ultimate result of all this is that the rural economy has been steadily declining over the years. Production of both export and food crops has at best stagnated and at worst declined absolutely. As can be seen on Tables IX, X and XI, while there was a small but gradual increase in the early 1970s, production of the major export crops (i.e. cotton, coffee, sisal, tea, cashew nuts, pyrethrum, and tobacco) has been on the decline ever since the villagisation measures of the mid-seventies. In some cases, in fact, the decline has been drastic. The sharpest decline has been in the case of sisal and pyrethrum, but even in the case of once popular crops like coffee and cotton, the general tendency has been one of decline. As a matter of fact, if we look at

TABLE VIII
PRICE STRUCTURE FOR MAIZE

	Shillings Per Ton	Percentage of Producer Price	Percentage of Consumer Price
1. Producer price:	750	100	37.50
2. NMC Milling costs:	690.28	92.04	34.51
3. Packing, admin. & finance charges:	117.29	15.64	5.86
4. NMC margin:	222.43	29.66	11.12
5. Wholesaler's margin	71.85	9.58	3.59
6. Retailer's margin	148.15	19.75	7.41
7. Consumer price:	2000	166.67	100

Source: Reconstructed from data in ILO, *Towards Self-Reliance, op. cit.,* p. 66.

TABLE IX
AGRICULTURAL PRODUCTION INDEX IN TANZANIA
(1969-71 = 100)

	Total Food Production	Total Agric. Production	Food Prod. per capita	Agric. Prod. per capita
1966	92	96	103	107
1967	90	92	98	100
1968	91	91	96	96
1969	96	96	98	99
1970	104	104	104	103
1971	101	100	98	97
1972	100	101	95	95
1973	109	107	100	98
1974	110	107	98	96
1975	115	112	100	97
1976	116	113	97	95
1977	118	113	96	92
1978	121	115	95	91
1979	122	116	93	89
1980	121	116	90	86
1981	124	120	89	86

SOURCE: Maeda, J.H.J. and Msambichaka, L.A., *op. cit.,* p. 65.

TABLE X
INDEX OF MAJOR EXPORT CROPS (1970 = 100)

Year	Index
1971/72	111
1972/73	119
1973/74	116
1974/75	122
1975/76	109
1976/77	118
1977/78	110
1978/79	98
1979/80	98

SOURCE: Quarterly Economic Reviews, op. cit.

TABLE XI

N.M.C. PURCHASE OF MAIN FOOD CROPS

(Thousands of Tons)

	1978/79	**1979/80**	**1980/81**
Maize:	223	160	105
Rice:	52	30	5
Wheat:	28	26	26
Millet:	40	17	-
Sorghum:	58	21	-

SOURCE: Ibid.

the performance of the agricultural sector as a whole for the entire independence period we see that its rate of development has declined from an average level of 4.0% between 1964 and 1967 to 2.6% between 1970 and to 1.5% between 1973 and 1975.[23]

While it is true that there are many reasons for this general tendency of decline in agricultural production, we think that it is also true that a kind of 'go-slow' exists in the rural areas in response to the unpopular policies that have been pursued by the authorities. Professor Mascarenhas who lauded the villagisation programme, and called it one of 'the most outstanding indigenous rural development policies in Africa' also could not but conclude that 'the present agricultural picture is one of a peaceful revolt, an unwillingness to produce, or to become part of the wider system. There has been a turning back to the small farm/small plot for survival-level farming'.[24]

As a result of all this, the state bourgeoisie has had to assume a more and more repressive posture. Confronted by the permanent problem of 'shortage of foreign exchange' at a higher and higher level, the authorities have had to use coercive means *vis-a-vis* the peasants to a greater extent. We alluded, for instance, to the tendency by peasants to ignore cashew nut weeding. The state has been waging a desperate struggle on this, using in many cases the courts to imprison and fine peasants as these quotes from the *Daily News* show:[25]

Six peasants in Mchauru Division in Masasi District has been fined 300/= each or six months imprisonment in default after being found 'guilty' of burning their cashew nut farms. They paid the find. Sentencing them, the Mchauru Primary Court magistrate, Ndugu C.K. Kamguna, warned against the offence and said it adversely affected the country's economy.

Two Nachingwea residents, Zuberi Chunga (45) and Vitus Juma (29) have been sentenced by the Nachingwea District Magistrate, Ndugu P.S. Litanda, to 12 months imprisonment each for setting fire to their cashew nut farms instead of weeding them. The prosecution alleged that the two set fire to their cashew nut plantations, but the fire extended to other plantations where it burnt several hectares of cashew nut trees.

Ten peasants from Mpeta village, Masasi District, have been fined 50/= each or one month in jail by a Chungutwa Primary Court for refusing to work on a communal farm belonging to the village.

It goes without saying that the basic reason why peasants do not pay attention to the cashew farms is that the return just does not justify the effort. The peasant is paid just too little for the nuts, and—what is more—the proportion that the peasant gets from the world market price has been declining every year, from 57% in 1974/75 to 29% in 1979/80. A larger and larger proportion of the turnover from cashew nut industry is appropriated by the state. As can be seen from Table XII below, the further the decline of the proportion that has gone to the peasant the further has also been the decline in total cashew nut production.

TABLE XII

OUTPUT OF CASHEW NUTS

Year	Producer Price as Percentage of Export Price	Index of Total Output
1974/75	57	100
1975/76	52	70
1976/77	42	82
1977/78	30	57
1978/79	44	50
1979/80	29	38

SOURCE: Quarterly Economic Reviews, op.cit.

At the social and political levels, the institutional changes that have been effected in the rural areas together with the economic malaise have contributed in the no small way to changes in the status of stability of the countryside. In many regions, social unrest has become a permanent feature, replacing the stability that was based on traditional communal relations that dominated the rural areas just a few years ago. Crime has for instance showed a marked increase recently.

In this regard, a dramatic experience is the unrest that has characterised the 'Western Cotton Zone' since the mid-seventies. As the people in the area are traditionally semi-agricultural and semi-pastoral, villagisation broke down many of the communal ties that bound villagers. Crime increased dramatically as people of distant clans found themselves living close together in a social situation where traditionally allegations of witch-craft are every day occurrence. In time, killings became the order of the day. Cattle rustling became so frequent and so violent that the youth in the one section of the area formed a semi-secret army to hunt down all cattle rustlers. The army went about burning down the houses and other property of all known and suspected cattle thieves. Naturally, this increased to an alarming rate the state of violence in the entire area for several months. By the time the security forces were able to control the situation—taking the unprecedented step of stationing units of the para-military police in each village—tremendous damage had been done on the social fabric. No wonder the cattle rustlers in 1981 publicly announced in Tabora the formation of an 'Association of Cattle Rustlers' and once again went on a rampage in the countryside. Since attempts by the authorities to control the situation absolutely failed, in late 1982 they allowed the formation of the un-official citizens' army (*sungusungu*) to begin operating officially.

This permission was obviously a clear admission that the police force and other state organs were no match for the social forces that had been unleashed by the growing contradictions in the rural areas.

Conclusion

In a nutshell, then, this is to some extent an indication of the intensity of contradictions in rural Tanzania today. It would be wrong to ascribe every incident or trend to any or all of the government policies that we have mentioned in this chapter. But definitely in the process of trying to bring about 'rural development' through the strategies that we have discussed, numerous contradictions have necessarily arisen and sharpened.

We have argued that neo-colonial situations basically continue the colonial policies in the economic area, and that as far as the rural areas are concerned such policies generally amount to an attempt to incorporate the peasantry further and further into the ambit of world capitalism. In countries like Tanzania which have never known feudalism in any real sense, and where uninhabited land is still available to a large extent, this process of integration is a long and arduous process. The peasantry can easily withdraw into subsistence, and it becomes necessary to institute control and domination over them. It was the aim of the colonial rulers to achieve this, but the very nature of colonialism militated against this, and it was thus left to the independence governments to complete the process. Given different exigencies, situations, and historical experience, different governments complete it at different periods using different methods. As we have seen in the case of Tanzania, the process has had to take numerous turns here and there.

What is to be emphasised is that the specific structures of control and domination over the peasantry that we have outlined here are the concrete forms of manifestation of capitalism in the rural areas of countries like Tanzania. Those who look for capitalism in rural Africa by merely counting the number of wage labourers have no understanding of socio-economic formations in the era of imperialism. For capitalism to exploit the peasantry it does not necessarily mean the peasants have to be turned off the land and made to look for wage employment. It is perfectly in accordance with the laws of capitalism on the world scale that the peasant form persists in the rural areas while the economic content changes. Through the mechanism of domination and control, the economic content of village life can change drastically as we have seen with reference to Tanzania while the smallholder form of production remains the same.

Needless to add, this domination and exploitation very much hampers the development of the productive forces—and productivity about which there is so much outcry by the authorities and establishment intellectuals. And that is the contradication in which underdeveloped capitalism is always entwined.

NOTES

1. See for instance Mwansasu, B.U. and Pratt, C. (eds.), *Towards Socialism in Tanzania* (Dar es Salaam: Tanzania Publishing House, 1979): Lofchie, M.F. 'Agrarian Crisis and Economic Liberalism in Tanzania', *Journal of Modern African Studies*, (Vol. 16 No. 3. (1978); McHenry, D., *Tanzania's Ujamaa Villages* (Berkeley: Institute of International Studies, 1979).
2. Coulson, A., *Tanzania: A Political Economy* (Oxford: Clarendon Press, 1982) p.260.
3. *Ibid.*, p.10.
4. Maeda, J.H.J. and L.A. Msambichaka, *Agrarian Transformation and Rural Development in Tanzania* (Dar es Salaam: mimeo) (1983) p.12.
5. Rodney, W., *How Europe Underdeveloped Africa* (Dar es Salaam: Tanzania

Publishing House, 1972).

6. Gwassa, G.C.K., (ed.) *Vita vya Majimaji* (Dar es Salaam: East African Publishing House, 1967).

7. Rodney, W., *op. cit.*

8. Iliffe, J., *Agricultural Change in Modern Tanganyika* (Dar es Salaam: East African Publishing House, 1967).

9. See for instance Cliffe, L., and Saul, J.S., (eds), *Socialism in Tanzania* (Dar es Salaam: East African Publishing House, 1973); Ruthenberg, H., (ed.) *Smallholder Farming and Smallholder Development in Tanzania* (London: C. Hurst and Co. 1968).

10. Chambers, R., *Settlement Schemes in Tropical Africa* (London: Routledge and Kegan Paul, 1969).

11. Cabral, A. *Revolution in Guinea* (London: Stage 1, 1969) p.81.

12. Babu, A.M., *African Socialism or Socialist Africa* (Dars es Salaam: Tanzania Publishing House, 1981).

13. .Cliffe, L., and Saul, J.S., (eds.) *op. cit.* p.136.

14. *Ibid.*, p.135.

15. Shivji, I., *Class Struggles in Tanzania* (Dar es Salaam: Tanzania Publishing House, 1976).

16. Mapolu, H., *The Social and Economic Organisation of Ujamaa Villages, M.A. Thesis, 1973 (University of Dar es Salaam).*

17. McHenry, D., *op. cit.*

18. Yeager, R., *Demography and Development Policy in Tanzania, Journal of Development Areas* Vol. 16 No. 4 (1982).

19. Lwoga, C.M., *Bureaucrats, Peasants and Land Rights*, (Mimeo) (1978); Matango, R. 'Operation Mara: The Paradox of Democracy,' *Majimaji*, No. 20.

20. Coulson, A., (ed.) *African Socialism in Practice: The Tanzanian Experience* (Nottingham: Spokesman Books, 1979).

21. *Ibid.*, p.277.

22. UR. of Tanzania, *Agricultural Census Report*, (Dar es Salaam: Government Printer, 1971).

23. *Quarterly Economic Review of Tanzania and Mozambique* (London).

24. Mascarenhas, A., 'After Villagisation, What?' Mwansasu, B.U. and Pratt, C., (eds). *op. cit.*

25. The quoted in Williams, D.V., 'State Coercion Against Peasant Farmers: The Tanzania State', *Journal of Legal Pluralism*, No. 20 (1982).

6. STATE CONTROL OVER COOPERATIVE SOCIETIES AND AGRICULTURAL MARKETING BOARDS

Shamshad Naali

Introduction

Part I of this Chapter deals with the objectives behind state control of agricultural surplus product of the farmer both by the British colonial and the Independence governments. Part II addresses the pre-Arusha Declaration period wherein state control over Agricultural Marketing Boards and Co-operatives is analysed. Part III discusses the post-Arusha Declaration period when Co-operative Unions were dissolved and their functions were taken over, first, by the Agricultural Marketing Boards, and then by the state monopoly organisations called Crop Authorities. This part analyses state control over the authorities through various state bodies, for example, the parent Ministry (that is, the Ministry of Agriculture), the Treasury, and so on. Part IV reveals that state controls over the producers' surplus product through the above mechanisms has had an adverse impact on the cash crop production in general. The state does not realise its goal of appropriating increased agricultural surplus product of the peasantry as hitherto anticipated. Consequently, the state considers the reinstitution of co-operative unions. Thus the enactment of the 1982 Co-operative Societies Act. Part V attempts to compare the 1982 Act with the 1968 Co-operative Societies Act and find out whether the new legislation caters for the interests of the producers or not.

Why State Control?

The objective of state control over the Agricultural Marketing Boards and Co-operatives is to enable tighter control of cash crops producers and appropriation of their agricultural surplus product. State control of the cash crop producers is not a new phenomenon. Control was exerted by the British colonial government mainly to expropriate cash crops which served as raw materials for the industries in the metropolis. During the post-War period cash crops exported to the metropolis helped to pay war debts incurred by the British government. The British colonial government continued to control the surplus agricultural product even after this period, as it provided the colonial government with revenue for running the colonial state, as well as for expropriation of both the raw materials and the cash from sale of such raw materials to the metropolis.

The independence government also needed to control the cash crops in exchange for industrial commodities for the development of the state. And since it got involved with the international lending agencies by accepting loans for the improvement of production of cash crops, the need for control of these crops became even greater for payment of debts. For example, in 1970, the World Bank gave a loan of $ 9 million for tobacco; in 1972, a $10.8 million loan for smallholder tea farmers, in 1973, in a loan of $18.5 million for livestock development for export, in 1974, a $17.5 million for cotton, and so on.[1]

Pre-Arusha Declaration Period
At the time of Independence, Tanganyika inherited the export-oriented economy from the British colonial government, depending heavily on the export of agricultural cash crops like coffee, cotton, tea, sisal, and so on. This is well demonstrated by Shivji in his *Class Struggles in Tanzania*.

TABLE I

EXPORT ORIENTATION: QUANTUM OF TOTAL PRODUCTION EXPORTED IN PERCENTAGE

Year	Sisal	Cotton	Coffee	Tea	Cashew nuts
1964	90.80	81.76	99.26	44.54	76.00
1969	81.89	81.89	100.01	86.94	76.35

SOURCE: (Tanzania) Statistical Abstract, 1966 and 1970 contained in Shivji's *Class Struggles in Tanzania* (Dar es Salaam: Tanzania Publishing House, 1976), p. 39.

With this economic system dominating at the time of Independence, the Tanganyika African National Union government's policy was no different from that of the British colonial government's namely legal and administrative control of cash crops, with the same instruments of control, that is, application of laws in controlling the peasants' produce through the Agricultural Marketing Boards and the Co-operative Unions, using extension services and District Councils.

The important legislation adopted at this time was the Agricultural Products (Control and Marketing) Act, 1962 (which repealed the African Agricultural Products (Control and Marketing) Ordinance of 1949, No 5 of 1949. This status applied mainly to food crops like maize, beans, cassava, sorghum, sun flower, etc.

Several Boards were established in different areas to control food crops grown in those areas. [2] The Minister for Agriculture was empowered to declare an area in which production, cultivation and marketing of agricultural products could be controlled and for every such area the Minister established a Board for the control and regulation of the specific agricultural products. [3] Members of the Board were appointed by the Minister.[4] Section 7 of the above mentioned Act provided for compulsory marketing orders, whereby peasants were compelled to market their produce to the Board. [5] Not only did this section compel the peasant to sell his produce to the established Board, it also specified what grade of crop the peasant must sell to the Board. The Boards however, were not autonomous bodies. They were subject to state control. For instance, the Minister could under s. 7(4) of the above Act, instruct the Board concerning matters to be taken into account in determining the price and the terms of payment for the producer. In addition to that, the Minister was empowered under s. 8(9) to give direction in writing to the Board as to the preparation of the ground, the cultivation, production, processing and marketing of any specific agricultural product. No directions of the Board were valid if they were at variance with the directions given by the Minister.

The state, therefore, exercised control not only over the quality and quantity of crops produced for procurement of the state; it even regulated the manner in which the peasant planted his crop.[6] Thus the state controlled the peasant both at the marketing and production level. An example is that of cashew nut, an important cash crop grown in Tanganyika. The state controlled the producers of this crop *vide* the Board established under the South Region Cashew Nut (Compulsory Marketing) Order No. 2 of 1962. All peasants producing cashew nuts in the Southern Region were compelled under the order to comply with any directions of the Board as to the sale of cashew nuts.

Other Boards were established to control specific cash crops under the National Agricultural Products Boards Act, 1964 (NAPB). This Act was to be read together with the Agricultural Products Boards

(Marketing and Control) Act, No. 56 of 1962 (to be called the principal Act). Among these Boards was the Tanganyika Tobacco Board.[7] The Boards were empowered to compel sale of produce by peasants to the Boards. It was the Boards which determined producer prices without the participation of the producers. To ensure punishment for the producers who did not follow orders of the Boards, the Independence government (like the colonial government) made it an offence under the Act to contravene the orders of the Boards. The offence was punishable by imprisonment not exceeding six months on conviction or a fine not exceeding shs. 2,000.[8] Intensive control by the state is further evidenced in the composition of all the Boards created under this Act. They were mostly composed of state functioneries. For example, by Government Notice No. 125 of 22/3/1963,[9] additional members to the National Agricultural Boards appointed under the Agricultural Products (Control and Marketing) Act, 1962 were the Minister for Agricultural or his representative; the Principal Secretary of the Ministry of Co-operatives and Community Development, and the Regional Commissioner of Dar es Salaam Region.

It would be expected that the peasants whose produce was marketed by these Boards would be the major component of the same Boards. However, this was not so. The main component of the Boards were state officials. Considering the composition of the Boards, decisions taken by the Boards were naturally in the interest of the state rather than that of the producers.

Intensive control by the state over cash crops producers was further manifested in the Tanganyika Coffee Board established under section 3 of the Coffee Industry Act No. 20 of 1961. The general functions of the Board as provided under section 5 of the same Act were to advise the Minister upon measures for the promotion and protection of the coffee industry, to promote the sale of coffee and encourage the production of good quality coffee, to arrange for the marketing of coffee in Tanganyika and to conduct research in connection with the industry. The Act further provided under section 6, for the sale, purchase, processing and export of coffee, and restricted sale and purchase of coffee and other dealings in coffee. It appointed designated agencies, the co-operative societies and unions, through which producers could sell their coffee. Section 9(ii) of the same Act provided for the control of quality processing of coffee. The Act thus empowered the coffee Board to give directives with regard to export and sale or delivery for export, and the Board was, under section 16 of the same Act, specifically empowered to purchase coffee.

The coffee Board also directly controlled the activities of the licensed dealers of coffee. It was further empowered to impose levy on the sale of coffee. [10] Section 2 of the Coffee Industry (Collection of Levy) Rules, 1965 specifically empowered the coffee Board to collect levy from the seller at the time of the sale of coffee, the rate of levies on different grades of coffee were also statutorily provided for. [11] The imposition of levy clearly shows the exploitation and alienation of producers who had no say whatsoever in the price of their produce. This exploitation is further discerned in the marketing activities of the Tanganyika Coffee Board. It collected coffee from the co-operative unions and the Tanganyika Coffee Growers Association (TCCA). It then sent raw coffee to the coffee curing and graded the coffee for bagging and for sale. The sale was conducted through weekly auctions at Moshi, and the levy was deducted from the proceeds of sale before it was sent to the unions to be handed down to the producers through their respective societies. The Tanganyika Coffee Board also deducted export tax introduced in 1960 on behalf of the Government. It further introduced the Coffee Berry Disease Control (CBD) programme in the 1970s for which it further deducted peasants' money from the sale price. The Coffee Board also took over the research centre at Lyamungu, near Moshi, which was formerly known as the coffee research centre. The running of this station also demanded a further deduction of the peasant's money from the sale of coffee.

Indeed, some years after independence we see that the coffee Board had powerful in controlling the peasant's activities in the production of coffee. This was typical of all the Boards dealing with specific crops like tobacco, cotton, cashew nuts, and so on.

The additional functions conferred by the state over the Agricultural Marketing Boards were a maneouvre towards greater control of the peasants' produce both at the production and marketing level. The fact that these Boards were the state's instruments of control over the peasants is confirmed by their composition. For example, both the chairman and vice-chairman of the coffee board were the Minister's appointees. [12] The producers had no say in the election of the above members. It was in the state's interest to ensure that whoever held these important positions were the state's representatives who would guard the interests of the state as against those of the peasants. Both the constitution of the Board and the Executive Committee consisted of representatives of the societies. [13] Nevertheless, the Minister had his own appointees who were not members of co-operative societies. Considering that the Minister's appointees were high officials from the government departments, one wonders whether an ordinary peasant could have a strong voice against them. Futhermore, even if the Board did represent the producers, it was not strictly autonomous. This is clearly seen in the Minister's wide ranging powers to issue orders and directives to the Board in almost every aspect of the functions of the Board. Whether the co-operatives were genuinely people's associations or they too catered for interests other than those of the peasants will be discussed presently.

In 1961, marketing co-operatives were important instruments for development in the agricultural sector. By this time co-operative unions were well established in the marketing of the peasant's agricultural products, as at the same time, they had the capacity to give out loans to the farmer for the purchase of agricultural inputs. It was easier to deduct the loans from the peasant's income as their cash crops were handled by the co-operatives. The importance of the co-operatives was officially recognized by the government in the Government Paper No. 4 of 1967, which said: "There is no other type of organisation which is so suited to the problems and concept of rural development ... it will be impossible for the Government administrative machinery to deal with numerous individuals requiring Government assistance and services, including credit for raising production and productivity without the use of co-operatives. The number of people wanting government help will make dissemination of government services and assistance financially very expensive and administratively almost impossible."[14]

It is evident in the above statement that the Independence government was aware that it could conveniently use the already established co-operatives as its agents to control the peasant's cash crops. So as to intensify its control, the post-Independence government set up a policy of expanding the co-operative movement by establishing co-operatives even in areas where co-operatives did not exist. And to have a strong controlling organization to co-ordinate all the activities of the co-operative unions, the government established the Co-operative Union of Tanganyika (CUT) in 1967. This expansion in the co-operative movement is clearly evidenced in the rapid upsurge in the number of co-operative societies in the country starting with a figure of 857 in 1961 to 1,616 in 1966.[15]

At this time, we witness the existence of two categories of co-operative societies. First, there were co-operatives which were formed voluntarily by farmers during the colonial times, for example the Kilimanjaro Native Cooperative Union Ltd (KNCU). And in the second category were co-operative societies, formed and registered without members' but with government's initiative. The Presidential Special Committee of Enquiry into the Co-operative Unions and Marketing Boards recognized this by reporting that "The political pressures were considerable and that societies were organised from the top without genuine local demand or even understanding".[16] The government extended state aid to the co-operatives with more incentives such as access to government credit schemes (at first the National Agricultural Agency and later the Rural Development Bank). This of course made it desirable and advantageous for many farmers to join co-operative societies.

Since the co-operative unions had accumulated surplus through society fees and levies, the government bureaucracy thought that there was a greater need for state control in the co-operatives lest the surplus accumulated be misused. This could be done through a slow penetration into the movement, which became possible earlier than envisaged, when inefficiency, corruption and deliberate misuse of funds had allegedly become rampant in the co-operative movement. Thus the above-mentioned Presidential Special Committee of Enquiry into the Co-operative Societies and Marketing Boards was appointed to look into the alleged defects in the movement. The Committee found that the allegations against the co-operative societies were to some extent true.[17]

Whether the above weaknesses did exist in the cooperative movement or not, the appointment of a special state body to look into these affairs reflected the government bureaucracy's desire to officially and justifiably oust the co-operative bureaucracy which was becoming a force to contend with. Before that, however, in 1966 about 16 co-operative unions and hundreds of co-operative societies were temporarily taken over by the state. The committee men in these co-operative societies were dismissed, and replaced by government officials. The official enquiry helped in emphasising the defects of the movement. One significant fact the Committee pointed out was that the co-operative movement was subjected to political interference which demanded premature registration of co-operative societies which was alleged to be the root cause of the problem.[18]

The Committee therefore put forward recommendations for the improvement of the co-operative movement. The recommendations reflected greater control by the state over the movement. One of its first recommendations was the formation of unified co-operative service which would become a central organisational instrument of the co-operative movement responsible for the engagement, discipline, terms of service and dismissal of all secretaries of societies, managers of unions and federation of unions.[19]

This removed legal control by the co-operative committee of employees of the societies and unions. This was one further step towards the state bureaucracy's control of the societies. The Presidential Special Committee pointed out that the unified co-operative service would diminish local responsibility and local accountability and that there was a greater need for central responsibility and central accountability.[20] This meant that the employees of societies being reduced by the government would have greater allegiance towards the state rather than the societies. The Committee further recommended that emergency powers be given to the co-operative development division (a state department) to take care of the interest of the farmers. It recommended that the Registrar of Co-operatives be empowered to take emergency steps with respect to any primary society whose costs of operation per unit of produce handled exceeded levels which the Registrar might fix in the Registration or which were incurring shortages of either produce or money to an extent which such officers were satisfied were not adequately explained.[21] The emergency steps could either be suspension or removal of the secretary of a society, committee or committee man or instruction to the union to which the society was affiliated to perform directly the services ordinarily performed by the society at the expense of the society.[22] The power of removal being in the hands of state officials reflected that the central government would have close control of the society and its members. The Committee reported that, "ordinarily we would not favour this degree of *Government intervention* in co-operative societies,"[23] (emphasis added). This was ostensibly an admission of the state control over the co-operative movement, which the government justified by stating that the rapid growth of co-operatives resulted in inadequate personnel to manage them. Thus it was desirable to have officials from the state to interfere until that time that the co-operatives were strengthened to perform their functions effectively and economically.

Following the Committee's report, the Co-operative Societies Act was passed in May 1968, which repealed the 1942 Co-operative Societies Ordinance. The Act was evidently passed for greater control of the societies by the state.[24] First of all, the Registrar of Co-operatives was an appointee of the President. The Registrar had powers to approve the registration of a society. He had vast powers in the amalgamation, division and dissolution of co-operative societies, (the Registrar exercised this power in the case of Bukoba Co-operative Union), to remove elected members of the committee,[25] and appoint officers to the society.[26] the Registrar further had powers to control the maximum liability a society could incur, he could also decide in which way the funds of the registered society were invested or deposited,[27] and he could disallow any item of the expenditure by a registered society. Further, the financial control of the society was entirely in the hands of the Registrar.[28] Furthermore, the Registrar could recommend that the by-laws of a society be amended so as to conform with such directions as he may give in that behalf.[29] There was the right to appeal to the Minister following the refusal of the Registrar to register such a society and the Minister's decision would be final.[30] The Registrar could also have the accounts of every registered society audited at least once a year on their behalf by persons authorised by a general or special written order.[31] This was to look into the financial affairs of the society and to ensure that there was no misappropriation by the committee men. The Registrar could also fix the remuneration payable to any person appointed by him.[32]

The Post-Arusha Declaration Period

Clearly, by mid-sixties, state control over agricultural marketing through co-operatives had expanded considerably. However, in the course of the societies' operations arose corrupt elements. During this period dishonesty and misappropriation of funds became rampant in co-operative societies and Union.[33] Hence the Presidential Special Committee which confirmed the allegations that corruption was widespread at every level in the co-operative movement. Following the Committee's report, as we have seen, the Government took steps towards greater control over the movement. Yet the alleged malpractices continued. Thus the state bureaucracy saw an opportunity to strengthen itself and weaken those who were opposed to control, namely the co-operative bureaucracy. At this juncture, it would seem that the state bureaucracy was no longer willing to let the co-operative bureaucracy get the lion's share of the peasant's agricultural surplus value. The state bureaucracy's contention was what the functional utility of the co-operatives had declined. That these institutions were becoming less satisfactory as government policy instruments. Consequently, it is not surprising that there should have been increasing state bureaucratic pressure to eliminate this particular "middleman". The aim was to bring the peasant under the direct control of the state through the crop authorities (wholly owned state organisations). In 1971, the Minister for Agriculture and Co-operatives, the late Dereck Bryceson stated that, "the structure of co-operative societies and unions was similar to middlemen, the present unions are just the people's creation of middle man. Through discussion with the peasants it has been found out that even the peasants know that. These unions are therefore bound to face the fate of other middle men".[34] During this time the villagisation programme had increased its tempo whereby most or all of the rural population was being settled in village units. These villages were given a marketing role in addition to the role of production. Under this programme the primary societies, which were the economic base of co-operative unions, were declared redundant within the contemporary socio-economic structure. It was from this perspective that dissolution of the unions in Tanzania became inevitable.

It is against this background that in 1976 the dissolution of the unions took place by a pronouncement of a government official, the then Prime Minister Rashidi Kawawa following a directive by the Party. The Agricultural Marketing Boards took over the functions of the co-operative unions handling the respective crops of such Boards. For example, the Tanganyika Coffee Board took over all the functions of the co-operative societies and unions of coffee producers.

It is contended that this was a blatant manoeuvre of the state bureaucracy to bring the cash crop producers into closer contact with itself. After the dissolution of the unions, the marketing boards undertook the collection of cash crops from the growers hitherto procured by the co-operative societies and unions. These marketing boards were, however, not structured and had no capacity to carry out the prescribed functions effectively. Consequently, the state decided to establish crop authorities where none existed, and confer necessary powers upon them. The main crop authorities were the Coffee Authority of Tanzania, the Tobacco Authority, the Cashew Nut Authority, the Cotton Authority, and so on. These authorities were however not autonomous entities. They were subject to government's control in line with the TANU guidelines under para 33 that, ''The conduct and activities of the parastatals must be looked into to ensure that they help further our policy of socialism and self-reliance. The activities of the parastatals should be a source of satisfaction and not discontent. The Party must ensure that the parastatals do not spend money extravagantly on items which do not contribute to the national economy as a whole''. The Party guidelines connote that it is the Party which has to ensure that parastatals help to achieve the national objectives. And it is upon the Party to see that the government exercises control over the principal means of production which facilitates the way to collective ownership of the resources of the country.[35]

The government endeavoured to control the crop authorities through various instruments. Primarily, control was exerted through Parliament *vide* the enabling Acts which empowered the government to issue directives, appoint and discuss members of the Boards of the authorities, and approve certain decisions of the Board in accordance with the provisions of the enabling statute. Parliamentary control could further be exercised through the debates and questioning in the Assembly, scrutiny of the authorities' accounts and reports and annual estimates. Other controlling agencies are the Treasury, the Tanzania Audit Corporation, the Standing Committee on Parastatal Organisations (SCOPO), the Bank of Tanzania and the Tanzania Rural Development Bank.

The enabling statutes establish effective control mechanism of the state over the authorities. For example, there is the Minister's control over the authorities and provisions for the President's power to appoint the important personnel of the authority.[36] The enabling Acts effectively establish the scope of functions and powers of the authorities which means that anything done beyond the scope and powers will be *ultra vires*. The enabling Acts however do not provide for growers' representation in the organisations. This means that the growers were being alienated from the organisations which were directly linked with their agricultural life.

The enabling Acts also provide for the powers of the authorities which means that the authorities have no other source of power except their establishing Acts.[37] Normally, the enabling statutes provide for the sources of finance.[38] They also provide for the establishment of the Board of Directors, the decision-making body.[40]

The enabling Acts also give the Minister powers to issue regulations for the better carrying out of objects and provisions of the Act and the management of the corporations. This clearly shows that control is imposed over the authorities through the enabling Acts. Further they provide for the conduct of the business of the authorities by the Boards and also for the duties of the chief executives.[41] The provisions of the Acts establishing the crop authorities are clear on the objects, powers, sources of finance, auditing and management of the same. In this connection, it is clear that the initial instrument to establish the control mechanism over the authorities are the enabling statutes.

The Minister for Agriculture is empowered to appoint Directors to the Board of the specific authority, and to give general and specific directives (e.g. investment and loan policies) to the authority. The strategy of the Minster to ensure that these directives are adhered to is through the power to both appoint and dismiss members of the Boards of Directors.

The Treasury is the most effective financial control mechanism over the authorities. First, the authorities are obliged to submit to the Treasury, through the Parent Ministry, their budget estimates for each financial year. On satisfaction that they are in conformity with the government annual economic development plan, the Treasury recommends the estimates for approval by Parliament. The Treasury, therefore, is the real force behind the control of allocation of government funds to authorities. Treasury also controls the investment projects of the authorities. Authorities have to submit to the Treasury their project plans, which only upon satisfaction that they are in conformity with the Treasury's laid down standards for public investments projects, that funds are released for implementation. Moreover, Treasury's department, the Public Investment Monitoring Unit (PIMU), ensures that the authorities do implement their projects.

Among other controlling government agencies are the Tanzania

Audit Corporation, the Standing Committee of Parastatal Organisations and the standing committee on Parastatal Organisations Technical Management Agreements.

The Bank of Tanzania effects control on the foreign exchange allocation to the authorities which have to first convince the Bank of the necessity of importing agricultural implements and inputs before it consents to allocate the foreign exchange. The Bank also scrutinizes the management agreements entered into by the authorities which are indefinite, and also ensure that the agreements provide for the proper training programme which would ensure adequate training of local personnel to enable the local company to function by itself.

In its endeavour to control public investment in agriculture, especially peasant farmers, the Tanzania Rural Development Bank (TRDB) was established. TRDB is mainly involved in the tobacco industry whereby it helps the farmers by supplying them credit or agricultural inputs. TRDB being part of the state's apparatus serves as a conduit pipe for international finance. TRDB ensures that loans advanced to farmers are paid back with interest. This is done through the crop authorities where the farmer must sell his crop.

Effect of State Control Over the Producers of Cash Crops

We have seen in the proceeding sections that control over the producers of cash crops is exerted both at the marketing and production level. Village governments are strong instruments of state control at the production level. Villagers are obliged to observe and implement decisions of their village councils. For example, the village council in Kimangara Village in Kilimanjaro region resolved that every villager must cultivate his shamba well, and if one habours weeds or pests in his shamba then he should be fined shs. 40 on the first and shs. 60 on the second occasion and be thrown off the land on the third occasion.[42] The village further resolved that any villager selling cash crops other than through the village council shall be dealt with (it was not specified how).[43] Similarly, a villager's shamba was confiscated by the village council in Hai district, Kilimanjaro Region, for lack of proper care of his shamba. Apart from the village directives the producer is also directed at the district level, whereby the district development councils issue by-laws to the producers as to the minimum acreage crop cultivation.[44] The reintroduction of minimum acreage provided the means of imposing closer control upon the producer by the state.

The crop authorities mainly control the producer at the market level. The village governments act as the authorities' agents for collection of cash crops, whereby the villages are paid levy by the authorities. For example, coffee authority pays village governments a levy of 25c/kg. of coffee purchased. The crop is then procured by the authorities who can make deductions from the producer's price as they deem fit. The producer has no say whatsoever as far as such deductions are concerned. Consequently, the producers have through deductions from producer price borne the burden of ever increasing administrative costs of the authorities. The escalating administrative costs have been due to higher overhead costs by the authorities in the maintenance of a large permanent work force at the authorities. Frank Ellis maintains that, "this is one of the reasons why contemporary parastatals have such higher overhead costs from the former marketing system".[45] The figure for persons employed in 1982 at the coffee authority, for example, was 2,000 but actual manpower strength was 1,393 or about 70% of the total manpower establishment.[46] Similarly, overheads of Tobacco Authority of Tanzania have been increasing, whereby administrative costs have increased by an average of 2.4% per year during 1979/80 and was budgeted for a 13% increase between 1982/83 and 1983/84. TAT headquarters consumed 45% of the total expenses in 1981/82 and 44% in 1982/83. On a per kg. basis Headquarter's expenses increased 14% between 1981/82 and 1982/83.[47] Apart from Crop Authorities' overheads other deductions are made from the producer price. The table below illustrates various deductions made by the Coffee Authority from the coffee growers' producer price.

In addition to the different costs deducted from the producer price, the increasing taxation by the state has also been added to the overheads. Ellis and Hanak conclude in their paper on coffee that the most important factor responsible for the declining share of the growers in the export price is the taxation of the industry by the Government.[48]

The Marketing Development Bureau (MDB) under the aegis of the Ministry of Agriculture acts as a regulatory agent as it makes its own estimates on the possible price each season. It acts as a basis of control on the crop authorities over estimation of deduction from producer price. It may be noted, however, that the cash crop producer is nowhere involved in the mechanism of fixing the producer price. There is thus an apparent communication breakdown between the producer and the crop authorities in the contemporary marketing system. The producers complain that they receive no information whatsoever regarding the deductions made by the authorities from the export price.

Although state control over the producer had comparatively increased during the co-operative unions times, the producer at least had a forum in the co-operative unions through which he could voice his grievances. For example, during the time of the KNCU, although

TABLE 2

SUMMARY OF CAT'S CONSOLIDATED BUDGET 1982/83

INCOME	SHS. 000
Levies from Growers	
CAT Levy @ shs. 3.02/kg.	161,306
CDC (1) Levy @ shs. 2.18/kg.	116,615
CIP (2) Levy @ 0.72/kg.	38,400
Development Levy @ shs. 040/kg.	21,671
Sub total	337,992
Sales of inputs	55,513
Government subventions (3)	71,033
EDF (4) contribution	66,563
Misc. CAT income (5)	30,900
Total	562,001
Expenditure	
CAT recurrent expenditure	192,206
CAT Capital expenditure	21,206
CIP/CDP recurrent expenditure	310,036
CIP/CDP capital expenditure	38,086
Total	562,001

NOTES

(1) Coffee Disease Control Levy.
(2) Coffee Improvement Programme.
(3) Including shs. 49.6 million for the cost of extension services.
(4) European Development Fund of EEC.
(5) Includes CAT Export Division, Coffee Bars, CAT farms, license fees and so on.

SOURCE: Marketing Development Bureau,
Price Policy Recommendations for 1982/83 Annex 7, p. 24.

the Tanganyika Coffee Board decided on the price to be paid to the producer, the KNCU could hold up auction until such a time when certain price was agreed upon between it and the buyer. Moreover, the producer could put forward his views before payments were made. He could also advise on the period when payment could be made according to his programme of expenditure. On the other hand, the centralised institutions of the state have completely alienated themselves from the producer of the crop it handles, thus, possible control from the grassroot level has been eliminated.

The increased state control over the producer has brought a negative result in that the state bureaucracy does not get hold of as much of the peasants' agricultural surplus product as it had anticipated. This is, for example, evident from the generally considerable fall in the cash crops production and a very little increase in production of coffee. Table 3 summarises the trend of production for some major cash crops in the country.

The general trend of fall in the total production (official) in the country has been noted with alarm by the government bureaucracy. The Minister of Agriculture stated that, "there are certain regions which are stagnating even though agronomic and climatic conditions would favour expansion. These include Arusha, Mbeya and Kagera while Kilimanjaro region is on the verge of decline."[49]

TABLE 3

**PRODUCTION TRENDS FOR SOME MAJOR EXPORT CROPS
1970/71—1982/83**

Year	Pyrethrum (000 Tons)	Cashewnut (Raw) (000 Tons)	Coffee (Clean) (000 Tons)	Cotton Bales ('000)	Tobacco (Leaf) (000 Tons)
1970/1971	2.7	112.5	46.8	429.5	12.0
1971/1972	4.3	126.0	52.4	363.4	13.1
1972/1973	4.0	125.5	47.5	424.0	12.7
1973/1974	3.3	145.1	42.5	359.1	18.3
1974/1975	4.7	119.0	52.1	393.6	14.2
1975/1976	3.9	83.7	55.4	234.6	19.1
1976/1977	3.3	97.6	48.9	369.8	18.3
1977/1978	2.5	68.4	51.9	278.6	17.1
1978/1979	1.6	57.1	49.6	310.2	17.3
1979/1980	1.6	41.0	48.0	334.1	16.8
1980/1981	2.0	61.0	66.8	324.0	11.7
1981/1982	2.4	72.0	55.5	325.0	15.4
1982/1983	2.5	53.8			13.1

SOURCE: Marketing Development Bureau
Price Policy Recommendations for 1982/83 Annexes 1,6,7,9 and 13.

The other variables accounting for the decline in the production are the fall in the world market price in the cash crops; increasing inflation reducing the producer price, which has been aggravated by high export tax by the state; fall in the extension services and the adverse climatic conditions. Other variables notwithstanding, one may conclude that the state's endeavour to closely control the peasant's agricultural surplus product has had a negative impact. The fall of cash crops production was noted by Party officials during the CCM National Executive Seminar held in Arusha in May 1980. Mwalimu Nyerere noted that, "the shortage of foreign exchange in Tanzania was primarily a result of a drastic drop in production of export cash crops such as coffee, cotton, sisal, cashew nuts".

The fact that the producer has been alienated from the organisation handling his produce, and the fact that the authorities do not offer any explanation to the producer on the increasing deductions which result in the decrease of the producer's price, made the producer lose confidence in such an organisation. This disregard of the producer's interests further aggravates the producer's suspicion of being exploited by the state's monopoly organisation. The producer needs a body whereby he can have a say and a sense of belonging by being involved in the important decision-making about the crop that he produces. This was succinctly pointed out by one of the participants in the same CCM Seminar at Arusha, that, " . . . in order for the peasant to contribute fully in agricultural production, they must have a body in which they can democratically participate in deciding on their development. It was perhaps time for reconsidering the co-operatives which in the past were peasant's units to which they felt a sense of belonging and acted as a guarantor of their own welfare."[55]

The state bureaucracy realized the anomaly of excluding peasants from participating in the important decisions on their own development. It also realized that it was a mistake, for example, to have dissolved the Co-operative Unions like the KNCU and the Bukoba Co-operative Unions. The government therefore appointed in October 1980 a commission to enquire into the possibility of reviving the co-operative unions in the country. The desire to see the reinstatement of co-operative unions was great amongst all the peasants in the country. The government bureaucracy also realised that the high export tax on cash crops did not help in getting higher revenues as the reduced producer prices resulted in the fall of production, which consequently reduced not only government revenue but potential foreign exchange earnings from the export of cash crops. Accordingly, the Minister for Finance announced the state's waiver of export tax on coffee, sisal and tobacco, hoping to give the farmer an incentive for producing more. The Ministry of Agriculture was accordingly advised to adjust the producer's price of the same crop.[51]

The Co-operative Societies Act, 1982

After the dissolution of the co-operative unions, the marketing boards and later the crop authorities purchased cash crops from the producers through the village government. The authorities, however, did not produce as much cash crops as envisaged. Overall production was generally on the decline for the past few years. The government bureaucracy realized the anomaly of having dissolved the unions. Thus in late 1980, it appointed a special commission to examine the possibility of reviving the co-operative unions. The commission submitted its report in early 1981 in which it recommended the reinstitution of co-operative unions. The government accepted the commission's recommendations. The 1982 Co-operative Act was therefore enacted to enable the implementation of the above recommendation.

The objects of the Co-operative Societies Act 1982 under section 2 are *inter alia* to accelerate the building of socialism by bringing about socialist development both in rural and urban areas and of foster development of co-operative farming in rural areas as a means of modernising and developing agriculture and of eliminating exploitation. The Act thus provides for "formation, constitution, registration and functions of the co-operative societies as instruments for the implementation of the policy of socialism and self-reliance, to repeal the Co-operative Societies Act 1968 and to provide for matters connected with these purposes". The role of the state under this Act is that of a protector by way of guidance and supervision.

Looking at the objects of the Act, it is evident that the co-operatives will again be used by the state for the achievement of its own goals—namely, control of co-operatives and ultimately control of producers of crops, even though provisions have been made for the co-operatives other than agricultural production and marketing co-operatives. The co-operative movement is certainly not intended to be an independent body as it is clearly stated that the state will have a supervisory role over the co-operatives.

Analysing the provisions of the Act, one may conclude that the new legislation is not much different from the preceding legislation as regards the power of the state apparatus. For example, the Registrar's powers have not been very much diminished as far as the operation of co-operative societies is involved. Therefore, we see that it is upon the Registrar's satisfaction that a co-operative society has complied with the provisions of the 1982 Act and of the rules and that its proposed by-laws are not contrary to the Act and the rules that the society may be registered (s. 70(1)). Before registering any society the Registrar may require that the by-laws of a society be amended according to his directions (s. 70(2)). The Registrar may, if he deems necessary, require any Bank to furnish any information regarding the transactions of any registered society with the Bank (s.89(9)). He can further under s. 90(1) bring to the notice of a society any defects in the working of such a society and may make an order directing the society or its officers to take such actions that he may specify in the order and within such time as he may direct in that order. If the Registrar is of the opinion that the committee of any registered society is not performing its duties properly, he may after giving an opportunity to the committee to state its objections, at a general meeting of the society summoned by him by order in writing, dissolve the committee and by the same or subsequent order direct the society, within such time as may be specified in the order, to elect a new committee in accordance with the by-laws of the society. The Registrar may of his own motion, or on the application of a majority of the committee or not less than a third of the members, direct some person authorised by him by order in writing in his behalf to hold an inquiry into the constitution, activities and financial affairs of a registered society (s. 133(1)). He may further, in the interest of two or more societies, amalgamate such societies as a single society (s. 137(1)). He may also divide a society if he is satisfied that it is in the interest of the society (s. 140). The Registrar, after an inquiry has been held or after inspection has been made or on receipt of an application made by three-quarters of the members of a registered society, is of the opinion that the society ought to be dissolved, may, by order in writing and after due consultation with the secretary general of the apex organization, has powers to make regulations prescribing the accounts and books to be kept by a society, the returns to be submitted by a society to the Registrar and the persons by whom and the form and language in which such returns are to be submitted, and the maximum loan which may be made by a society to any members thereof without prior consultation.

The difference between the 1982 Co-operative Societies Act and the 1968 Act is that the important role of the apex organisation is recognised.[52] That is, the registrar is required to gradually delegate his duties of promoting and giving advice to co-operative societies to the apex organisation. And as seen above, the registrar does not have absolute discretion to dissolve the committee of a society neither can he dissolve societies without consulting the secretary general.[53] Even the power of making rules and regulations has to be shared with the secretary general.[54]

One wonders, however, whether the delegation of these powers to the apex organization will mean powers in the hands of the members of co-operative societies. Looking at the constitution and the proposed by-laws of the apex organisation, it is evident that it is one of the instruments of the state. The apex organisation is first and foremost one of the organs of CCM. It is envisaged to comprise of all co-operative societies and unions in the country. One of the prerequisites for a leadership position in the organisation is Party membership.[55] Before a person is considered for a leadership position in the apex organisation he will be screened and recommended by the Party. In accordance with clause 69 (9) (g) of the CCM constitution, the secretary general of the apex organisation will be appointed by the national executive council pursuant to clause 71(4) of the CCM constitution.[56] The general meeting of the apex organisation at the national level will comprise of representatives from co-operative societies at regional level and representatives from the Party at the regional level and a representative from each of the other party organs. Similarly, general meetings of the apex organisation at regional level will also comprise of party secretaries from the relative areas and representatives from the other organs of the party and representatives from co-operative societies.

The 1982 Co-operative Societies Act provides for the establishment of different types of co-operative societies both in the urban and rural areas: Section 24 of the Act compels all persons who have attained the age of fifteen years and who are residents and in occupation of land or those who qualify to form a co-operative group to be members. The anamoly here is that, open membership is not given due consideration for rural co-operatives. When the Bill was being passed members of Parliament demanded that the above important principle be adhered to, and that the element of compulsion should be removed.

The Act also provides for the establishment of co-operative development committee for every rural co-operative society which is the managing and the executive agency of the society, (s.28). Conditions for membership to the committee are spelt out in a circular by the Registrar sent to all Regional Co-operative Officers which makes reference to a Party directive. The conditions are that all elections of societies' leaders must be approved by the Party. Further, that whereas committee members can be non-Party members, the chairman and secretary and any representative in Party meetings must be CCM members.

It is evident from above that the Party tends to impose itself at the initial state of co-operative activities by having a say in the leadership of such co-operative societies.

The co-operative development committee is further subjected to state control from the central government whereby the Minister for

States has general powers under the Local Government Act No. 7 of 1982 of approving by-laws of local authorities, and of issuing directives to such authorities. Since co-operative development committees as economic entities are committed to the village governments, they will automatically be subject to such directives.

Hand in hand with the Co-operative Act is the Co-operative Audit and Supervision Act (No. 15 of 1982), which under s. 3 established the co-operative audit and supervision corporation as another state controlling instrument over the co-operative movement. The functions of the corporation (s.4) are to provide audit and services to co-operative societies, to give advice on audit and accounting procedures and to formulate audit and accounting policy for adoption by the societies. The corporation is also to audit accounts of any co-operative society, or such other body as may be prescribed by the Minister or Registrar as the case may be, (s.4(2)). The Director of the Corporation may summon any officer of a co-operative society to give material information in regard to any transactions or the management of its affairs or to require the production of any books or documents of the society, (s.6). The Registrar, on the other hand, may require the Director or any other employee of the Corporation to hold a special inspection into the activities and financial affairs of a registered society, (s.7(1)).

We have seen in this section that the 1982 Co-operation Act is not fundamentally different from the previous co-operative legislation as far as control by the state is concerned. The Registrar still has considerable powers over the activities of the societies, although he is purported to delegate such powers to the apex organisation of the co-operative societies. However, the apex organisation is also another controlling instrument of the state. The co-operatives are further subject to other state controlling agencies namely the Minister for Local Authorities through the village governments and also vide the co-operative audit and supervision corporation. All in all, one may conclude that the new co-operative legislation is the case of old wine in new bottles.

Conclusion

The motive behind state control over the co-operatives and Agricultural Marketing Boards and later, the crop authorities, is to control the agricultural surplus product of the peasantry. Increased controls as seen in this chapter gradually alienated the producer from the organisations marketing his crop and his participation in the decision-making on the important factors affecting his agricultural life has declined. As a result, the producer's interests do not get due consideration. The peasant thus gets minimal price for his produce. This in turn acts as a disincentive to the production of cash crops, which in turn has an adverse effect on the overall production of cash crops in the country.

The Chapter looks at the trend towards centralization of state control over the co-operatives and agricultural marketing boards. This control was effected through legislation and administrative devices. Both the Minister for Agriculture and the Registrar of Co-operatives had vast regulatory powers to control the Marketing Boards and the co-operatives. The latter were agents of the former for the procurement of the peasant's agricultural surplus product, which was possible through the co-operative legislation, 1968. The co-operative bureaucracy, however, seemed to have retained a large share of the agricultural surplus value, which the government bureaucracy resented. With the Arusha Declaration and the advent of Ujamaa Villages, co-operatives lost importance in the contemporary socio-economic structure of Tanzania. The co-operative unions were thus officially dissolved in May 1976. The Agricultural Marketing Boards, and shortly thereafter, the crop authorities, took over the functions of the co-operatives. This trend depicts a steady increase and centralisation of state control over the production and marketing of cash crops. To effectively control the agricultural surplus value of the peasant, the state evolved proper mechanism to control the state monopoly organisations handling cash crops, namely the crop authorities. Control has been effected through Parliament, through the enabling statutes, through the Minister for Agricultural who is empowered *vide* the enabling statutes to issue directives to the authorities, through the Treasury, the Bank of Tanzania, the Tanzania Rural Development Bank, and so on. Administrative devices like the District Councils and village governments have been used to effect direct control over the producers, especially at production level.

Increased state control among other factors resulted in the fall of overall cash crops production in the country. The government bureaucracy therefore thought it prudent to reinstitute co-operative unions as one of the steps towards encouraging peasants to produce more cash crops and market them through these bodies. This will be effected through the 1982 co-operative legislation. A study of the above legislation however reflects that the role of the new co-operative societies will not be much different from its predecessors; namely, that they are envisaged to be instruments of control of the state. Thus the idea that cash crops producers would have their own bodies free from state control and that the co-operatives would be an independent movement is a far off cry.

NOTES

1. *New Africa Magazine* (London) June 1980, p.77.
2. For example, under Government Notice No. 325 of 1963 an Agricultural Board was established in Tabora Region to control beans, finger millets, groundnuts, etc: under Government Notice No 142 of 1963, the Southern Region Marketing Board was established to control cashew nuts, groundnuts, castor and sunflower; under Government Notice Nos. 377, 503 and 521 of 1963, the Central Region Marketing Boards were established for the control of beeswax, castor seed, groundnuts and sunflower.
3. The Agricultural Products (Control and Marketing) Act, No 56 of 1962, s. 3(2) (9).
4. *Ibid.*, 1st schedule.
5. For example, Government Notice No. 7 of 1963 published on 4-1-63, established the Lake Region Agricultural Products Board; Government Notice No. 251 published on 31-5-63 established the Southern Region Agricultural Board, Government Notice No. 250 published on 31-5-63, established the National Agricultural Products Board controlling maize and maize flour in Tanganyika.
6. The Agricultural Products (Control and Marketing) Act, 1962 s. 10.
7. Established by Government Notice No. 117 of 1963 which replaced the Native Tobacco Board established under the African Agricultural Products (Control and Marketing) Ord. of 1930, cap. 284.
8. The National Agricultural Products Act, No. 39 of 1964, s. 9 (2).
9. The Agricultural Products (National Agricultural Products Board) (Amendment) Order 1963 to be read with the Agricultural Products (National Agricultural Products) Order, Government Notice No. 250 of 1962.
10. The Coffee Industry (Collection of Levy) Rules, 1965, Government Notice No. 243, of 6-8-1965.
11. Schedule to G.N. No 345 of 6-8-1965.
12. G.N. No. 289 of 29-6-1962.
13. Refer to composition of Board under Government Notice No. 247 of 28-6-1968, under the Coffee Industry Act, para 2.
14. United Republic of Tanzania, Government Paper No. 4 of 1967 (Dar es Salaam: Government Printer, 1967), p. 15.
15. Union of Co-operative Societies, Dar es Salaam, May 1968.
16. Report of the Presidential Special Committee of Enquiry into the Co-operatives and Marketing Boards (Dar es Salaam: Government Printer, 1966), para 28, p. 5.
17. *Ibid.*, para 5 pp 9 and 10.
18. *Ibid.*, para 51, p. 10.
19. *Ibid.*, para 57, p. 13.
20. *Ibid.*, para 58, p. 13.
21. *Ibid.*, para 73, pp. 15 and 16.
22. *Ibid.*, para 75 p. 16.
23. *Ibid.*, para 73 (4), p. 16.
24. The Co-operative Societies Act, No. 27 of 1968, s. 3(1). 25. *Ibid.*, ss. 39 and 40.
26. *Ibid.*, ss. 109 ans 110.
27. *Ibid.*, s. 45 (2)
28. The Co-operative Societies Rules, 1968 Supp. 38 of 1968, Rules 29,32,35,36, and 39.
29. The Co-operative Societies Act, ss. 10-12.
30. *Ibid.*, s. 10(3)
31. *Ibid.*, s. 21(1).
32. *Ibid.*, s. 39.

33. *Daily News* (Tanzania), 3 July 1976, for example, reported that losses were incurred by the Nyanza Co-operative Union which reported a loss of shs. 2,918,877/95 during 1972/73; the Central Region Co-operative Union was reported to have lost shs. 2.5 millions; the Tanga Region Co-operative Union reported a misappropriation of shs. 9.6 million, and the Mbeya Co-operative Union had never presented its accounts and yet it was reported to have been operating on a shs. 21 million bank overdraft.

34. *Daily News* (Tanzania), 31 October 1971.

35. CCM Constitution Articles 5(12) and (13).

36. For example, sections 5(2) para 1(1) (a) and para 1(1)(b) of the Coffee Industry Act.

37. *Ibid.*, ss. 9(1), (2), (3); 10(1), (2); and 12(1).

38. *Ibid.*, s 23 whereby 'The funds and resources of the Authority shall consist of sums provided by Parliament, and what the Authority could borrow in accordance with this Act, or any such sums which may become payable to the Authority under this Act or which may vest in the Authority in the performance of its functions'.

39. Coffee Industry Act, ss. 27 (1) and (2).

40. *Ibid.*, 1st Sch. para 1(1)(c).

41. *Ibid.*, s. 39(2).

42. Village Councils Rules 10 and 12 of 12th November, 1978.

43. Village Council Resolution No. 9 of 2nd July, 1979.

44. For example, G.N. No. 65 published on 9-5-1980 under the Decentralisation of Government Administration (Interim Provisions) Act.

45. Ellis Frank, 'Cashewnuts' (University of Dar es Salaam, mimeo), 1980, p. 33.

46. Marketing Development Bureau (MDB), *Price Policy Recommendations for 1982/83*, Annex 7, p. 10.

47. *Ibid.*, Annex 9, p. 18.

48. Ellis and Hanak, "An Economic Analysis of the Tanzania Coffee Industry 1969/70: Towards a Higher and more stable producer price", (University of Dar es Salaam) September, 1980, p. 14.

49. Ministry of Agriculture "A Summary of the Present Position of Kilimo Parastatals: A Review of Critical Problems and Issues", (Dar es Salaam: 1980), p.18.

50. *Daily News* (Tanzania), 8th May, 1980.

51. *Daily News* (Tanzania), 22nd January, 1981.

52. The Co-operative Societies Act, No. 14 of 1982.

53. *Ibid.*, Part XVI.

54. *Ibid.*, Part XVII.

55. The Co-operative Union of Tanzania By-laws R. 11. (1).

56. *Ibid.*, clause 13(1).

7. THE STATE AND THE STUDENT STRUGGLES

Chris Peter
Sengondo Mvungi

Introduction

This Chapter attempts to review briefly student struggles against the post-Independence neo-colonial state in Tanzania. It does not attempt to review the role of the student movement (if there was any such movement) in the anti-colonial struggles. The dearth of documentation of any student activity during this period would have made any meaningful discussion impossible. Again, although the Chapter was meant to cover both Mainland and Isles, the authors have limited their review to the Mainland due to unavoidable circumstances which made research on Zanzibar student movement difficult. In this chapter the authors intend to discuss the rise and fall of an independent student movement in Tanzania after Independence. This will be attempted as an aspect of the general process of development of an authoritarian neo-colonial state in the country.

The major thrust of the chapter will be to show that in the process of its development into an authoritarian state, the neo-colonial state in Tanzania worked tooth and nail to destroy the organisational initiative of the Tanzania people. This has been done by clamping down upon all forms of independent civil organisations capable of articulating a dissenting political opinion, one of which is a student organisation.

Pre-Independence Background

When Tanganyika became independent on 9 December, 1961 little or nothing at all was known about the student movement. This was not an accident. The colonial education system had no place for student politics, just as colonialism did not have a place for democracy for the colonised. Colonies did not have democratic constitutions and its inhabitants were not entitled to enjoy the democratic rights which inhabitants of the colonial power enjoyed. Although it is now common knowledge that colonialism is the process whereby one nation conquers and rules another for purposes of economic exploitation and plunder, this definition hardly explains the other more subtle aspect of this process which involves colonisation of the mind of the colonised. Education was a tool with which the colonial state undertook this task of mental colonisation of the native. The culture, values and tastes of the race of the coloniser were inculcated in the colonised and viewed as superior while African race, culture, values and tastes were discouraged for being 'inferior', 'primitive', 'barbaric' and 'unchristian'. This kind of cultural domination meant the inculcation of attitudes of inferiority and shame of everything African.

The colonial state however did not consider education a crucial ingredient in its primary objective of economic exploitation. This was because it did not envisage establishing in the colony a developed modern agro-industrial economy which would require skilled labour. What is required was primitive and cheap labour for production of cheap raw materials and a market for dumping its excess industrial production. Consequently it built very few primary schools and still fewer secondary schools and colleges. Thus the bulk of the task of education was left in the hands of philanthropic organisations, religious denominations, and private entrepreneurs.[1] Since it was the religious denominations which built most schools, the inculation of western religious beliefs underlined the ideological perspective of the colonial education. The converts to Christianity were also converted to a bourgeois world outlook. The total effect of this was denial of opportunities of education to non-believers and production of an elitist and subservient clerical cadre for the colonial state apparatus and the production sector.

It is important to note that colonial education was imparted in a structure which ensured the breaking of the African and his personality so that he may fit in the scheme of reducing him into a robot for economic exploitation. The structure of the school system, for example, was woven in a way so that racial superiority of the Europeans was emphasized while the inferiority of the African was encouraged. This was effected by the establishment of separate schools for Europeans, Asians and Africans. The best schools in terms of buildings, environment facilities and teaching staff were reserved for whites. Asians were given second class quality while Africans, who were considered third class, received the worst.[2]

Naturally, an education system of this nature created a hostile environment for the germination and growth of a strong student movement. Although a national student organisation is reported to have come into existence by 1958 under the name of Pan African Student Association of Tanganyika (PASAT), active student politics can only be meaningfully discussed in the period after Independence.[3] The uneventful history of PASAT notwithstanding, it remains a credit to the founders of PASAT that an.attempt was made to organise students for national and international politics independent of the colonial state. The low profile which PASAT assumed towards nationalist struggles for independence is however noticeable. It may well be argued that a docile or relatively submissive student movement is what could have been expected of the colonial education system we have just described. This is partly true, but that is not all. The absence of institutions of higher learning which could expose the students to liberating ideas as are ordinarily found in Universities was the greatest weakness in the constitution of the student body. This, coupled with the fact that the struggle for Independence concentrated much on constitutional changes rather than mobilisation of all sections of the population for mass struggle, denied the student movement a revolutionising environment. The non-antagonistic strategy which underlined the relationship between TANU and the colonial state, and the fabianist inspired tactic of separation of politics from other forms of mass struggles like trade unionism, could hardly have inspired to action the technical-oriented student body like PASAT devoid of University radicalism. These were some of the limitations of the student movement during the colonial period and a background upon which post-independence student struggles may be viewed.

The Anatomy of the Neo-colonial State

The student politics during the post Independence period cannot be properly understood without locating the position occupied by the student movement in the structure of the state. The state has been defined as an institution of the society which arises out of the development in society of irreconcilable antagonisms among social classes with conflicting economic interests. The state is the institution which the dominant social class creates to wield coercive power over other classes it seeks to rule, dominate and exploit. It is an institution conceived to look as if it stands above class conflict so that it may keep the conflicts within the bounds of law and order. The prime object of the state however is to enable the dominant class to establish, protect and enhance their economic, political and cultural interests and suppress those of the ruled.[4]

In the structure and composition of the state, the executive, the parliament and the judiciary form the most essential components of the secular state. One of the most essential social institutions which the executive controls besides the coercive apparatuses of state is the school system. Education, which the school system aims at imparting, is considered part of the super-structure whose primary role is supportive of the economic base. Any consideration of the anatomy of social classes in a neo-colonial state must therefore take into account the part played or which can be played by the students in the socio-economic and political dynamics of that state. Within the class structure of the neo-colonial state it is suggested that students as a transitional stratum of the intelligentsia should be considered as forming part and parcel of the petty bourgeoisie. It is understood that despite their preparation as the future intelligentsia of the society, students do not occupy any position in the production system of any society. This enables them to be relatively open-minded to diverse ideas and schools of thought. Taking into account the fact that in a neo-colonial situation, the bulk of the students come from the under-privileged classes, their sympathies with the plight of the working peoples cannot be discounted. In fact available historical evidence shows that students in neo-colonies constitute a potential radical force capable of making considerable contribution to the struggles of the working peoples.[5]

The other class which must be considered is the petty bourgeoisie or the middle class which, it has been suggested, the students are part and parcel of. This has to be done for quite different reasons, one of which is the fact that it is this class which came to power at independence. Its characteristics, interests and political programme has profound influence on student politics. The other equally important reason is that the transition from colonialism to neo-colonialism meant the transition of the petty bourgeoisie which formerly was part of the ruled classes to a ruling class. Its numerical smallness, economic weakness and political bankruptcy meant that this class could not remain in power except by overcoming these weaknesses. Bound by its own limitations as a class the petty bourgeoisie became transformed into a client class in service of imperialism. This client class has come to be known as comprador bourgeoisie.

Frantz Fanon's critique of the neo-colonial state remains the most outstanding treatise of the phenomenon of neo-colonialism to date. In his *The Wretched of the Earth*, Fanon argues:

> The national middle class which takes over power at the end of the colonial regime is an underdeveloped middle class. It has practically no economic power, and in any case it is no way commensurate with the bourgeoisie of the mother country which it hopes to replace. In its willful narcissism, the national middle class is easily convinced that it can advantageously replace the middle class of the mother country. But that same independence

which literally drives it into a corner will give rise within its ranks to catastrophic reactions, and will oblige it to send out frenzied appeals for help to former mother country.[6]

In his critique of the neo-colonial state in Uganda Mahmood Mamdani makes a similar observation. He notes that the greatest weakness of the petit bourgeoisie was that although it managed to articulate popular demands of the masses during independence struggle, it had no clear ideological direction capable of stirring the under-developed nation out of the lethargy of underdevelopment. Mamdani argues that this class was so bankrupt that it did not even understand that the real power behind the colonial state was British imperialist interests. It did not even notice that the system of oppression and exploitation these interests had built remained unscathed by the independence struggles. When imperialism withdrew physically it left the system of oppression and exploitation intact under the supervision of new agents now in the form of the militant nationalists.[7]

It is here that the legalistic approach by which bourgeois jurisprudence has attempted to explain the process of transition to neo-colonialism had been proved to be inadequate. The positivists under the leadership of H.L.A. Hart for example admit the subordinate status of the legal system of the colony to that of the colonising power. However, positivists do not see the inextricable link and the subtle subordination of the neo-colony not only to the former colonial power but to the new array of imperialist powers. They fail to see this link because the legalistic approach which positivists are fond of employing is taken in isolation from the socio-economic relations from which the legal relations arose.[8] It is suggested therefore that in studying the neo-colonial state in Tanzania and the student struggles against the state, the socio-economic relations which give rise to different classes of people and the state must be taken into account.

It is common knowledge that the petit bourgeoisie which took over state power at independence was numerically a very small class. Although Tanganyika African National Union (TANU), the political organisation of this class, was led by a highly educated leadership by the 1960 standards, the Tanganyika petty bourgeoisie was in the main illiterate. This weakness did not deprive this class of the capability to mobilise the entire population irrespective of class, sex or colour for national independence. The devastating effects of the second imperialist world war and the counter-productive and costly peasant war in Kenya taught British imperialism that colonialism was detrimental to its objective of economic exploitation. Quickly the old agents of colonialism, the chiefs, akidas and liwalis who manned the indirect rule system, were thrown overboard and a new class of British educated elite was appointed to the legislature of the colonial state. These were later bequeathed with a tailor made state at independence.

The petty bourgeoisie was the only class organised well enough for seizure of political power at Independence. The working class was too weak and small, while the peasants had never risen out of the defeat and organisational disintegration sustained during the anti-colonial struggle in the late 19th and early 20th centuries into an organised political force except in some few areas where passive and active resistance to colonial policies subsisted during the entire colonial period. [9]

The British educated petty bourgeoisie which took power at independence had serious ideological weakness. It lacked a practicable philosophy of development capable of solving the problem of underdevelopment. The African socialism or *Ujamaa* which TANU propagated was a product of the training which its leadership had acquired from the Fabian society of England which toes a petty bourgeois brand of socialism. In fact the ideological bankruptcy of Fabian socialism was reflected in the non-antagonistic strategy which TANU adopted *vis-a-vis* the colonial state. [10] This strategy coupled with the limitations of the petty bourgeoisie in conducting a protracted revolutionary pedagogy among the masses; caused the failure by TANU to establish in the public memory a continuity of mass struggle from where Maji-Maji and all previous anti-colonial struggles had reached. The petty bourgeoisie failed to erase in the public memory the notion that organised coercive force of the state was too powerful to be combated by mass struggle. [11] The impression decolonisation through constitutional changes created on the general public was that rights of a people can be won by negotiations between the transgressor and the transgressed. These then are some of the same elements which underlie the seemingly timorous and submissive psychology of the Tanzanian nation *vis-a-vis* the development of authoritarian tendencies in their neo-colonial state.

With these comments in mind it goes without saying that the character of student politics after Independence reflected the on-going struggle of the state-based petty bourgeoisis to establish its dictatorship politically, economically and culturally. In view of the inherent weakness of this section of the petty bourgeoisie, it is clear that such an undertaking was simply inconceivable if the state-based petty bourgeoisie was to pursue the path of popular democracy. In fact it has been proven by historical practice, that petty bourgeois dictatorship and democracy are contradictory in terms. Haunted by its numerical smallness and its lack of confidence due both to its economic weakness and its utopian political philosophy, the petty bourgeois state in Tanganyika found itself increasingly isolated from the popular masses. Its widespread corruption, conspicuous consumption exemplified by extravagent and pompous style of life became the breeding spots of dissatisfaction with its rule by even the most naive nationalist.

An ex-student of the University College of Dar es Salaam during the early years of independence recapitulated the situation in the following words:

> The government was simply out of touch with common sentiments. The ministers and top civil servants had stepped into the shoes of the colonial officers. They had joined the Dar es Salaam club, an exclusive club of top officials of the colonial state. They competed with each other in divorcing their old wives and marrying young modern ones and were identified with riding 'Humber', 'Roho' and 'Mercedes Benz' saloon cars. They were nicknamed 'Wakenzi' which means those who drive in Mercedes Benz cars. It was a state of exploiters fattening up on people's sweat. It was also a directionless government without a concise political philosophy. As you may know, we didn't have Arusha Declaration then.[12]

An opulent, corrupt and self-aggrandising ruling class of this nature could hardly have escaped criticism. However, its weakness and isolation from popular mass support made it impossible for its state to respond tolerantly to criticism from the popular masses. The state sought ways of silencing the people rather than responding creatively to their criticism. Discontent simmered in all facets of national life and the state tried frantically to eliminate all forms of organised dissent.

When Tanganyika Rifles mutinied in 1964 over bad working conditions including low pay and slow pace of Africanisation, Nyerere not only called in the armed forces of the former colonial masters to quell the rebellion and disarm his forces but he seized the opportunity to clamp down upon the independent trade union—Tanganyika Federation of Labour (TFL). TFL represented one form of independent civil organisations capable of articulating popular dissent.

The student movement which had recorded a steady growth ever since independence could hardly remain unaffected by these developments. It may be recalled that one of the first actions of the independence government was the establishment of the University College of Dar es Salaam as part of the University of East Africa. As could have been expected, no sooner had the new college been opened than the students formed their organs of representation. One such student organisation which was formed in order to take care of students' affairs, interests and problems, was the University College of Dar es Salaam Student Union (USUD). It was formed in October, 1961 and drew its membership from the whole of the student body in the University.

USUD was a petty bourgeois student organisation *par excellence*. It was elitist and petty bourgeois in form and outlook. A report of its early activities by its first president, G. James Miruka, boasted of successful hosting of dances and balls. It also depicted student participation in the mayoral procession around Dar es Salaam during the ceremony of vesting upon the municipality of Dar es Salaam the status of being a city, as a very significant activity of the student organisation. It lauded USUD's participation in a begging-for-the-poor-programme and also taking part in TANU sponsored self-help schemes.[13]

Another student organisation during this time was the Tanganyika University Students Association (TUSA) formed in 1963 with Joseph Warioba as its Secretary General. TUSA was an organisation of Tanganyika nationals in the University of East Africa. It had three units in each of the three campuses, Makerere, Nairobi and Dar es Salaam. According to Warioba TUSA had close and cordial connections with the state. It held consultations, discussions and debates with the government on many issues one of which was an all University of East Africa student seminar on the first five year plan.[14]

What should be observed with regard to both USUD and TUSA is that they were both limited to University student membership. The University being new and small, such movements or organisations could hardly make an impact on students at territorial level. It was only after the formation of the National Union of Tanzanian Students (NAUTS) in April 1964 that active student politics can be said to have begun in Tanzania. It is to the evenful history of NAUTS that we now turn.

The Politics of NAUTS and the 1966 Crisis
NAUTS was a nation-wide student organisation which drew its membership from secondary schools, colleges and the University. It led active student politics and represented the student body at both national and international levels. Two events stand out prominently in the history of NAUTS. The first was the demonstration by the students against the Unilateral Declaration of Independence by Ian Smith in Rhodesia. The second and the last major event in the history of NAUTS was the demonstration against the government's refusal to amend its controversial compulsory National Service programme for students. We pursue each event in turn.

The UDI Demonstration
The reaction of the state towards the student demonstration against

the Unilateral Declaration of Independence by Ian Smith in Rhodesia was just as dramatic as it was unexpected. The government's position on UDI was clearly negative. Students had therefore no reason to doubt the response of the state to a demonstration in solidarity with the black majority in Rhodesia. Both the students and the state shared the view that the people of Zimbabwe had been deprived of their right to independence by high handed political brigandage of the settlers.

Students sought police permission to hold the demonstration but permission was not granted. In the event, students decided to proceed with their demonstration without police permission. They took to the streets of Dar es Salaam and went down to the British High Commission where they ransacked the British Council Library, burnt the Union Jack and destroyed a High Commission vehicle. Following these actions the government ordered the students to be rounded up and some were severely punished. This reaction by the state was unexpected in view of the government's opposition to Ian Smith's UDI in Rhodesia. Students had defied the Police, or to put it more concisely, they had ignored the police decision to reject their request for permission. Even then no one had expected that the state would react as high-handedly as it did. Looking back at the totality of events which shaped Tanzanian political history in the first years of Independence two factors seem to have influenced the government's reaction.

Firstly, the 1964 army mutiny seemed to have shaken up the neo-colonial state in Tanganyika. The ruling section of the petty bourgeoisie realised for the first time how vulnerable their state was to the armed forces. It became clear that any breach of law and order could create confusion which could easily lead to the overthrow of the government. It seems the ruling petty bourgeoisie failed to create, both at the level of production and constitutional framework of their state, a democratic process which could ensure maintainance of the rule of law. Instead it introduced an authoritarian process aimed at suppression of dissent. Existing forms of civil organisations which were independent of the state but which were capable of expressing a dissenting political view had to be destroyed. The capability that students had shown by demonstrating without state's approval proved to the government that students were developing into a harbinger of an organised political force independent of the state. Although in this issue students and the state were defending the same principle, the government could hardly rejoice at the emergence of a powerful and radical *independent* student movement.

The other factor was the element of violence which students had displayed during the demonstration. In the circumstances, Britain may have deserved the treatment it received from the students. Its refusal to quell the Smith rebellion showed how irresponsible colonialism could be to the rights of the colonised and how imperialism was incapable of a principled stand. The state did not seem to interpret the element of violence in student politics merely in terms of what British imperialism deserved. It saw the use of violence not only as impolitic diplomatically but as a bad precedent.

Orders to have students rounded up and punished even by caning seem to have been a calculated political act aimed at putting an end, once and for all, to the use of violence in political struggles in Tanzania. It is hardly plausible to entertain the view that the illiberal neo-colonial state which Tanzania state had proved to be, could have watched the dangerous precedent of violence being set, its hands akimbo. Even in the disadvantageous situation the state was in (students were demonstrating in support of a principle endorsed by the government hence could not be easily isolated from popular sentiment through the usual misinformation) it still found it sensible to clamp down upon the students. The reason stemmed from the government's own weakness. Its expanding and bourgeoning bureaucratic complex, inefficiency, corruption and naked exploitation accompanied by the growth of an liberal legal system had begun to push the whole state apparatus into isolation and unpopularity. A scape-goat was needed. The state failed to find a scape-goat in the students' anti-UDI demonstration. A cooked up story on what students were up against could not have been believed. Issues were too clear to be manipulated. But it was not long before the state hit a gold mine. On 22 October 1966, students came out against the government-proposed compulsory national service programme.

The National Service Demonstration

It is common knowledge that by 1966 the state exhausted almost all the political and economic ammunition in its command *vis-a-vis* the growth of a neo-colonial capitalist economy in Tanzania. Although the state had failed to attract substantial foreign investment due to the poor infrastructure, the growth of import-substitution industries, real estate, agricultural and service sectors implied concomitant growth of social classes corresponding to the social and production relations arising therefrom.

The transformation of the ruling petty bourgeoisie into a comprador bourgeoisie both at state and economic levels was a new and interesting phenomenon which found inadequate expression in the terms 'Wabenzi' or 'naizi'. The pioneering work in this area by Franz Fanon ably describes and analyses the reasons for this phenomenon.[15] The weakness in Fanon's work is that it did not see that the national middle class which came to power at independence had only one destiny, which was its transformation into an economically strong class nationally but a dependent class *vis-a-vis* international imperialism.

In this transformation the petty bourgeoisie entered into a crisis of capital accumulation, something comparable to the primitive accumulation of capital in Europe by the merchant class which was in the process of becoming a bourgeoisie. David Williams had dealt at length with this aspect and has concluded that the emergence of the comprador bourgeoisie as the new ruling class in the neo-colony is accompanied by the re-organisation of the state and law into an authoritarian legal system.[16] The 1966 student struggles provided the petty bourgeoisie with a scapegoat with which to divert the growing opposition to the state within the working people. As it will be explained later, the crisis forced the emergent comprador bourgeoisie to awaken to reality. Its radical faction which had state power in its hands worked to purify petty bourgeois socialism into an ideology of the new ruling class in Tanzania. This ideology has ever since become the ideology of many ruling classes in Africa.[17]

Events began in early February 1966 when the government published its proposal of an intended compulsory National Service programme. The service was to include students completing their high school or institutions of higher learning. It was proposed that the duration of the service would be two years. The servicemen would receive Shs. 20 per month in the months they would be in camps and be paid 40% of their salaries during the 18 months of service while in their respective places of employment.[18] The programme was to be run by Israeli trained military instructors many of whom were notorious for their immoral behaviour towards service girls and for perpetrating many forms of torture and cruelty to the servicemen.

The proposal generated heated discussion among students and members of the public. Students and members of the public including members of the Parliament criticised various aspects of the proposed compulsory national service programme. When Rashidi Kawawa, the then 2nd Vice President, tabled the government white paper on the subject of October 1966, he told the Parliament that the students had accepted the principle of compulsory national service but had raised objections to various aspects of the programme. According to Kawawa, students wanted the proposed two year programme to be shortened to a total of six months or less. They also objected to the 60% cut in their salaries during the 18 months they were to serve as servicemen. Students had demanded further that deductions from their salaries of business and other loans incurred by students during their courses, should be postponed until after national service. Other suggestions made by students included postponement of national service programme for any student who was awarded a scholarship while in national service and provision of good living conditions.[19]

Students' organisations, NAUTS, TUSA and Teachers Colleges Student Association met with the 2nd Vice President to present and argue the student's position and had three other meetings with the President on the same issue.[19]

The protracted consultations with the government yielded little result. Inconsequential demands like postponement of deduction of bursaries and other loans until the national service period elapsed and postponement of national service until completion of studies for scholarship holders were accepted by the state. Major demands were rejected and it seemed no effort was made by the state to meet student demands halfway. The questions which the government never took trouble to ask itself before rejecting student demands was why it had failed to convince the educated elite to serve in the voluntary national service programme? Was it due to arrogance and attitudes of superiority? Did this reflect lack of patriotism on the part of the students or was it a reflection of alienation of the state from the masses?

Given the socio-economic dynamics we have described above the government could hardly have asked itself such questions. Its alienation from the popular sentiments was so absolute that it could hardly see the sense embodied in students' resistance. Kawawa admitted in Parliament that the proposed amendment of the National Service Act, 1964 was a result of failure of the Government to sell the students the idea of voluntary national service. "Only 25 have joined national service under the voluntary scheme so far," he told the Parliament.

The voluntary national service programme started in 1964. By October 1966 only 25 students had volunteered to join it. The state made no effort to clear national service of the bad name it had acquired through those who served in it. Claims of torture, moral corruption, humiliation and inhuman treatment by those who had passed through it had spread all over the country and there was no point for the government to ignore them. It seemed as though by introducing a compulsory programme without improving the voluntary programme, the government had set itself on a path of inevitable blunder. Furthermore, for a country purporting to be following a socialist path training its cadres in Israel, a zionist state which thrives on the annihilation of millions of Palestinian people, was contradictory in terms. This was a fundamental mistake which had ideological and technical ramifications. Israel is a neo-fascist state which can never be an ally of a democratic socialist nation. It could only be an ally of countries like South Africa. The fact that the government chose Israel as the training ground for its military officers was a reflection of a serious ideological bankruptcy in view of its purported socialist path. Technically, the fascist militarism of the Israeli state was imported wholesale by the local military instructors who ran the National Service. Claims of torture, moral corruption and humiliation by those who attended the voluntary programme could only have been ignored, as they were, by a state in transition to authoritarianism.

Again, behind the student resistance, lurked a feeling of remorse and victimisation. Most of the state functionaries at middle and top level and the political leadership in general were young people who should have volunteered into national service to show the example of commitment and patriotism. There was hardly any who did so. It was pointless telling students to volunteer and worse to submit themselves for a compulsory national service programme which excluded this bulk of eligible youth who then held positions in the party and the state.

The feeling that students were being victimised by the semi-literate 'Wabenzi' can be well appreciated if the whole question of the purpose of higher learning in any state is taken into consideration. The running of the modern state is a monopoly of the elite section of the ruling class. The elite which in the modern bourgeois states are picked on the basis of their qualifications, become absorbed by the ruling class and there is hardly a dividing line between the ruling class and its intelligentsia. In Tanzania, the semi-literate and sometimes absolutely illiterate political elite which came to power at independence was rallied by a very minute group of western educated elite a few of whom were university graduates. The first locally educated university graduates graduated in 1964.

The new breed of qualified, articulate but poor elite posed a challenge to the 'Wabenzi' who laboured to make up for their low level of education by showing-off, of power and conspicuous spending on new cars, mansions and girl friends. The 'Wabenzi' felt their position threatened and in the ensuing one or two years after the 1964 graduation, there was widespread abusive talk by the state and political functonaries directed against the educated elite. Talks like: "*Kusoma siyo hoja, hata ukiwa na digirii mtatufanya nini wakati tuna majumba, magari, vipusa na madaraka tunayo?*" which literally means 'being educated does not matter; even if you have a degree, what match can you be to us when we have mansions, cars, beautiful women and power' are said to have gained currency and wide usage during this period.[21] When therefore the government rejected the students demand that the national service period be reduced from a period of two years to six months and that the 60% salary deduction during the 18 months of servicemanship be stricken off the programme, students suspected bad faith on the part of the government. They felt that the jealous 'Wabenzi' were up to humiliating them through this programme. The more radical among them began questioning the legitimacy of the state itself. They felt the 'Wabenzi', whose business was fattening themselves up by syphoning the sweat of the working people, were only being hypocritical by insisting that the 60% deduction and the long national service period was part of socialism.

In fact more enlightened members of Parliament like Nicholas Kuhanga were quick to grasp the ridiculous situation the government was muddled in when he told the Parliament that the youth could not be taught discipline and sacrifice by being oppressed. He pointed out that those who were arguing for the 60% deduction on students salaries during the 18 months of servicemanship on the grounds that it was socialism forgot that they were the same ones who lived opulently with mansions for renting and posh cars like Benzes, Kaddets, and so on. He concluded that those who advocated such views should first show that they were socialist before they could tell students to be socialist.[22] But as the Kiswahili saying goes *sikio la kufa halisikii dawa* that is, "an ear destined to die responds to no medicine"! The government plugged its ears and refused to open its mind to reason. The result was that it opened the floodgates of social turmoil and resistance. Frequent visits by state officials ot the University during this period failed to win student accord. In fact it was one such visit by Junior Minister of Defence and National Service Mr. R.S. Wambura on 18 October, 1966 which prompted the student demonstration. Ex-students who were involved in these struggles assert that after Wambura's speech, which was nothing less than a 'disaster', students were left with no doubt in their minds that the compulsory national service programme was a malicious project aimed at frustrating and humiliating them, for the only reason that they were educated. After Wambura's speech NAUTS called an emergency students' assembly of all students. This assembly decided *inter alia* to hold a mass demonstration protesting against the mishandling of the national service issue by the government.

A committee was sent to meet the President and another to seek permission from the central Police to hold the demonstration. The police refused permission and students met in an emergency meeting again on 21 October 1966 to receive reports from the committees. Those who had been sent to meet Mwalimu at Msasani reported that Mwalimu seemed unsure of what was going on and had stuck to explaining the principle of national service and had dismissed their demands as 'details'. Another committee which had met D. Wilbert Chagula, the Principal, reported failure. Students decided to demonstrate despite refusal of permission . A committee led by Luke Mkoka was charged with drafting the memorandum to be read to the Vice President. NAUTS prepared its official placards, one of which said clearly *Fumechoka kutumikia Wabenzi* meaning, "we are tired of serving Wabenzi". The class content of the student resistance was clear. Now it turned out that there were many placards, some of which were made by individual students. These were not endorsed by NAUTS. One such placard read *Afadhali wakati wa ukoloni* meaning "colonialism was better".

Unknown to the students however, Nyerere knowing clearly that students were dissatisfied and would demonstrate had called an emergency cabinet meeting on 22 October which decided the way to deal with the students. It was decided that they would be led by the Police into the state house[23]. It turned out however that the demonstration was unprecedentedly huge. It included students from secondary schools, colleges and the University, large number of people including civil servants, other public officials and common people also joined this popular enterprise. Many of them, especially those who looked old and possibly secondary school students who looked too young to be University students, were weeded out at the state house gates. Only those who appeared to be University students were allowed in.

Students were received by the President and they read to him their wordy memorandum. According to one participant, the memorandum contained all basic points which students had agreed upon although not all students agreed with the excessively arrogant language the drafting committee had used. Words like "This is an ultimatum" clearly reflected infantilism which always accompanies petty bourgeois student radicalism.

Students argued that they saw no rationale in 60% salary deductions while in the national service. They at least did not think it was proper for the state to discriminate as to who should serve under the compulsory programme. Those enjoying the sweat of the peasants and workers in the state bureaucracy, politicians and those in the public sector should also serve under the programme, they thought. They questioned the propriety of the fat salaries politicians, civil servants and those in the management of public enterprises were drawing, while the peasantry was barely surviving and the proletariat was living below poverty datum line. Finally they decried the fascist militarism in national service but their souls would remain outside the programme.

The President rose up and delivered an emotionally charged speech in which he employed his extraordinary power of speech to turn the nation against the students. By appealing to narrow nationalism that the students were ungrateful elements who had managed to belittle the struggles which the nation waged against colonialism, Nyerere managed at the end of the day to scandalise the students. Students, who saw better life under colonialism than under independence, were shown as the enemies of the people. Their objections to some aspects of the compulsory national service programme were construed as an attitude of arrogance and superiority. The President ordered them to be rounded up and to be sent down to their respective 'homes' where they were supposed to learn how to be useful and selfless to the community.

More than 400 students from Muhimbili Medical School, Teacher's Training College Chang'ombe, College of Business Education, Ex-Aga-Khan Secondary School, Aga Khan Secondary Centre and the University College of Dar es Salaam were sent home. Foreign students who participated in the demonstration were de-registered and declared *persona non grata*.

It was not immediately clear however whether the students sent down had been expelled or had only been temporarily suspended. In fact the use of the term "students whose bursaries have been withdrawn" created a confusion as to whether the students could come back and continue with their studies if they could pay for their own fees. The principal, Dr. Wilbert Chagula, wrote to the Ministry of National Education for clarification and the Principal Secretary replied that the sent-down students could neither come back and pay for their tuition and residential fees nor resort to the same facilities in the Nairobi or Kampala campuses of the University College of East Africa.[24]

Later the sent-down students were advised to initiate reconciliation. The sent-down students resident in Dar es Salaam wrote a joint letter of apology to the President on 29 October 1966. It was a very funny letter of apology which addressed the President "Father of the nation". They said they were sorry for what they had done and had "realised that such behaviour is not expected from youths to their elders".[25] So the whole thing had reached the core of African politics. The President, though a modern ruler, still expected to be respected as an elder or head of a family or clan. Following this apology Leonce Ruta, Secretary for National Affairs of NAUTS, wrote to the rest of the sent-down students informing them of the communication and requesting them to apologise if they so wished as quickly as possible.

On 28 October 1966 the University College of Dar es Salaam Student Union (USUD) apologised through a letter signed by John Mbithi, the Acting President of USUD. Four other students, Mohamed Mullani, R. Wambaa, J.R. Menezes and Joshua Angatia pleaded with the President to use his wisdom to pardon the sent-down students. Another interesting fact which emerged from all letters of apology including the last one sent by remaining students on the campus on 30 October 1966 was that students felt that their protest had been grossly mishandled and misconstrued. They underlined the point that the protest had never been intended to act as an opposition to the state or working to overthrow the state. This was significant because one placard the students had held read "Remember Indonesia" emphasizing the power of students at this point should not be underestimated. When Rashid Kawawa addressed the remaining students on the College campus on 14 December 1966 he said, *inter alia:*

> It is not part of the University to constitute itself into unofficial opposition to the government. The people of this country have thrown their support behind TANU and have rejected the idea of disunity...Constructive criticism is welcome but opposition for opposition's sake has no sympathy with the people of the country.[26]

Finally the President agreed, after considerable pressure, to pardon the sent-down students.[27] Three hundred and ninety-two students were allowed to return and resume studies from July 1967, but twenty, whom the state considered leaders of the October crisis, were not pardoned. They were advised to apologise again to the President and their cases were to be dealt with on individual basis. Those not allowed to return included Sanwel Sitta who is currently a Minister in Nyerere's government. They were finally pardoned after they had satisfied the President that they had repented and had proved to be useful to the community.[28]

It has been argued by a number of scholars, a view which even the Academic Board of the University College of Dar es Salaam shared, that the 1966 student struggles constituted "a profound alienation of the students and the college life from the needs of the nation".[29] The state held and propagated a view that students were against national service. This was not true in the light of Kawawa's statements in Parliament. The state was well aware that in fact the President had discussions with student representatives on three occasions. So even the President could not plead ignorance of the students' position. It was unfair and dishonest on the part of the state to depict the students' demands out of context so that they were seen as enemies of the people.

Students had made significant arguments which Nyerere ought not to have glossed over using his extraordinary power of oration. Their attack of the expanding state bureaucracy which was drawing fat salaries and fringe benefits could not be simply brushed aside as student radicalism. It was a question which had far reaching class implications. Not many ordinary Tanzanians would have thought this as being elitist, arrogant or selfish on the part of the students as it has always been asserted by officials of the state and intellectuals of similar outlook.[30] In fact not many who had undergone national service and faced the unnecessary torture, humiliation and degradation perpetrated by the Israeli trained instructors could have thought the statement "let our bodies go but our souls will remain outside the scheme" as being outrightly outrageous.

Nyerere had no answer to the question of the emergence of his regime as a state of the exploiting class. He glossed over it by ordering the slashing of his own salary and the salaries of his top state officials. That was a populist reply to the question and it left the question unsolved. It is true that in 1966 students were defending what they believed to be their rights. Struggling to protect one's salary is not equivalent to a struggle to defend unjustified privileges. A salary is a legitimate gain which everyone entitled to can fight to protect or to have increased. A salary is never a privilege as some scholars believe.[31] The state had a democratic obligation to seek the accord of the students before going into the exercise of deducting 60% of their salaries. The fact is that the state has never considered salaries and wages as rights of its people.

The other aspect of this argument centres on the attempt by the state to isolate the students from the masses by depicting them as selfish, elitist and arrogant. By doing this the state sought to gain cheap popularity that it was working in the interests of the people. For a regime which had lost popular support such gimmicks were necessary to be able to divert the wrath of the toiling masses. The argument that national service would expose the students to national reality was ill-conceived both in form and content, for, although students were to be subjected to the peasant-style of life, students were not being prepared to be peasants or even to live like them. Their imitation of peasant life would therefore remain a mere mockery of the peasants. The belief that it is modesty and revolutionary to don peasant garb, imitate their style of life and help them build mud huts was a horribly backward ideological position. National service was to entrench backwardness rather than working to transform the peasantry into modern agriculturalists.

It may be true that the 1966 University College of Dar es Salaam was a bourgeois University. The majority of the students and teaching staff may have been bourgeois in orientation. However, the student struggles could not be generalised as a purely bourgeois affair. Professor T.O. Ranger in a letter to Miss Joan Wickens, noted that some sent down students considered it "unfair to be used, as they saw it, as scapegoats for an establishment which was itself growing fat".[32]

Professor Ranger was writing to persuade Miss Wickens to use her influence to make the President pardon the sent down students. By then Nyerere had awakened to reality, thanks to student radicalism. He had promulgated a socialist blue print which came to be known as the Arusha Declaration. Professor Ranger argued that the reasons Nyerere had advanced for sending down students had been watered down if not nullfied by the Arusha Declaration. He noted that although the crisis between students and the state had become a constant feature in East Africa, in Congo, Malawi, Zambia and in Tanzania, it was only Tanzania which had developed out of this crisis and ideological position radical enough to be capable of attracting student support. He suggested that students could even become part of the vanguard of the revolution in Tanzania. Nyerere backed down. We have noted how after subjecting the students to humiliating apology, all but twenty were pardoned.

All in all, the 1966 student crisis was a turning point in the history of student struggles in Tanzania. It was also the turning point in the politics of TANU. Thereafter, both the students and state entered a period of radical politics. Our discussion turns to these with a view to establish whether the Arusha Declaration meant the same thing for the student and the state.

The Arusha Declaration and After

It is conceivable that the Arusha Declaration came as a result of the interplay of many factors among which failure by the state to attract adequate foreign investments and the development of antagonistic social classes in society at an unprecedented pace, seem to have exerted significant influence. Nyerere's elaborate assurance given to foreign investors that Tanzania would protect their investments and allow them to repatriate their profits seemed to have made little impact, if any, on finance capital.[33]

The failure of the village settlement scheme, which was part of the World Bank package, and inadequate foreign aid and loans were reflected in Nyerere's castigation of over-dependence on foreign aid and emphasis on the role of money in stimulating development.[34] Nyerere and his men who drafted the Arusha Declaration seemed to have refused to make a clear class analysis of the Tanzanian society as Fabian socialists always fail to do. The Arusha Declaration simply stated four class categories, the working class (Wafanyakazi), and peasants (Wakulima) on one hand as the exploited and the capitalists (Mabepari) and feudalists (Makabaila) on the other as the exploiters.

Despite this confusing categorisation which included the top section of the petit bourgeoisie in the state sector in the working class, by 1966 several indicators had shown clearly that class contradictions in the society had reached a breaking point. The outcome of the Presidential Commission on the Co-operative Movement had shown that the peasantry saw the co-operative as exploiters just as the Indian middlemen had been.[35] The students had pointed fingers at Nyerere and his government as a bureaucratic outgrowth which was getting fat at the expense of the toiling masses. It is submitted that these factors, rather than any other factor prompted radicalisation of the state based comprador bourgeoisie.

A shift to the left was an inevitable development following the October 1966 student struggles. No sooner had the last student been sent down, than the academic members started a soul searching study of the crisis. One of these efforts was the seminar held at the Institute of Adult Education to discuss the role and function of University education in the social transformation of the society. Among the prominent attending members of the University staff was the outstanding Guyanese marxist, Walter Rodney. When therefore Nyerere announced the Arusha Declaration on 5 February 1967, radical students at the University College of Dar es Salaam received a powerful political boost. They immediately formed a socialist club for purposes of initiating, organising and carrying out socialist debate.

The club membership was made up of progressive students while progressive members of staff were made associate members. The club became the nucleus of the students left in the University. Its limitation as a debating club soon became apparent and its members transformed it into a broader organisation of the student left in the University which they called University Students African Revolutionary Front (USARF). USARF was intended to translate socialist debate into socialist revolutionary action.[36] The objects for which USARF was formed can be grouped into three categories. The first was to disseminate marxist-leninist ideas among students and to raise ideological consciousness and enthusiasm among the students in the University. The second was to contribute positively to the ideals of African Revolution and people's struggles elsewhere. The third was to identify the students with the cause of the toiling masses in Tanzania, Africa and the world.

In practice USARF was a very militant organisation. Its membership was open to students of all nationalities in the University. The only limitation in this regard was that USARF was a university and not a nation-wide organisation. Its ambitious objectives became advantageous to University students only, leaving out teachers' colleges and secondary schools. Whatever the case may be, USARF was qualitatively a better organisation compared to NAUTS or USUD.

It implemented its objectives by employing a variety of methods in order to create socialist revolutionary consciousness among the students. USARF started by ideological cultivation of its own members through constant and systematic study of marxist-leninist thought in weekly ideological classes. These were organised and conducted by students themselves and had the advantage of contributions by seasoned marxists like Walter Rodney who was one of the associate members of USARF.

USARF ideological classes were then supplemented by public lectures, symposia and seminars which the organisation organised for the entire student community. Among the prominent speakers in some of these lectures were black power militants like Stokely Carmichael, and socialists like Gora Ibrahim, Cheddi Jagan, Abdul Rahman Mohamed Babu and C.L.R. James. These lectures helped to stimulate revolutionary spirit and activism among the students and provided a positive contrast between socialist thought and bourgeois thought, the later being the dominant school of thought at the University. The effect of this drive could be easily seen when bourgeois scholars like Professor Ali Mazrui visited and delivered public lectures or when some bourgeois professors openly showed contempt to revolutionary theory, as it happened during the "Singleton affair".

Singleton, an American Visiting Professor had made abusive remarks in a political science class on Franz Fanon's contribution to revolutionary theory. This offended some USARF militants in his class and they immediately took him to task for it. Not satisfied with the debate in the class the militants organised a public USARF symposium on Franz Fanon's contribution to revolutionary knowledge. They invited the Professor to come and defend his views, but the Professor declined under the pretext that what he had said should have been confined to the classroom. The symposium went on with its business all the same and Singleton's views were thoroughly discredited. A proposal was made to contribute money towards Singleton's return to the United States. But when the money had been collected the symposium dismissed Singleton's one-track mindedness as not worthy of their money and voted that the money be donated to the liberation movements.

USARF augmented its efforts further to sow revolutionary consciousness among students and to participate in the African Revolution by conducting a constant vigil against imperialist ideologies and activities. It took an active part in analysing current events and taking position on all such events at national and international level. It published these analyses in leaflets, handouts and in its theoretical organ "Cheche". Such events were like condemnation of Russian invasion of Czechoslovakia and condemation of American imperialism in Asia. USARF also made clear its position on the banning of Kenya People's Union (KPU) and the decision by Karadha Company to issue loans for purchase of personal effects (cars and refrigerators) for the petty bourgeoisie.

USARF did not hesitate to combat reactionary or imperialist supported activities which enhance idealist outlook of society. It effectively demonstrated its commitment in this when it sabotaged a World University Service (WUS) activity called the Rag Day. This was an annual University student activity when students put on rags in order to look like the poor and solicit offerings from the rich in order to donate such returns to the poor by way of charity or philanthropy. WUS had a national committee whose first patron was Mwalimu Nyerere. This committee sought a Police permit to undertake this begging circus in the city on 9 November 1968. It instructed students to "dress in rags of every colour and description" and to rehearse their calls and songs for soliciting offerings. Students were required to make as much noise as possible.[36]

USARF militants organised a public discussion on the role of charity and philanthropy in society and in the discussion it was agreed that University Rag Day should be combated because it reduced students into a laughing stock by causing them to participate in mockery of the poor. Philanthropism was defined as an "euphemism for those who plunder by the ton and give by the ounce". Following this unanimous decision USARF militants punctured the tyres of the vehicles which had been brought to transport students to town and erected barricades across the exist from the square where they had been parked. The militants managed to mobilise and win over both the guards and the police who had been sent to help WUS against USARF militants. The Police subsequently withdrew its permit and Rag Day become erased from the life of the University. The square in which the WUS vehicles had been parked was thereafter called the 'Revolutionary Square'.

The third objective of identification of students with the struggles of the working people against imperialism gave USARF militants practical experience of working among the people. They participated in communal self help projects in Ujamaa Villages like cashewnut picking and such related activities. Their analysis of the government policies like the Karadha issue, tourist debate,[37] and finally the debate on disengagement from imperialism which precipitated into what has now been called the "Imperialism debate"[38] have gone down in history as part of the countribution to the stuggles of the working peoples in Tanzania, of which USARF was the spring board. Before we deal in detail with these debates, it is suggested that a review of USARF's impact in the life of the University during this period be attempted.

Events which took place in the Faculty of Law during the months of February and March, 1969 show that USARF's influence did not end with the activities in which it had a direct and dominant participation. Its militants had penetrated various institutions in the University and were engaged in a struggle to have bourgeois traditions, style of work and syllabus changed for socialist ones. One such area penetrated was the Faculty of Law where USARF militants had got elected into leadership positions. The Faculty was then under very heavy American influence and control. They formed a vigilance committee which led the struggle against the bureaucratic style of running the affairs of the university, and the growing influence of imperialism in the Faculty. They demanded participation in the decision-making process and questioned the way in which the teaching staff was being recruited.

In this struggle student demands aimed not only at having a university which was manned by East Africans but one which belonged to and served the interests of the people. Essentially their struggle was anti-imperialist. Students argued: "the real issue at stake is a fundamental one concerning the ownership of this unversity college: whether the college will ultimately belong to the people of Tanzania and East Africa or to Imperialism".[39]

In the event, students opposed a new syllabus of the Faculty of Law which was being adopted. The syllabus, when introduced, would inculcate American bourgeois liberalism as opposed to the existing one which was based on British legal conservatism.[40] The new syllabus also included a new subject on military law which students in their narrow nationalist phobia thought would endanger the 'socialist Revolution' in Tanzania. In their memorandum to the visitation committee, appointed by the President to recommend how a national university could be established, students argued:

we maintain that the way we train our lawyers will of necessity determine the legal system we shall have. We cannot train bourgeois lawyers and expect to have a socialist legal system.[41]

The vigilance committee demanded therefore East Africanisation of the teaching staff, involvement of students in decision-making process, Tanzanianisation of the office of the Dean of the Faculty of Law and recruitment, where necessary, of teaching staff from socialist countries. Although the student demands seemed reasonable and progressive, it was clear that their ideological development had not reached the point of disengagement from the *status quo*. They suffered from an erroneous belief that the legal system and education which are all part of the superstructure, can determine the economic base. They believed that the Arusha Declaration constituted a socialist revolution and that what then remained was creating conditions for socialist construction. Socialist law and a socialist legal system are not in the final analysis determined by the type of education given to functionaries of the system but rather by the creation of a socialist economic base.

Therefore although most of the student demands were met, Issa Shivji, one of the participants in these struggles, admits that they did not go far beyond intense nationalism. Their demands did not attack the root of the neo-colonial state in Tanzania. Their demands were in fact complimentary to it. Issa Shivji explains:

> However, within a very short period the students realised that Tanzanianisation of the Deanship did not necessarily mean that Deanship would be progressive nor did the East Africanisation of the staff mean that the Faculty of Law would be the leading light of radicalism. In fact the student body as a whole began to realise that the fact that the University had become a national university did not mean that it was a people's University.[42]

In so far as the anti-imperialist student struggles in the Faculty of Law were remotely controlled by USARF, the criticism that ideologically students had not moved out of the Fabianist snare and tutelage applies also to USARF. Although USARF's function was to inform the students of the tactics of imperialism and to oppose and combat imperialist manipulations, it could not have successfully undertaken such a task without having clarified itself on the basic question of the nature, character, function and form of the neo-colonial state. Had USARF been clear on this basic question, the substance of the student demands in the Faculty of Law crisis could have been completely different. The results of their struggles could have also been different also.

USARF militants took up this challenge and started serious study of the socio-economic formation of the neo-colonial state in Tanzania. The results of these efforts were so rewarding that path-breaking theoretical works *The silent class struggle in Tanzania* and *Class struggle continues* by Issa Shivji saw the light of the day in USARF's theoretical organ *Cheche*. These works generated an intense theoretical debate on imperialism and the state during which the left in Tanzania split into two warring camps, and the publication of "Silent Class Struggles in Tanzania" in *Cheche* prompted the state to ban both USARF and its theoretical organ *Cheche*. We shall deal with the highlights of the debate later. For a moment let us review this regrettable ban.

On Monday, 9 November 1970, the Vice Chancellor summoned the TANU Youth League (TYL) committee on the University Campus and informed it that USARF had been instructed by the State House to wind up its activities and that its theoretical organ *Cheche* should cease publication. The reason given for the ban was that USARF had become a redundant organisation since TYL was supposed to exercise a monopoly of all political activities on the campus. USARF, the Vice Chancellor explained, had been meddling in the political affairs of Tanzania by its mordant commentaries on various issues without any specific *locus standi* since it represented no recognized national body inside Tanzania or abroad.

Cheche was on the other hand banned for a very funny reason— its name. The authorities said that *Cheche*, which is the Kiswahili translation of ISKRA (The spark), the leninist theoretical journal of the Russian Bolsheviks, tended to give the impression that Tanzania was building Russian socialism and not the true Tanzanian socialism. Authorities stated that TANU and TYL had always been ideologically self reliant, thus such borrowing from foreign ideologies could not be tolerated.[43] It is common knowledge that there is no such thing as Russian or Tanzanian socialism. The truth was that *Cheche* had developed into too powerful a theoretical journal exposing the neo-colonial character of the Tanzania state. Together with *Cheche*, USARF was asked to wind up its activities because all political activities in the University were a monopoly of the TANU Youth League. Of course this also was untrue. Underneath these subtle manoeuvres appealing to narrow nationalism was the growth of an authoritarian state in the neo-colonial Tanzania. The state had already banned the independent working-class trade union TFL in 1964, the independent student union (NAUTS) in 1966 and was now encroaching upon academic freedom in the University College of Dar es Salaam. USARF's statement on being banned however, gave a resounding rebuff to these manoeuvres. It asked:

> Can a magazine be banned just because of its name? *Cheche* no doubt means the same thing as *Iskra*. But how original is *The Standard*, *The Nationalist* or *The Echo*? or is it the con-tents of *Cheché* that are pricking someone's conscience? If what *Cheche* published are fabrications, then why not disprove them with counter facts and figures. After all this University is sup-posed to stimulate debate within the socialist context. Can socialism be built without sincere and vigorous discussion? Are there as many varieties of socialisms as there are nations? If people will think we are building 'Russian Socialism' because of the name *Cheche*, then will they not also think we are building 'American Socialism' since our nationalized institutions get advice from American Management consultancy agencies! Or perhaps we are building 'British socialism' since Kivukoni College—the party school—is modelled after Ruskin College. If we want to be totally self reliant, then why not invent Tanzania

political science, sociology, economics, physics, and mathematics?

We do not have answers to any of these questions. Yet we do not doubt the wisdom prompting our ban. But one thing must be remembered. Organisations can be banned, individuals can be liquidated, but ideas live on. *Revolutionary ideas never die. That is our last stand!*[43]

The death of USARF and its theoretical organ *Cheche* nipped in the bud the growth of a real revolutionary left in Tanzania. It destroyed the embryonic organisation which could have enabled the left in Tanzania to operate in an organised form. It should be emphasized that one of the salient characteristics of the development of the left in Tanzania is its inextricable link with the student movement and struggles especially in the University of Dar es Salaam. This is understandable if one notes that marxism-leninism was not an established stream of thought in Tanzania before the arrival of marxist academics like Walter Rodney and others in the mid-sixties. Although, for example, the student crisis in 1966 had a radical content, its ideological articulation lacked the sharpness of a marxist conception of society.

The lack of a tradition of revolutionary struggle, and the regrettable lack of a tradition of organisation for political struggle, made it possible for the state to throw into disarray the budding Tanzanian left with the banning of USARF and *Cheche*. In truth therefore, the Tanzanian left is a conceptual usage rather than a description of what actually exists. Ever since the death of USARF leftists in Tanzania have remained scattered, each indulging in self-styled activities while their ideological development has remained a sphere of speculation. In the absence of any concrete organisational form, the Tanzanian left has become an easy tool for ideological manipulation of the masses in the hands of the crafty Fabian faction of the ruling petty bourgeois class which has wielded state power since 1961. It has played the role of ideological mercenaries whose duty is to pre-empt crises by intoxicating the people with a lot of revolutionary hot air.

USARF had represented the highest form of student militant organisation outside the control of the state. It represented genuine attempts by the student left in Tanzania to organise for political action. In the brief period of its existence, USARF developed from a lower to higher level of political and ideological consciousness. Its rigorousness in ideological debate gave it some flexibility and capability required for internalisation of the salient features of the events of the day. Its critical attitude towards the practice and approach of the TANU/Afro Shirazi parties to the problems of underdevelopment and strategies for national liberation from the shackles of neo-colonialism enabled it ot expose slowly but surely the real nature and character of the neo-colonial state in Tanzania.

Of course USARF started as an off-shoot of the Arusha Declaration. It therefore proceeded from the false premise that the process of socialist revolution was in progress, and that the revolution had triumphed over neo-colonial socio-economic formation. It believed, though erroneously, that the capitalist and the comprador bourgeosie had been overthrown by the mere nationalisations which followed the Arusha Declaration. USARF's involvement in national political process became an eye opener to some of its most committed militants. They began to see the fallacy of the belief held by marxists during this time that the system could be changed from within by getting involved in it and transforming it into a revolutionary socialist system. Like the communards of the classical Paris Commune, the Tanzania Left made the error of believing that the state of the oppressor can be taken over and used by the oppressed. To them the state, and the political party, were mere tools which could be used by anyone who handled them.

We have noted in the preceeding discussion that this realisation came as a result of the process of ideological self clarification within USARF, militants through study, debates and attempts at analysing the nature and character of the neo-colonial state. We have noted also that one of the results of this process was the publication of two major theoretical works on the neo-colonial state, *Silent Class Struggles in Tanzania* and *Class Struggle Continues* by Issa Shivji. The debate stimulated by these works split the Left in Tanzania into two camps. One camp identified itself with Issa Shiviji's proposition which avers that the ruling petty bourgoisie (Shiivji called it bureaucratic bourgeoisie) was the local manifestation of imperialism which should be seen as the immediate enemy of the working peoples in their struggles against imperialism. The other camp identified itself with Professor Dan Nabudere's proposition that the ruling class in a neo-colonial economic formation is the international financial oligarchy and that a broad front of anti-imperialist forces was the essential pre-requisite for combating imperialism.

This debate has been called a confused debate. It diverged from theoretical analysis and indulged in name-calling. Comrades starting tagging each other names like 'trotskyite', 'neo-marxist' and many other such names. The debate aside, an assessment of the contribution made by USARF to the development of revolutionary consciousness among the Tanzanian youth cannot be over-emphasized. USARF was a militant student organisation in the University of Dar es Salaam and it will be remembered in history as such.

Despite all this however, it should be noted that the death of

USARF meant also a draw back on the quality of the student struggles in Tanzania. The Akivaga crisis, for example, was the best example of the deterioration in the content of student struggle. One should have expected that happening in 1971, the Akivaga crisis would have reflected the lessons which students had learnt from the Faculty of Law crisis in 1969. This was however not the case as the record of the events reveals.

In July 1971, Akivaga, the President of DUSO, the student organisation of the University of Dar es Salaam, wrote an open letter to the Vice Chancellor challenging the University authorities for running the University bureaucratically without consulting the students on their interests. He emphasized the democratic right of students to be involved in making major decisions in the running of the University. Students were of the view that if the University was to serve the interests of the people, then it must be run democratically. It must involve in its decision making process the majority of those people it directly served, that is the students.

The university authorities felt offended, and their positions challenged. They decided to rusticate Akivaga. Students saw the most naked misuse of coercive power of the state when armed riot police (there was no riot on the campus then) drove into the campus in full gear, armed to the teeth, to escort the unarmed Akivaga away. Students boycotted classes demading the return of their leader and the granting of their demands. Members of staff met and discovered that the crisis was in fact a result of the undemocratic way the University was being run. They were never involved nor or consulted by the administration in the issue until Akivaga had been rusticated. The members of staff therefore came out in support of student demands. The student struggles had opened the eyes of the staff to the reality of the day. In a joint staff-student meeting called to discuss Akivaga's rustication, it transpired that the members of staff and not only the students had no say in the running of the University. Members of staff could not even meet without the permission of the administration because they had no organisation of their own. They therefore supported student demands and demanded for an academic assembly and an academic staff association.

Students held their ground, continuing to boycott classes. They however failed to involved in their struggle the workers and members of staff who had similar grievances against the University bureaucracy. Their resistance had no articulate and deep going analysis of the events. So when it became clear to the bureaucracy that the issue had been reduced to that of readmitting Akivaga, it backed down and allowed Akivaga back. This diffused student resistance. Student did not press further their demands for democratisation. The only highlight of the

Akivaga crisis was that the University changed its administrative system into a committee system. This was a democratic form far better than the bureaucratic one in which decisions were made by one individual. The content of the University administration however, remained unchanged. This derived from the fact that students had failed to cross the borders of their petit bourgeois frame work and involve the working class who were then involved in post-Mwongozo class struggles. This limitation became the major weakness of student movement because soon, the opportunistic faction of the student movement rose and overthrew Akivaga's government on parochial nationalism (Akivaga was a Kenyan!)

The coup was blessed by the Vice Chancellor and ever since the state moved to control the student organisation by sponsoring reactionary bootlickers into the student leadership. In fact as days went by student community became infested with members of the intelligence service and these elements went to control the student leadership. This brings us to a new phase of the student movement in Tanzania.

Musoma and After: 1972-1984

The interesting feature of the Akivaga crisis was that students rose against the University bureaucracy just as the workers were doing at the same time in production centres. The weakness of the students' struggle arising from their failure to reach out to join their struggle to that of the workers notwithstanding, their theme was in tune with the current stage reached in the working people's struggles against the neo-colonial state and economic formation in Tanzania.

The insensitive, rigid, corrupt and inefficient state bureaucracy had reached a stage where it could not see beyond its parochial class interests. It responded against any challenge to its hegemony with excessive use of force. When for example, workers in Mount Carmel Rubber Factory rose up demanding their right to take over and run the factory, the state moved in the process subjected them to harassment as if they were common criminals. Finally, the state returned the factory to the capitalist who had owned the rubber factory. It was the state and not the working people who should determine the extent of socialism Tanzania should have!

The period following the Akivaga crisis saw a cooling off of student dissent in the University of Dar es Salaam. TYL militants had established a new theoretical organ called *Majimaji*. Unlike its predecessor *Cheche*, *Majimaji* succumbed to censorship and allowed publication of apologetic articles on the Tanzania state and economy. On the other hand DUSO became an organisation rife with corruption and embezzlement of student funds. The struggle shifted to secondary schools and the whole of 1972, 1973 and 1974 saw students in various secondary schools, Mkwawa, Mzumbe, Musoma, Pugu, Kirakala and many others rising up against maladministration, bureaucratism, appalling conditions of life and lack of education facilities. Above all secondary school students rose up against lack of involvement in decision-making in the running of schools, self reliance projects, and embezzlement of self reliance funds by their teachers. In all these struggles however the state unleashed violence on the student community under the pretext of quelling indiscipline. One interesting case is the Mzumbe Secondary School—April 1973 —crisis examined below.

This was a crisis emanating purely from bureaucracy on the part of the teachers. The teachers decided that partitions in the dormitories in the Shaaban Robert Area should be removed because they were old and were made out of cardboard. This decision was taken without involving the students. The result was that students refused to remove the partitions. Teachers anticipated riots, therefore one of them telephoned the Police Station that students had rioted and were causing a lot of damage to the school. When armed riot police drove into the school, they found that everything was normal and students were peacefully attending a Saturday flag raising ceremony. The police demanded an explanation. The headmaster was panic striken and had to take the riot police to Shaaban Robert area. The Police demanded that students resident in that area should be assembled and after issuing a number of threats, the commander of the riot Police ordered the students to remove the wooden partitions in their dormitories. Students resisted and the commander ordered the Police squad into action.

The result of this incident was that a number of students were injured. Following this incident the whole student leadership resigned except for a few puppets. The headmaster decided to expel the 28 student leaders. An emergency school assembly was called during which the Headmaster read out the names of the 28 students leaders and declared them expelled. Students were told to go back to their dormitories but instead they re-assembled and marched to Morogoro town 10 miles away to present their grievances to the regional authorities. They were intercepted by the riot Police and told to go back to school where the Regional Education Officer had agreed to meet them. Students went back to school but were informed by the headmaster that a decision had been reached to close down the school. Students went back to their dormitories to prepare their homeward journey. The following morning however, the headmaster ordered them to classes, saying he had announced closure of the school only in order to pre-empt a full scale disorder. Students felt that they were being treated like children so they boycotted classes.

The Headmaster went ahead and expelled more than 187 students who had boycotted classes. The students including the 28 student leaders were pardoned and allowed to resume their studies three months later. Fourteen students were however arbitrarily expelled allegedly because they had been found to have been ring leaders. The Mzumbe Secondary School crisis represented one clear example of bureaucratic arrogance on the part of teachers in a period when the syllabus had managed to mould radical students who could not accept the old fashioned master-pupil relationship.

The Mzumbe Secondary School crisis followed a stream of other school crises like the 1972 Musoma Secondary School crisis in which 370 students were expelled after rising against the bad food. The students had been subjected to continuous routine of *ugali* and nothing had been done to explain the reasons for the monotonous diet. After the Mzumbe crisis, there developed a serious crisis in Mkwawa Secondary School in 1975. This crisis dragged on for more than six months. Although originally the crisis had been sparked off by bad diet, it later turned out that teachers had barred students from buying shares in the school co-operative shop, and were still getting bread from the school bakery while they had told the students that they could not get bread because the bakery had closed down due to the bad economic situation in the country. The Ministry of Education finally decided to demobilise the staff and students by transferring them to other schools in the country.

The astounding rise of student struggles in secondary schools prompted the state to consider methods of curbing their radicalism so that it would not spill into colleges of higher learning and the University. By the end of 1974 the Minister of National Education Mr. Israel Elinawinga announced that disciplinary measures would be taken against teachers who sided with students in school riots. He said that the government would not hestitate to dismiss teachers proved to have been behind unrest and riots in schools. In fact the state was also contemplating denying those students who had been involved in unrest, University entrance. Finally, however, the state went forward to restructure the eduction system in a move calculated to forestall student radicalism in post-secondary school education. TANU National Executive Committee met at Musoma early 1975 and resolved that after secondary school education students should go to National Service for one full year and then work for a period of two years before joining higher institutions of learning. The reasons given to explain these changes were that the party felt that it was time the education system merged theory and practice. Higher education should only be given in order to enable the students who had already acquired skills in their working places to advance his or her acquired skills for better performance and productivity. Secondly, subjecting students to two years of work would allow them to sober up and acquire a mature attitude during their higher learning.[44]

The whole scheme was of course misconceived and it collapsed even before it started. Immediately, the women's organisation UWT started struggling for exemption of girls from the Musoma Resolution due to their special maternal duties. This was granted. Again there were not enough candidates eligible to enrol in the scientific fields, especially in engineering, so the government had to exempt students eligible to enrol in those fields from the Musoma Resolution. Finally no jobs were available according to specializations which students would pursue in the University. As a result the two year work period become an expensive waste since it delayed skilled manpower for almost three years running, while the ineligible mature entrants recorded mass failure in most institutions of higher learning. Finally the higher education bill became too heavy for the government to sustain. The government realised its mistake so NEC session of June 1984 decided to reintroduce the old direct entrance system.

The government had aimed at elimination of student radicalism in institutions of higher leaning. The argument was that mature students had a sober look at life and had other interests to protect so they would not jump into any radical bandwagon against the state. This was a total misconception of the neo-colonial state of the socio-economic dynamics and the historically determined role of student community in any class society. Despite the relative privileges of the student life, and the aspiration to join the system, students remain a potentially revolutionary stratum which easily assimilates new ideas. In the neo-colonial context students can hardly avoid sympathies with the working people's struggles since they are still not totally cut off from them.

In Tanzania, the influx of University graduates into secondary schools brought into the secondary schools teachers with progressive ideas and these brought a new quality of radicalism unknown in the secondary school student politics. When these were later subjected to the harsh militarism of National Service and the empty reality of two years of work, they become even more hardened in their radicalism. But even before these breed of students entered institutions of higher learning the University exploded under the excessive build up of privileges of the state-based section of the ruling class. It is interesting to note that the petty bourgeoisie which had taken over power in 1961 had now transformed itself into a strong comprador bourgeoisie permeating both state and private sectors. This transformation reflected itself in the new structure of salaries and fringe benefits of party and government leaders which prompted the 1978 student struggles.

The 1978 Student Struggle

Two events mark the coming of age of the ideological crystalization of the student radicalism in Tanzania. The first was the Shaba Province crisis of 1977 and the second was the March 1978 demonstration against the introduction of new terms and conditions of service for ministers, members of parliament, government and party political leaders at various levels.

The Shaba Province crisis was prompted by the incursions made by one General Nathaniel Mboumba from the Angolan border with a view to overthrow the pro-imperialist regime of General Mobutu Sese-Seko from March 8 to May 13 1977. Mobutu called French forces to his aid. His indisciplined army and the French gendarmes perpetrated acts of violence and breaches of human rights and dignity against the Zairean people in repulsing General Mboumba's forces. Although Tanzania was not interested in the internal dimensions of the conflict, it expressed its indignation at the gross violation of human rights and the involvement of imperialist forces to protect anti-people governments from being overthrown by the people. It rejected the proposal to create a continental peace keeping force whose duty would be to protect African governments from being overthrown. French Foreign Minister Louis de Guiringand visited a number of African states to sell his country's proposition to create in Africa a continental peace keeping force. On his arrival in Tanzania students met him at the airport and snubbed him. They had failed to secure a police permit to stage the protest but had ignored this predicament and arranged protest rallies at the airport and the Kilimanjaro Hotel where the Foreign Minister was to be put up. When De Guiringand asked for an apology, the foreign office declined and he left in anger and embarrassment with his mission unaccomplished.

Student protest against De Guiringand's tour was not just in support of the official stand on the role of foreign forces purporting to police Africa, but a total identification with the people in asserting their right to struggle against neo-colonial regimes. With this perspective in mind the student struggles against the neo-colonial state in Tanzania in 1978 can be properly understood. It so happened that the Parliament which sat in February in Wete Pemba considered among other matters new terms and conditions of service for political leaders including members of parliament. These were released on 7 January 1978. They stipulated, *inter alia*, that effective from 1 January, 1978 government would foot water and electricity bills for Regional Commissioners and would pay the salary of one domestic servant in the Regional Commissioner's residence. It was revealed that these privileges had been introduced since 1972.

As regards members of parliament their salaries would be 36,000 shs. per annum but for nominated members of parliament, formally employed in the public sector or civil service, the member of parliament could choose whichever salary was bigger. The Parliament also endorsed gratuity and pension terms for members of parliament. Accordingly, a member of Parliament who served two consecutive terms would be pensionable while one who served only one term would be entitled to a gratuity amounting to 25% of his gross salary for five years. The pension and gratuity was non-taxable and payable in a lump sum. These terms and conditions were published by the government daily, *The Daily News*, on 27 February 1978.

Students were infuriated. By then the country was in grave economic problems and cholera had spread almost over the entire country. Due to difficult economic conditions it had become necessary to shelve the third five year development plan which the Wete Parliamentary session had been scheduled to consider. It occurred to students that the state had absolutely sold out to imperialism and the socialist revolution had been betrayed both by the CCM Party and the government.

Students demanded an explanation and they sought audience with the Chancellor Mwalimu Nyerere. Negotiations for the audience were being conducted by the Vice-Chancellor, Ibrahim Kaduma, in consultation with student organisations of the three institutions of learning, the Ardhi Institute (Ardhi), the Water Resources Institute (Maji) and the University of Dar es Salaam CCM Youth League, University District. It happened however that Kaduma had wanted the students to meet Party Executive Secretary Pius Msekwa and not Mwalimu Nyerere. Nyerere said that he was ready to meet the students. Kaduma knew that the students were highly inflamed by the new terms and conditions of service of political leaders and were considering a protest demonstration, yet he chose to sit on the information. In the event, Dar es Salaam University Student organisation and student organisations of Ardhi and Maji believed that the Chancellor had refused to see them so they spilled into the city.

Riot police Field Force Unit intercepted the students at Manzese with a view to disperse them or to order them back to their respective campuses. Students resisted both. The police unleashed violence. Students regrouped and continued their demonstration which ended at the government newspaper, *Daily News*. There they read their memorandum which analysed the neo-colonial state and the economy of Tanzania and how CCM as a party had failed in practice to lead the working people to socialism. They argued *inter alia* that:

> Just as it is important to distinguish in a person's life between
> what he professes and what he does in practice, similarly in

a revolutionary struggle it is necessary to distinguish between what a party professes in its constitution, guidelines, declarations and other pronouncements and what the party does in practice in order to evaluate its successes or failures.

In accordance with this, it is now time to evaluate what the party has done or has allowed to be done in view of its professed ideology of socialism and self reliance. The act of the members of Parliament of increasing their salaries and fringe benefits announced in the government *Daily News* paper of 27/2/1978 has shocked peasants and workers especially when one takes into consideration the difficult economic problems of this country, which leaders of the party and government explain to us. It is clear that the economy of this country has stagnated. Prices of essential commodities for peasants and workers have sky-rocketed, low income earners are living in squalor and deprivation. We also know that 20% of the work-force has been laid off due to economic recession. Amidst all these, and when the country is suffering from a cholera epidemic which has spread like bush fire all over the country, our leaders chose this critical time, to sit at Wete Pemba and endorse a scheme to double their salaries and fringe benefits when the peasants and workers expected them to safeguard their interests. To show their jubilation for this, they were seen riding aboard children seesaw (translation ours).

In their memorandum students questioned the practice of making membership of Parliament a job paid by way of salary drawn out of state coffers. They challenged the rationale of turning a people's representative into a paid servant of the state.

If membership of Parliament is a salaried job, what is the meaning of having had to elect them? If membership of Parliament is a salaried job then it is only logical that aspirants should apply for it as it is done for other salaried jobs. Accordingly, if a member of Parliament will be an employee of the state, then he or she will fail to represent the interests of the people. This practice did not start with members of Parliament but with elected representatives at various levels of the Party like District Executive Committee of the party and central committee members.
    Therefore the question of being an elected representative at various levels in the party and as members of the Parliament has become a question of exploitation and establishing economic

power of those so elected (translation ours).

Students complained further that the Party and governmen† had abandoned socialism. They charged that the increasing indebtedness of the country to imperialism, and the practice of entrusting development of the nation to imperialist powers by dividing the country into zones each with one imperialist power—for example Kilimanjaro to Japanese, Tanga to Canadians, Coast to Sweden, and so on—was detrimental to socialism and had completely derailed the efforts of the nation to build a socialist economy.

Students rightly concluded that Tanzania had been sold out to imperialism and there was no use hiding behind hackneyed anti-imperialist slogans to deceive the people. They demanded that the new terms and conditions for political leaders should be stopped at once and that the practice of paying salaries and fringe benefits to elected party and government officers should be re-considered. They further demanded raising of minimum wages and prices of food and cash crops and government subsidy on commodities essential to workers and peasants. They also warned against the practice among senior party and government officials of discouraging revolutionary activities which were genuinely in the interest of socialism in Tanzania.

These demands of the students never reached a receptive ear. The President ordered the police to round the students up and a total of 350 students from the University of Dar es Salaam, Ardhi Institute and the Water Resources Institute were expelled and their student organisation banned. The government issued a fabricated account of the student struggle. Its statement released to the state-controlled press charged that students had been expelled because they had engaged themselves in acts of hooliganism and had tried to cause chaos contrary to national ethic.[46]

The statement further charged that "the students were protesting against the government programme of sending experts to the rural areas and the new terms and conditions of service of members of Parliament, Ministers and Party leaders at different levels of leadership".

It alleged that students had earlier on been given an opportunity to meet the Chief Executive Secretary of the Party and had been informed that the Chairman of the Party was willing to listen to their complaints but had chosen to stage an illegal demonstration. This, the statement charged, indicated that their purpose was not to present their complaints to the Party Chairman or to get an explanation of the government decisions but to cause chaos.

It may be true that the state never anticipated a student protest or even a heated debate on the issue. The University had a majority of mature entrants who were hardly expected to entertain radical ideas such as opposing a raise of salaries and fringe benefits for party and government leaders. As mature entrants, the students had a stake in such changes and had other interests to protect.

When therefore the University and the Colleges erupted so suddenly, the state was caught with its pants down. As could be expected of an authoritarian legal system, the gendarmerie was used once it was put on the anti-people carpet. The table it had set for itself as a pro-people regime in 1966, when it sent down students protesting against certain aspects of compulsory national service programme, had now been turned against it on 5 March 1978. Students demonstrated squarely in defence of popular interest and the government was clearly isolated. Fearing the worst, the usual scare of the University students being manipulated against the state by foreign powers was sold to the rumour mills of Dar es Salaam to justify the clamp down on students. Of course students had neither a sympathetic press nor armed might as the state had at its disposal.

The introduction of the issue of government programme to send experts to the rural areas was clear fabrication and contradictory. How could the students oppose going to work in villages and demonstrate at the same time in defence of the interests of workers and peasants?

Nyerere realised his mistake. Students demonstrated not because they wanted to cause chaos but because Kaduma had sat on the vital information which could have diffused the crisis. Nyerere pardoned the students, and later when he held a public question answer session with them in July 1978, he admitted the error and swore it would never happen again. In this session students blatantly told Nyerere that he was presiding over a police state. Startled, Nyerere replied "you want your freedom on a silver platter. No state will give you that. Freedom must be fought for".[47] When requested to lift the ban an DUSO, the student organisation, Nyerere backed down. He said the ban would not be lifted because the CCM Youth League could run student affairs in the University.

So with DUSO dead, the Youth League appointed a caretaker government and later that year at a conference held in Iringa, *Muungano wa Wanafunzi Tanzania* (MUWATA) was conceived as a pan-territorial student organisation under the control and supervision of the Youth League. A tailor-made constitution was adopted without students having been consulted. MUWATA was imposed on the unwilling student community. Its opportunistic stand notwithstanding MUWATA has since then tried to win student support. These efforts have never come to fruition because MUWATA is considered a sellout organisation which works at the behest of the state. The constant attempt by student members of the intelligence service to take over and run MUWATA has made MUWATA's acceptability a far-off dream.

When therefore MUWATA made highly derogatory statements about DUSO in March 1983, it completely smeared the little name it had managed to acquire as a respectable student organisation. Students refer to MUWATA officials as "hogs", a metaphor for sell-outs derived from George Orwell's *Animal Farm*. By creation of MUWATA the state has at long last crushed the student movements. Students can no longer organise for political action without consent of the Youth League which is part and parcel of the state. The torch of knowledge and revolutionary activism which the University of Dar es Salaam had won by hard struggle has finally been extinguished. There is no longer a revolutionary square where students met at the call of their organisation DUSO to discuss affairs related to their organisation and the revolution. When Walter Rodney was assassinated by Burnham's authoritarian state in Guyana, revolutionary activists in Dar es Salaam, members of the academic staff and radical students met at a symposium organised by the History Department in honour of Walter Rodney. The symposium resolved unanimously to erect a plaque in the memory of Walter Rodney at the centre of the Revolutionary square. Money was to be donated by all who subscribed to the revolutionary ideas which Rodney taught, pursued and died for. The resolution has remained a dead letter to date. A radical student organisation could never rest until this aspiration is achieved. But MUWATA cannot indulge in such enterprises. It is controlled by the state and can hardly stand firm against the University authority. It cannot therefore be expected to stand and challenge an authoritarian state it is so much part and parcel of.

All in all, one thing is clear. By destroying the initiative of the masses to organise themselves, politically independent of the state, the state closed the doors of peaceful change in Tanzania. People cannot rise up to meet the challenge of underdevelopment in the absence of democracy, for in the final analysis, no people will ever release its creative capacities for productivity and development without being meaningfully involved in the democratic process. A nation will acquire the capacity for its development and self-reliance only to the extent of democratic latitude it enjoys. May be this is the lesson many ordinary Tanzanians have come to learn the hard way but which may cost their nation blood and iron to achieve. Students will undoubtedly have their share in the next phase of the struggle.

NOTES

1. Van de Laar, A.J.M; "Towards a manpower development strategy in Tanzania", Cliffe, L., & Saul, J.S. (eds.) *Socialism in Tanzania,* Vol.2, Nairobi: East African Publishing Housing, 1973), p.226. Van de Laar mentions the Tanganyika Episcopal Conference, the Christian Council of Tanganyika, the Education Secretary of the Aga Khan, Tanganyika African Parents Association and East African Muslim Welfare Society as the most important educational agencies during the colonial period.

2. *Ibid.* The racial education system was abolished in 1961 by an ordinance of Parliament which made provision for a single education system in Tanganyika, Ordinance No. 37 of 1961.

3. Interview with Joseph Warioba, who was a PASAT executive committee member in 1959.

4. Engels, F., *Origin of Family Private Property and the State* in Marx, K., Engels, F.,*Selected Works,* Vol. 3 (Moscow: Progress Publishers, 1966)p. 327. Lenin V.I., *The State.,* (Peking: Foreign Landuage Press, 1970), p.14.

5. Makene, S., "Student Radicalism: The Politics of Change". An article published in the Mzumbe Institute Students Organisation Annual Magazine, 1978.

6. Fanon, F., *The Wretched of the Earth,* (London: Penguin Books, 1963), p. 120.

7. Mamdani M., *Imperialism and Fascism in Uganda,* (Nairobi: Heineman Educational Books, 1983), p. 17.

8. Hart H.L.A. *The Concept of Law,* (London: Oxford University Press, 1961), p. 116.

9. Komba B.M.L. *Maji Maji Research Project, Collected Papers* (1968) University College of Dar es Salaam, Department of History (mimeo)

10. See generally Nyerere J.K. *Freedom and Unity,* (Oxford University Press, Dar es Salaam (1966).

11. *Ibid.,* pp.40-41.

12. Verbatim record of an interview made by the authors with one ex-student of the University College of Dar es Salaam who participated in 1966 student struggles. His identity has been concealed at his request.

13. Report published in the Student Union's bulletin *The Watchtower,* May 1962 issue.

14. Authors' interview with Joseph Warioba, the first Secretary General of TUSA.

15. Fanon F., *The Wretched of the Earth, op.cit.*

16. Williams, D.V., "State Coercion Against Peasant Farmers: The Tanzania State", *Journal of Legal Pluralism,* No. 20, (1982).

17. Coulson, A., *A Political Economy of Tanzania,* (Oxford: Clarendon Press, 1982), p.5.

18. Kawawa, R., *Hansard* Sept 22-11 Oct., 1966 at p. 249.

19. *Ibid.,*p.249

20. *Ibid.*

21. *Ibid.*

22. Kuhanga N., *Hansard op.cit.,*p.256.

23. Authors' Interview with the participants.

24. Letters by Principal Secretary of the Ministry of National Education Mr. F.K. Burengelo to the Registrar of University of East Africa, ref. No. EDC/13/41/35 of Oct. 1966.

25. Letter by sent-down students resident in Dar es Salaam, 29/10/1966.

26. Kawawa, R., Press release issued to and published by the Information Service Division, Ministry of Information and Tourism P.O. Box 9142, Dar es Salaam, 180/66; IT: 302.

27. It seems there was unanimity among University Council and the Academic Board

that students behaviour on the 22nd October deserved punishment but many also appealed for clemency on behalf of the students so that the University could return to normality and be allowed to reform. A letter by Professor T.O. Ranger of the University College of Dar es Salaam to Miss Joan Wickens, the personal assistant to the President, written on 2nd March 1967 (c3/5A.13) shows that at least some scholars had gone beyond the official propaganda to grasp the real issues which had been raised by the students. In this letter Professor Ranger noted: "even the students who were sent down had a certain radicalism; some at least of their case was that it was unfair for them to be used, as they saw it, as a scapegoat for an establishment which was itself growing fat".

28. Chagula W., "Circular letter to all sent down students", Ref. C3Sa.13 of 9th Jan., 1967.
29. Circular dated 25th Oct., 1966 to all Senior Staff of the University College of Dar es Salaam. On 13 Dec., 1966 also the Academic Board noted with concern the divergence of student attitude from the social and political ideals of the nation.
30. Coulson, *op.cit.,* p.225.
31. Coulson, *ibid.,* p.230
32. See footnote 27 above.
33. Nyerere J.K., *op.cit.,* p. 209-211.
34. Nyerere J.K., *Freedom and Socialism,* (Oxford: Oxford University Press, 1968), pp.230-250.
35. Mhaville Report, *Report of the Presidential Committee of Enquiry into the Co-operative Movement and Marketing Boards,* (Dar es Salaam: Government Printer, 1966).
36. USARF mobilisation leaflet entitled "University College Rag Day: Hark! Wus is speaking!", also quoted by Issa Shivji in "Rodney and Radicalism on the Hill 1966-1974", paper published in the special Issue of *Maji Maji,* no. 45, p.32.
37. A USARF/TYL sponsored Press debate on the "Role of Tourism in Socialist Construction", now published: See Shivji, I. (ed). *Tourism and Socialist Development.* (Dar es Salaam: Tanzania Publishing House, 1973).
38. *Cheche* published Issa Shivji's "Silent Class Struggles" in Tanzania in a special issue. This article was later published in a book which together with another work by the same author also published as a book *Class Struggle Continues* sparked off a lengthy debate on 'State and Imperialism'.
39. Students Vigilance Committee Memorandum, August 1969.
40. Ibid.
41. Ibid.
42. Shivji, I., "Walter Rodney and Radicalism on the Hill 1966-1974", *Maji Maji* No. 43.
43. USARF Statement "Our Last Stand" dated 12/11/1970.
44. *Daily News,* Editorial 21/4/75.
45. Musoma Resolution.
46. *Daily News* 6/3/78.
47. Authors' verbatim record of the question answer session.